HEALTHY
family
FAVORITES

TASTE OF HOME BOOKS • RDA ENTHUSIAST BRANDS, LLC • MILWAUKEE, WI

Taste of Home

For other Taste of Home books and products,
visit us at tasteofhome.com.

International Standard Book Number: 978-1-61765-719-1
Library of Congress Control Number: 2017952629

Cover Photographer: Grace Natoli Sheldon
Set Stylist: Pam Stasney
Food Stylist: Kathryn Conrad

Pictured on front cover: **Texas Tacos** page 53; **Applesauce Brownies**
page 201; **Turkey Medallions with Tomato Salad** page 70
Pictured on title page: **Potato-Topped Ground Beef Skillet** page 59
Pictured on back cover (from left): **Skillet Blueberry Slump** page 232;
French Dip Sandwiches page 244; **Zucchini Crust Pizza** page 154

Printed in China.
1 3 5 7 9 10 8 6 4 2

GET SOCIAL WITH US

To find a recipe tasteofhome.com
To submit a recipe tasteofhome.com/submit
To find out about other *Taste of Home* products shoptasteofhome.com

 **LIKE US**
facebook.com/tasteofhome

 **PIN US**
pinterest.com/taste_of_home

 **FOLLOW US**
@tasteofhome

 **TWEET US**
twitter.com/tasteofhome

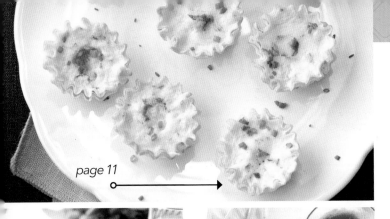

page 11

page 166

page 119

CONTENTS

page 60

REAL HOME COOKING

With **Healthy Family Favorites,** you can use what's in your pantry to prepare better-for-you meals.

As a working mom of two little ones, my life can get pretty hectic; I'd be lying if I said I never took advantage of pizza delivery. As a registered dietitian, though, I care about my family's diet and want to be sure they're eating healthy, nutritious meals—at least most of the time.

That's why I'm excited about this brand-new cookbook, **Healthy Family Favorites.** We set out to prove that eating healthy doesn't mean scouring the store for exotic foods or paying top dollar for fancy products. The recipes that follow come from today's home cooks and use practical ingredients in a way that's not only creative but also delicious and good for you.

Do your kids love spaghetti and meatballs? For a lighter riff on the classic comfort food, **Courtney Stultz** of **Weir, Kansas,** replaces the pasta with spaghetti squash and tosses in a bounty of veggies in her **Spaghetti Squash Meatball Casserole (page 60).** In **Kelso, Washington, Candace Clark** whips up **Makeover Beef Stroganoff (page 57, pictured at right)** for a hearty meal that won't weigh her family down. And in **Upper Sandusky, Ohio, Jean Gottfried** turns to colorful **Turkey Salsa Bowls (page 75)** when teaching the youngsters in her church's Junior Chef classes the basics on cooking healthy meals.

These snapshots bring our recipes to life, and you will find hundreds more in the pages that follow, along with fun facts and handy kitchen tips. And to help you make the best choices

possible, we offer Nutrition Facts with every recipe, icons to identify what's low-fat, low-sodium, low-carb and/or meatless, and diabetic exchanges for recipes that are diabetes-friendly.

We also test every recipe in our test kitchen, so we're confident it will be a success in your kitchen, too!

Now with hundreds of healthy and simple-to-prepare recipes to choose from, it's easier than ever to serve your family real meals you can feel good about, all year long.

Happy Cooking,

Peggy

Peggy Woodward

P.S. Would you like to see one of your family's favorite healthy dishes featured in a *Taste of Home* collection? Visit **tasteofhome.com/submit** to share your story and recipes.

Nutritional Guidelines

All of the recipes in **Healthy Family Favorites** fit the lifestyle of a health-conscious cook and family.

FACTS

- Whenever a choice of ingredients is given in a recipe (such as 1/3 cup of sour cream or plain yogurt), the first ingredient listed is always the one calculated in the Nutrition Facts.
- When a range is provided for an ingredient (such as 2 to 3 teaspoons), we calculate the first amount given.
- Only the amount of a marinade that is absorbed during preparation is calculated.
- Garnishes listed in recipes are generally included in our calculations.

DIABETIC EXCHANGES

Each recipe in this collection was reviewed by a registered dietitian. Diabetic Exchanges are assigned to recipes in accordance with guidelines from the American Diabetes Association and the Academy of Nutrition and Dietetics.

The majority of recipes in this cookbook are suitable for diabetics, but please check the diabetic exchanges to make sure the recipe is in accordance with your doctor's instructions and fits your particular dietary guidelines.

SPECIAL DIET INDICATORS

To help those on restricted diets easily find dishes to suit their needs, we clearly

indicate recipes that are particularly low in fat, sodium or carbohydrates as well as those that contain no meat. You will find these colored icons directly above the recipe title where appropriate.

F One serving contains 3 grams fat or less

S One serving contains 140 milligrams sodium or less

C One serving contains 15 grams carbohydrates or less

M Recipe contains no meat

FAST FIX Dish is table-ready in 30 minutes or less

SMART CHOICES, MADE EASY

Let the recipes in this book help you and your family eat great the whole day through.

Feast on hearty, veggie-packed **Skinny Cobb Salad** from *Taylor Kiser.* It serves up a powerhouse of nutrients from fresh produce and packs 23 grams of satisfying protein. See page 171.

Indulge in rich, velvety **Light Cheesecake** from baker *Diane Roth.* Once your gang sinks their teeth into this dessert, they'll have a hard time believing it's light! Check it out on page 223.

For a comforting meal without all the fat, serve your family *Rhonda Zavodny's* **Asparagus Ham Dinner.** The one-skillet favorite won't derail healthy eating habits. Find the details on page 94.

Healthy Makeovers

Get inspired! Use some of Peggy's favorite tricks to make your family faves healthier. See how quickly the savings add up!

	ORIGINAL	SUBSTITUTE	SAVE (per serving)
Spaghetti	1 pound Italian turkey sausage; *4 servings*	• ½ pound Italian turkey sausage • ½ pound lean ground turkey • 1 teaspoon Italian seasoning	200mg sodium
Tacos	1 pound lean ground beef; *4 servings*	• ½ pound lean ground beef • 1 can black beans (rinsed and drained)	5g fat (2g sat. fat) (+4g fiber)
Chili	2 cans tomatoes and 1 can tomato sauce; *8 servings*	• No-salt-added versions in the same amounts	400mg sodium
Cream Soup	2 cups half-and-half cream; *8 servings*	• 2 cups reduced-fat evaporated milk	30 calories, 5g fat (4g saturated fat)
Pancakes	4 tablespoons melted butter; *8 servings*	• 2 tablespoons melted butter • 2 tablespoons canola oil	2g saturated fat
Brunch Bake	12 large eggs; *8 servings*	• 4 large eggs • 2 cups egg substitute	42 calories, 5g fat (2g saturated fat)
Quick Breads	1 cup each chocolate chips and chopped pecans; *12 servings*	• ½ cup each in the bread • 1 tablespoon each sprinkled on top	57 calories, 5g fat
Cupcakes	1 cup canola oil; *24 servings*	• ½ cup canola oil • ½ cup applesauce	36 calories, 5g fat

Buffalo Chicken Meatballs
page 15

SNACK TIME

It's true! You can enjoy savory hot bites, meal starters, dips and spreads, munchies and other snacks without feeling an ounce of guilt. Try these simple, fun recipes the next time guests visit or whenever a craving calls.

C

TORTELLINI APPETIZERS

These kabobs will lend a welcome Italian flavor to any get-together. Cheese tortellini is marinated in salad dressing, then skewered on toothpicks along with stuffed olives, salami and cheese.
—Patricia Schmidt, Sterling Heights, MI

Prep: 25 min. + marinating
Makes: 1½ dozen

- 18 refrigerated cheese tortellini
- ¼ cup fat-free Italian salad dressing
- 6 thin slices (4 ounces) reduced-fat provolone cheese
- 6 thin slices (2 ounces) Genoa salami
- 18 large pimiento-stuffed olives

1. Cook tortellini according to package directions; drain and rinse in cold water. In a resealable plastic bag, combine the tortellini and salad dressing. Seal bag and refrigerate for 4 hours.
2. Place a slice of cheese on each slice of salami; roll up tightly. Cut into thirds. Drain tortellini and discard dressing. For each appetizer, thread a tortellini, salami roll-up and olive on a toothpick.
Per 1 appetizer: 63 cal., 4g fat (1g sat. fat), 10mg chol., 267mg sod., 4g carb. (0 sugars, 0 fiber), 4g pro.

F **S** **FAST FIX**

ICED HONEYDEW MINT TEA

I grow mint in the garden on my balcony. In this minty tea, I blend two of my favorite beverages— Moroccan mint tea and honeydew agua fresca.
—Sarah Batt Throne, El Cerrito, CA

Start to Finish: 20 min.
Makes: 10 servings

- 4 cups water
- 24 fresh mint leaves
- 8 individual green tea bags
- ⅔ cup sugar
- 5 cups diced honeydew, divided
- 3 cups ice cubes, divided
  Additional ice cubes

1. In a large saucepan, bring water to a boil; remove from heat. Add mint leaves and tea bags; steep, covered, 3-5 minutes according to taste, stirring occasionally. Discard mint and tea bags. Stir in sugar.
2. Place 2½ cups honeydew, 2 cups tea and 1½ cups ice in a blender; cover and process until blended. Serve over additional ice. Repeat with remaining ingredients.
Per 1 cup: 83 cal., 0 fat (0 sat. fat), 0 chol., 15mg sod., 21g carb. (20g sugars, 1g fiber), 0 pro.
Diabetic exchanges: 1 starch, ½ fruit.

PEANUT CARAMEL CORN

Here's a lighter alternative to traditional caramel corn that's just as tasty. This can't-stop-eatin'-it treat won't stick to fingers or teeth and it makes a fun edible gift, too.
—Lois Ward, Puslinch, ON

Prep: 20 min. • **Bake:** 45 min.
Makes: 2 quarts

- 8 cups air-popped popcorn
- ½ cup salted peanuts
- ½ cup packed brown sugar
- 3 tablespoons light corn syrup
- 4½ teaspoons molasses
- 1 tablespoon butter
- ¼ teaspoon salt
- ½ teaspoon vanilla extract
- ⅛ teaspoon baking soda

1. Place popcorn and peanuts in a large bowl coated with cooking spray; set aside.
2. In a large heavy saucepan, combine the brown sugar, corn syrup, molasses, butter and salt. Bring to a boil over medium heat, stirring constantly. Boil for 2-3 minutes without stirring.
3. Remove from the heat; stir in vanilla and baking soda (mixture will foam). Quickly pour over popcorn and mix well.
4. Transfer to a 15x10x1-in. baking pan coated with cooking spray. Bake at 250° for 45 minutes, stirring every 15 minutes. Remove from pan and place on waxed paper to cool. Store caramel corn in an airtight container.
Per 1 cup: 181 cal., 6g fat (2g sat. fat), 4mg chol., 155mg sod., 30g carb. (18g sugars, 2g fiber), 3g pro.
Diabetic exchanges: 2 starch, 1 fat.

C S CATHERINE'S GUACAMOLE

Get the scoop on making a bang-up guacamole that is sure to impress.
A big handful of chopped celery adds fun crunch to this avocado dip—everyone's favorite fiesta starter.
—Catherine Cassidy, Milwaukee, WI

Prep: 15 min. + chilling
Makes: 2½ cups

- 3 medium ripe avocados, peeled and pitted
- ⅓ cup chopped sweet onion
- 1 small tomato, seeded and chopped
- 1 celery rib, finely chopped
- 2 garlic cloves, minced
- 2 tablespoons lemon or lime juice
- 2 teaspoons Worcestershire sauce
- ½ teaspoon salt
- ¼ teaspoon pepper
- ¼ to ⅓ cup chopped fresh cilantro, optional
     Tortilla chips

In a small bowl, mash avocados. Stir in onion, tomato, celery, garlic, lemon juice, Worcestershire, salt, pepper and, if desired, cilantro. Chill guacamole 1 hour before serving. Serve with chips.
Per ¼ cup without chips: 75 cal., 6g fat (1g sat. fat), 0 chol., 136mg sod., 5g carb. (1g sugars, 3g fiber), 1g pro.
Diabetic exchanges: 1 fat.

F S C M FAST FIX

BLUE CHEESE-STUFFED STRAWBERRIES

I was enjoying a salad with strawberries and blue cheese when the idea hit me to stuff the strawberries and serve them as an appetizer. It worked out perfectly, and the flavors blend nicely.
—Diane Nemitz, Ludington, MI

Start to Finish: 25 min.
Makes: 16 appetizers

- ½ cup balsamic vinegar
- 3 ounces fat-free cream cheese
- ½ cup crumbled blue cheese
- 16 large fresh strawberries
- 3 tablespoons finely chopped pecans, toasted

1. Place vinegar in a small saucepan. Bring to a boil; cook until liquid is reduced by half. Cool to room temperature.
2. Meanwhile, in a small bowl, beat cream cheese until smooth. Beat in blue cheese. Remove stems and scoop out centers from the strawberries; fill each with about 2 teaspoons cheese mixture. Sprinkle pecans over filling, pressing lightly. Chill until serving. Drizzle with balsamic vinegar.
Per 1 stuffed strawberry: 36 cal., 2g fat (1g sat. fat), 3mg chol., 80mg sod., 3g carb. (2g sugars, 0 fiber), 2g pro.
Diabetic exchanges: ½ fat.

C

ROASTED FRESH PUMPKIN SEEDS

I learned how to roast pumpkin seeds from my mother, who learned it from her mother. It's a wholesome, healthy snack and fun to make after you finish carving Halloween jack-o'-lanterns.
—Margaret Drye, Plainfield, NH

Prep: 20 min. + soaking
Bake: 1½ hours + cooling
Makes: 1½ cups

- 2 cups fresh pumpkin seeds
- 1 teaspoon salt
- 1 tablespoon olive oil
- ¾ teaspoon kosher or fine sea salt

1. Place seeds in a 1-qt. bowl; cover with water. Stir in salt; let stand, covered, overnight.
2. Preheat oven to 200°. Drain and rinse seeds; drain again and pat dry. Transfer to a 15x10x1-in. baking pan. Toss with oil and kosher salt; spread in a single layer.
3. Roast 1½-1¾ hours or until crisp and lightly browned, stirring occasionally. Cool completely. Store in an airtight container.
Per ¼ cup: 115 cal., 6g fat (1g sat. fat), 0 chol., 248mg sod., 11g carb. (0 sugars, 4g fiber), 4g pro.
Diabetic exchanges: 1 fat, ½ starch.

ROAST BEEF AIOLI BUNDLES

Everyone will want to try these colorful bundles of fresh veggies and deli roast beef. They look impressive, but they're quite easy!
—*Taste of Home* Test Kitchen

Start to Finish: 30 min.
Makes: 16 appetizers

- 16 fresh asparagus spears, trimmed
- ⅓ cup mayonnaise
- 1 garlic clove, minced
- 1 teaspoon Dijon mustard
- 1 teaspoon lemon juice
- ⅛ teaspoon ground cumin
- 8 thin slices deli roast beef, cut in half lengthwise
- 1 medium sweet yellow pepper, thinly sliced
- 1 medium sweet orange pepper, thinly sliced
- 1 medium sweet red pepper, thinly sliced
- 16 whole chives

1. In a large skillet, bring 1 in. of water to a boil. Add asparagus; cover and cook for 3 minutes. Drain and immediately place in ice water. Drain and pat dry.
2. In a small bowl, combine the mayonnaise, garlic, mustard, lemon juice and cumin. Place roast beef slices on a work surface; spread each slice with 1 teaspoon aioli. Top each with an asparagus spear and pepper strips. Roll up tightly; tie bundles with chives. Serve immediately.
Per 1 appetizer: 52 cal., 4g fat (1g sat. fat), 6mg chol., 74mg sod., 2g carb. (1g sugars, 1g fiber), 2g pro.
Diabetic exchanges: 1 fat.

GARLIC-HERB MINI QUICHES

These lightened-up quiche tartlets make the perfect finger food for a luncheon or brunch. The recipe makes a big batch, so it's ideal when you need to feed a crowd. Feel free to add chopped imitation crabmeat to the filling if you like.
—Josephine Piro, Easton, PA

Start to Finish: 25 min.
Makes: 45 mini quiches

- 1 package (6½ ounces) reduced-fat garlic-herb spreadable cheese
- ¼ cup fat-free milk
- 2 large eggs
- 3 packages (1.9 ounces each) frozen miniature phyllo tart shells
- 2 tablespoons minced fresh parsley
  Minced chives, optional

1. In a small bowl, beat the spreadable cheese, milk and eggs. Place tart shells on an ungreased baking sheet; fill each shell with 2 teaspoons of the cheese and egg mixture. Sprinkle with parsley.
2. Bake at 350° for 10-12 minutes or until filling is set and shells are lightly browned. Sprinkle with chives if desired. Serve warm.
Per 1 mini quiche: 31 cal., 2g fat (0 sat. fat), 12mg chol., 32mg sod., 2g carb. (0 sugars, 0 fiber), 1g pro.

S

APPLE SALSA WITH CINNAMON CHIPS

Try this appetizer for a fun treat that's sure to be requested at all your parties. The salsa offers good-for-you fruits, and the home-baked chips are healthy alternative to commercial snacks.
—Courtney Fons, Brighton, MI

Prep: 25 min. • **Bake:** 10 min.
Makes: 12 servings

- 3 tablespoons sugar
- 1 teaspoon ground cinnamon
- 6 flour tortillas (8 inches)
  Cooking spray

SALSA
- 4 cups finely chopped tart apples (about 2 large)
- 1 medium ripe pear, finely chopped
- ½ cup quartered seedless red grapes
- ½ cup chopped celery
- ¼ cup chopped walnuts
- 2 teaspoons grated orange peel
- 3 tablespoons orange juice
- 1 tablespoon brown sugar

1. Preheat oven to 350°. Mix sugar and cinnamon. Spritz both sides of tortillas with cooking spray; sprinkle with sugar mixture. Cut each tortilla into eight wedges. Spread wedges in a single layer on baking sheets. Bake until lightly browned, 10-12 minutes, rotating pans as needed.
2. Place salsa ingredients in a bowl; toss to combine. Serve with chips.
Per serving: 154 cal., 4g fat (1g sat. fat), 0 chol., 123mg sod., 28g carb. (12g sugars, 3g fiber), 3g pro.
Diabetic exchanges: 1 starch, 1 fruit, ½ fat.

F **FAST FIX**
PARTY PRETZELS

Turn pretzels into instant party food with garlic, dill and lemon-pepper seasoning. This recipe also works with pretzel sticks.
—Carrie Shaub, Mount Joy, PA

Start to Finish: 25 min.
Makes: 12 cups

- 1 package (16 ounces) fat-free miniature pretzels
- ¼ cup canola oil
- 3 teaspoons garlic powder
- 1 teaspoon dill weed
- ½ teaspoon lemon-pepper seasoning

1. Preheat oven to 350°. Place pretzels in a 15x10x1-in. baking pan. In a small bowl, mix oil and seasonings; drizzle over pretzels and toss to coat.
2. Bake, uncovered, 12 minutes, stirring twice. Cool on a wire rack. Store in an airtight container.
Per ½ cup: 89 cal., 2g fat (0 sat. fat), 0 chol., 290mg sod., 16g carb. (1g sugars, 1g fiber), 2g pro.
Diabetic exchanges: 1 starch, ½ fat.

F S C
THYME-SEA SALT CRACKERS

My homemade crackers are light, crispy and spiked with flavor from fresh thyme. They are great on their own, paired with a sharp white cheddar or crumbled over soup or chili.
—Jessica Wirth, Charlotte, NC

Prep: 25 min.
Bake: 10 min./batch
Makes: about 7 dozen

- 2½ cups all-purpose flour
- ½ cup white whole wheat flour
- 1 teaspoon salt
- ¾ cup water
- ¼ cup plus 1 tablespoon olive oil, divided
- 1 to 2 tablespoons minced fresh thyme
- ¾ teaspoon sea or kosher salt

1. Preheat oven to 375°. In a large bowl, whisk flours and salt. Gradually add water and ¼ cup oil, tossing with a fork until dough holds together when pressed. Divide dough into three portions. On a lightly floured surface, roll each portion of dough to ⅛-in. thickness. Cut with a floured 1½-in. round cookie cutter. Place 1 in. apart on ungreased baking sheets. Prick each cracker with a fork; brush lightly with remaining oil. Mix thyme and sea salt; sprinkle over crackers.
2. Bake 9-11 minutes or until bottoms are lightly browned.
Per 1 cracker: 23 cal., 1g fat (0 sat. fat), 0 chol., 45mg sod., 3g carb. (0 sugars, 0 fiber), 0 pro.

F S C
GRILLED LEEK DIP

Smoky leeks from the grill add punch to this creamy appetizer with veggies and chips. I use baby Vidalia onions when available.
—Ramona Parris, Canton, GA

Prep: 10 min.
Grill: 10 min. + chilling
Makes: 2½ cups

- 2 medium leeks
- 2 teaspoons olive oil
- ½ teaspoon salt, divided
- ¼ teaspoon pepper
- 2 cups (16 ounces) reduced-fat sour cream
- 2 tablespoons Worcestershire sauce
  Assorted fresh vegetables

1. Trim and discard dark green portions of leeks. Brush leeks with oil; sprinkle with ¼ teaspoon salt and pepper. Grill leeks, covered, over medium-high heat 8-10 minutes or until lightly charred and tender, turning occasionally. Cool slightly; chop leeks.
2. In a small bowl, combine sour cream, Worcestershire sauce and remaining salt; stir in leeks. Refrigerate, covered, 2 hours before serving. Serve with vegetables.
Per 2 tablespoons without vegetables: 43 cal., 2g fat (1g sat. fat), 8mg chol., 93mg sod., 3g carb. (2g sugars, 0 fiber), 2g pro.

F S C
BUFFALO CHICKEN MEATBALLS

PICTURED ON PAGE 6

These appetizer meatballs have a nice flavor kick. To temper the heat, I serve them with blue cheese or ranch dressing for dipping. If I make them for a meal, I skip the dressing and serve the meatballs with blue cheese polenta on the side. Yum!
—Amber Massey, Argyle, TX

Prep: 15 min.
Bake: 20 min.
Makes: 2 dozen

- ¾ cup panko (Japanese) bread crumbs
- ⅓ cup plus ½ cup Louisiana-style hot sauce, divided
- ¼ cup chopped celery
- 1 large egg white
- 1 pound lean ground chicken
  Reduced-fat blue cheese or ranch salad dressing, optional

1. Preheat oven to 400°. In a large bowl, combine bread crumbs, ⅓ cup hot sauce, celery and egg white. Add chicken; mix lightly but thoroughly.

2. Shape into twenty-four 1-in. balls. Place on a greased rack in a shallow baking pan. Bake 20-25 minutes or until cooked through.

3. Toss meatballs with remaining hot sauce. If desired, drizzle with salad dressing just before serving.

Per 1 meatball: 35 cal., 1g fat (0 sat. fat), 14mg chol., 24mg sod., 2g carb. (0 sugars, 0 fiber), 4g pro.

F S C M FAST FIX ▶
DEVILED EGGS

These deviled eggs are nicely flavored with a tang of mustard and a sprinkling of paprika. This slimmed-down version uses only half the egg yolks of the original recipe and calls for fat-free mayo and reduced-fat sour cream.
—*Taste of Home* Test Kitchen

Start to Finish: 10 min.
Makes: 16 servings

- 8 hard-cooked large eggs
- ¼ cup fat-free mayonnaise
- ¼ cup reduced-fat sour cream
- 2 tablespoons soft bread crumbs
- 1 tablespoon prepared mustard
- ¼ teaspoon salt
  Dash white pepper
- 4 pimiento-stuffed olives, sliced
  Paprika, optional

Slice eggs in half lengthwise and remove yolks; refrigerate eight yolk halves for another use. Set whites aside. In a small bowl, mash the remaining eight yolks. Stir in the mayonnaise, sour cream, bread crumbs, mustard, salt and pepper. Stuff or pipe into egg whites. If desired, sprinkle eggs with paprika. Garnish with olives.

Per 1 half: 50 cal., 3g fat (1g sat. fat), 95mg chol., 133mg sod., 1g carb. (1g sugars, 0 fiber), 3g pro.

EASY BUFFALO CHICKEN DIP

Everyone will devour this savory dip full of hearty shredded chicken. The spicy kick makes it perfect game-day food, and the recipe always brings raves.
—Janice Foltz, Hershey, PA

Start to Finish: 30 min.
Makes: 4 cups

- 1 package (8 ounces) reduced-fat cream cheese
- 1 cup (8 ounces) reduced-fat sour cream
- ½ cup Louisiana-style hot sauce
- 3 cups shredded cooked chicken breast
  Assorted crackers

1. Preheat oven to 350°. In a large bowl, beat cream cheese, sour cream and hot sauce until smooth; stir in chicken.
2. Transfer to an 8-in. square baking dish coated with cooking spray. Cover and bake 18-22 minutes or until heated through. Serve warm with crackers.
Per 3 tablespoons: 77 cal., 4g fat (2g sat. fat), 28mg chol., 71mg sod., 1g carb. (1g sugars, 0 fiber), 8g pro.

STRAWBERRY CORN SALSA

All the colors of summer are captured in this fresh, light salsa. It can be served with chips, as a side dish or as a garnish to any grilled meat.
—Catherine Goza, Charlotte, NC

Prep: 15 min. + chilling
Makes: 5½ cups

- 2 cups fresh strawberries, chopped
- 2 cups grape tomatoes, chopped
- 1 package (10 ounces) frozen corn, thawed
- 2 green onions, chopped
- 3 tablespoons minced fresh cilantro
- ⅓ cup olive oil
- 2 tablespoons raspberry vinegar
- 2 tablespoons lime juice
- ½ teaspoon salt
  Baked tortilla chips

In a large bowl, combine the first five ingredients. In a small bowl, whisk the oil, vinegar, lime juice and salt. Drizzle over strawberry mixture; toss to coat. Refrigerate for 1 hour. Serve with chips.
Per ¼ cup without tortilla chips: 49 cal., 3g fat (0 sat. fat), 0 chol., 56mg sod., 5g carb. (1g sugars, 1g fiber), 1g pro.

F S C
RICOTTA SAUSAGE TRIANGLES

Stuffed with cheese, sausage and seasonings, these pockets are hard to put down! If you end up with leftovers, they freeze well.
—Virginia Anthony, Jacksonville, FL

Prep: 1 hour
Bake: 15 min./batch
Makes: 12 dozen

- 1 carton (15 ounces) part-skim ricotta cheese
- 1 package (10 ounces) frozen chopped spinach, thawed and squeezed dry
- 1 jar (8 ounces) roasted sweet red peppers, drained and chopped
- ⅓ cup grated Parmesan cheese
- 3 tablespoons chopped ripe olives
- 1 large egg
- 1 tablespoon minced fresh basil or 1 teaspoon dried basil
- 1 teaspoon Italian seasoning
- ¼ teaspoon salt
- ¼ teaspoon pepper
- 1 pound bulk Italian sausage
- 1 medium onion, chopped
- 96 sheets phyllo dough (14x9-inch size)
  Olive oil-flavored cooking spray
  Warm marinara sauce, optional

1. In a large bowl, combine the first 10 ingredients. In a large skillet, cook the sausage and onion over medium heat until the meat is no longer pink; drain. Stir into cheese mixture.

2. Place one sheet of phyllo dough on a work surface with a short end facing you; spray with cooking spray. Top with a second sheet of phyllo; spray again with cooking spray. (Keep remaining phyllo covered with plastic wrap and a damp towel to prevent it from drying out.) Cut layered sheets into three 14x3-in. strips.

3. Place a rounded teaspoonful of filling on lower corner of each strip. Fold dough over filling, forming a triangle. Fold triangle up, then fold triangle over, forming another triangle. Continue folding, like a flag, until you come to the end of the strip.

4. Spritz end of dough with spray and press onto triangle to seal. Turn triangle and spritz top with spray. Repeat with the remaining phyllo and filling.

5. Place triangles on baking sheets coated with cooking spray. Bake at 375° for 15-20 minutes or until golden brown. Serve warm with marinara sauce if desired.

Freeze option: Freeze unbaked triangles in freezer containers, separating layers with waxed paper. To use, bake triangles as directed, increasing time as necessary until golden and heated through.

Per 1 appetizer: 42 cal., 2g fat (0 sat. fat), 4mg chol., 64mg sod., 5g carb. (0 sugars, 0 fiber), 2g pro.
Diabetic exchanges: ½ starch.

TEST KITCHEN TIP
Phyllo is a tissue-thin pastry that's made by gently stretching the dough into fragile sheets. It can be layered, shaped and baked in a variety of ways. Handling it quickly is the key!

2 tablespoons plus ¾ cup sour cream, divided
¼ cup minced fresh cilantro
3 plum tomatoes, chopped
¾ cup peeled, seeded and finely chopped cucumber
¾ cup finely chopped zucchini
¼ cup finely chopped red onion
Cucumber slices

1. Pulse beans, cumin, paprika, cayenne and ⅓ cup water in food processor until smooth. Add salt and pepper to taste.

2. In a small saucepan, cook the quinoa with remaining 1⅓ cups of water according to package directions. Fluff with fork; sprinkle with 2 tablespoons lime juice. Set aside. Meanwhile, mash together avocados, 2 tablespoons sour cream, cilantro and remaining lime juice.

3. In a 2½-qt. dish, layer bean mixture, quinoa, avocado mixture, remaining sour cream, tomatoes, chopped cucumber, zucchini and onion. Serve immediately with cucumber slices for dipping, or refrigerate.

HEALTH TIP Quinoa is a gluten-free, high-protein grain that looks a little like couscous. It's an excellent source of trace minerals, such as manganese and copper, that help the body convert carbohydrates into energy.

Note: Look for quinoa in the cereal, rice or organic food aisle.

Per ¼ cup without cucumber slices: 65 cal., 3g fat (1g sat. fat), 4mg chol., 54mg sod., 8g carb. (1g sugars, 2g fiber), 2g pro.

Diabetic exchanges: ½ starch, ½ fat.

F S C M
SKINNY QUINOA VEGGIE DIP

Quinoa is a super grain that's packed with protein and vitamins, so it's a great addition to this good-for-you dip. We use crunchy cucumber slices for dippers.
—Jennifer Gizzi, Green Bay, WI

Prep: 20 min. • **Cook:** 15 min.
Makes: 32 servings

2 cans (15 ounces) black beans, rinsed and drained
1½ teaspoons ground cumin
1½ teaspoons paprika
½ teaspoon cayenne pepper
1⅔ cups water, divided
Salt and pepper to taste
⅔ cup quinoa, rinsed
5 tablespoons lime juice, divided
2 medium ripe avocados, peeled and coarsely chopped

F S C

HOT CRAB PINWHEELS

A friend gave me the recipe for these crabmeat bites. They're delish! What amazes me the most is my husband, who doesn't like seafood, can't stop eating them.
—Kitti Boesel, Woodbridge, VA

Prep: 15 min. + chilling
Bake: 10 min.
Makes: 3 dozen

- 1 package (8 ounces) reduced-fat cream cheese
- 1 can (6 ounces) crabmeat, drained, flaked and cartilage removed
- ¾ cup diced sweet red pepper
- ½ cup shredded reduced-fat cheddar cheese
- 2 green onions, thinly sliced
- 3 tablespoons minced fresh parsley
- ¼ to ½ teaspoon cayenne pepper
- 6 flour tortillas (6 inches)

1. Beat cream cheese until smooth; stir in crab, red pepper, cheese, green onions, parsley and cayenne. Spread ⅓ cup filling over each tortilla; roll up tightly. Wrap in plastic, twisting ends to seal; refrigerate at least 2 hours.

2. To serve, preheat oven to 350°. Unwrap rolls; trim ends and cut each into six slices. Place on baking sheets coated with cooking spray. Bake until pinwheels are bubbly, about 10 minutes. Serve warm.

Per 1 pinwheel: 44 cal., 2g fat (1g sat. fat), 10mg chol., 98mg sod., 3g carb. (0 sugars, 0 fiber), 2g pro.

thickened. Add meatballs; heat through, stirring gently.

Freeze option: Freeze cooled meatball mixture in freezer containers. To use, partially thaw in refrigerator overnight. Microwave, covered, on high in a microwave-safe dish until heated through, gently stirring and adding a little water if necessary.

Per 1 meatball: 42 cal., 1g fat (0 sat. fat), 9mg chol., 93mg sod., 4g carb. (3g sugars, 0 fiber), 3g pro.

C M FAST FIX

FAMILY-FAVORITE TACO DIP

I've tasted many different taco dips, but this one is my favorite. It's colorful, creamy and light!
—Laurie Ellsworth, Tully, NY

Start to Finish: 10 min.
Makes: 3 cups

- 2 packages (8 ounces each) fat-free cream cheese
- 2 tablespoons reduced-sodium taco seasoning
- 1 tablespoon fat-free milk
- 1 cup shredded cheddar cheese
- 1 medium tomato, diced
- ¼ cup sliced ripe olives, drained
- ¼ cup pickled jalapeno pepper
  Baked tortilla chips

In a small bowl, beat the cream cheese, taco seasoning and milk until blended. Spread mixture into a 9-in. pie plate. Sprinkle with cheese, tomato, olives and jalapenos. Serve with chips.

Per ¼ cup without chips: 81 cal., 4g fat (2g sat. fat), 13mg chol., 393mg sod., 5g carb. (1g sugars, 0 fiber), 8g pro.

F S C

BARBECUE-GLAZED MEATBALLS

Stock your freezer with these meatballs and you'll always have a hearty appetizer available when unexpected guests drop by. We also enjoy them with noodles or rice as a main dish on weeknights.
—Anna Finley, Columbia, MO

Prep: 30 min.
Bake: 15 min./batch
Makes: 8 dozen

- 2 cups quick-cooking oats
- 1 can (12 ounces) fat-free evaporated milk
- 1 small onion, finely chopped
- 2 teaspoons garlic powder
- 2 teaspoons chili powder
- 3 pounds lean ground beef (90% lean)

SAUCE
- 2½ cups ketchup
- 1 small onion, finely chopped
- ⅓ cup packed brown sugar
- 2 teaspoons liquid smoke, optional
- 1¼ teaspoons chili powder
- ¾ teaspoon garlic powder

1. Preheat oven to 400°. In a large bowl, combine the first five ingredients. Add beef; mix lightly but thoroughly. Shape mixture into 1-in. balls.
2. Place meatballs on greased racks in shallow baking pans. Bake until cooked through, 15-20 minutes. Drain on paper towels.
3. In a Dutch oven, combine sauce ingredients. Bring to a boil over medium heat, stirring constantly. Reduce heat; simmer, uncovered, 2-3 minutes or until slightly

ASPARAGUS WITH BASIL PESTO SAUCE

Add zip to your appetizer platter with an easy asparagus dip that can also double as a flavorful sandwich spread.
—Janie Colle, Hutchinson, KS

Start to Finish: 15 min.
Makes: 12 servings

- ¾ cup reduced-fat mayonnaise
- 2 tablespoons prepared pesto
- 1 tablespoon grated Parmesan cheese
- 1 tablespoon minced fresh basil
- 1 teaspoon lemon juice
- 1 garlic clove, minced
- 1½ pounds fresh asparagus, trimmed

1. In a small bowl, mix the first six ingredients until blended; refrigerate until serving.
2. In a Dutch oven, bring 12 cups water to a boil. Add asparagus in batches; cook, uncovered, until crisp-tender, 2-3 minutes. Remove and immediately drop into ice water. Drain and pat dry. Serve with sauce.
Per serving: 72 cal., 6g fat (1g sat. fat), 6mg chol., 149mg sod., 3g carb. (1g sugars, 1g fiber), 1g pro.
Diabetic exchanges: 1½ fat.

S

CHEWY HONEY GRANOLA BARS

There's so much to love about these homemade granola bars—sweet honey, chewy raisins, a hint of chocolate and cinnamon and bit of crunch. To save a few for later, wrap individual bars in plastic wrap and place in a resealable freezer bag. Pull one out whenever you crave a satisfying snack.
—Tasha Lehman, Williston, VT

Prep: 10 min.
Bake: 15 min. + cooling
Makes: 20 servings

- 3 cups old-fashioned oats
- 2 cups unsweetened puffed wheat cereal
- 1 cup all-purpose flour
- ⅓ cup chopped walnuts
- ⅓ cup raisins
- ⅓ cup miniature semisweet chocolate chips
- 1 teaspoon baking soda
- 1 teaspoon ground cinnamon
- 1 cup honey
- ¼ cup butter, melted
- 1 teaspoon vanilla extract

1. Preheat oven to 350°. In a large bowl, combine the first eight ingredients. In a small bowl, combine honey, butter and vanilla; pour over oat mixture and mix well. (Mixture will be sticky.)
2. Press into a 13x9-in. baking pan coated with cooking spray. Bake 14-18 minutes or until set and edges are lightly browned. Cool on a wire rack. Cut into bars.
Per 1 bar: 178 cal., 5g fat (2g sat. fat), 6mg chol., 81mg sod., 32g carb. (17g sugars, 2g fiber), 3g pro.
Diabetic exchanges: 2 starch, ½ fat.

Garden Veggie Egg Bake
page 35

EYE-OPENING BREAKFASTS

Rise and shine for one of these tempting breakfast specialties. Lower in sugar and carbohydrates, yet big on flavor, each one is guaranteed to start the day off right!

HAWAIIAN BREAKFAST PIZZA

My tropical creation is a fun spin on pizza. Kids love layering the toppings, and it's a great way to use up leftover ham. Try it for breakfast, lunch or dinner.
—Holly Ciani, Taberg, NY

Start to Finish: 30 min.
Makes: 6 slices

- 1 prebaked 12-inch thin whole wheat pizza crust
- 6 large eggs
- ¼ teaspoon pepper
- 1 cup cubed fully cooked ham
- 1 cup unsweetened pineapple tidbits, drained
- ¾ cup shredded cheddar cheese
- 1 tablespoon minced fresh parsley
  Salsa and reduced-fat sour cream, optional

1. Place crust on an ungreased 12-in. pizza pan; set aside.
2. Whisk eggs and pepper; stir into a large nonstick skillet coated with cooking spray. Cook and stir over medium heat until almost set. Transfer to pizza crust. Top with ham and pineapple. Sprinkle with cheese.
3. Bake at 400° for 9-12 minutes or until cheese is melted. Sprinkle with parsley. Serve with salsa and sour cream if desired.

Per 1 slice: 294 cal., 12g fat (6g sat. fat), 240mg chol., 688mg sod., 28g carb. (6g sugars, 4g fiber), 20g pro.

C M FAST FIX ▶
SHAKSHUKA

Shakshuka is a dish of poached eggs with tomatoes, peppers and cumin. I learned how to make it while traveling and it's been my favorite way to eat eggs since.
—Ezra Weeks, Calgary, AB

Start to Finish: 30 min.
Makes: 4 servings

- 2 tablespoons olive oil
- 1 medium onion, chopped
- 1 garlic clove, minced
- 1 teaspoon ground cumin
- 1 teaspoon pepper
- ½ to 1 teaspoon chili powder
- ½ teaspoon salt
- 1 teaspoon Sriracha Asian hot chili sauce or hot pepper sauce, optional
- 2 medium tomatoes, chopped
- 4 large eggs
  Chopped fresh cilantro
  Whole pita breads, toasted

1. In a large skillet, heat oil over medium heat. Add onion; cook and stir 4-6 minutes or until tender. Add garlic, seasonings and, if desired, hot chili sauce; cook 30 seconds longer. Add tomatoes; cook 3-5 minutes or until mixture is thickened, stirring occasionally.
2. With back of spoon, make four wells in vegetable mixture; break an egg into each well. Cook, covered, 4-6 minutes or until egg whites are completely set and yolks begin to thicken but are not hard. Sprinkle with cilantro; serve with pita bread.
Per serving: 159 cal., 12g fat (3g sat. fat), 186mg chol., 381mg sod., 6g carb. (3g sugars, 2g fiber), 7g pro.
Diabetic exchanges: 1½ fat, 1 medium-fat meat, 1 vegetable.

Ⓜ SWEET ONION PIE

Chock-full of sweet onions, this creamy pie makes a scrumptious addition to the brunch buffet. I cut calories and fat from this tasty dish by using less butter to cook the onions and substituting lighter ingredients for full-fat ones.
—Barbara Reese, Catawissa, PA

Prep: 35 min. • **Bake:** 30 min.
Makes: 8 servings

- 2 **sweet onions, halved and sliced**
- 1 **tablespoon butter**
- 1 **frozen deep-dish pie shell**
- 1 **cup egg substitute**
- 1 **cup fat-free evaporated milk**
- 1 **teaspoon salt**
- ¼ **teaspoon pepper**

1. In a large nonstick skillet, cook onions in butter over medium-low heat for 30 minutes or until very tender. Meanwhile, line unpricked pastry shell with a double thickness of heavy-duty foil.
2. Bake at 450° for 6 minutes. Remove foil; cool on a wire rack. Reduce heat to 425°.
3. Spoon onions into pastry shell. In a small bowl, whisk the egg substitute, milk, salt and pepper; pour over onions. Bake until a knife inserted near the center comes out clean, 30-35 minutes. Let stand 5-10 minutes before cutting.
Per 1 piece: 169 cal., 7g fat (2g sat. fat), 5mg chol., 487mg sod., 21g carb. (8g sugars, 1g fiber), 7g pro.
Diabetic exchanges: 1 starch, 1 lean meat, 1 fat.

Ⓕ Ⓢ Ⓜ FAST FIX ▶ YOGURT & HONEY FRUIT CUPS

Dress up fresh fruit in a sweet and creamy homemade sauce. This medley will disappear as fast as it comes together.
—*Taste of Home* Test Kitchen

Start to Finish: 10 min.
Makes: 6 servings

- 4½ **cups cut-up fresh fruit (pears, apples, bananas, grapes, etc.)**
- ¾ **cup (6 ounces) mandarin orange, vanilla or lemon yogurt**
- 1 **tablespoon honey**
- ½ **teaspoon grated orange peel**
- ¼ **teaspoon almond extract**

Divide fruit among six individual serving bowls. Combine the yogurt, honey, orange peel and extract; spoon over the fruit.
Per ¾ cup: 97 cal., 0 fat (0 sat. fat), 2mg chol., 22mg sod., 23g carb. (9g sugars, 2g fiber), 2g pro.
Diabetic exchanges: 1 fruit, ½ starch.

M

BANANA FRENCH TOAST BAKE

Who says you can't wake up to a comforting meal while you're watching your weight? You won't be able to get enough of this make-ahead family favorite.
—Nancy Zimmerman
Cape May Court House, NJ

Prep: 20 min. + chilling
Bake: 55 min. + standing
Makes: 8 servings

- 6 whole wheat hamburger buns
- 1 package (8 ounces) reduced-fat cream cheese, cut into ¾-inch cubes
- 3 medium bananas, sliced
- 6 large eggs
- 4 cups fat-free milk
- ¼ cup sugar
- ¼ cup maple syrup
- ½ teaspoon ground cinnamon

1. Preheat oven to 350°. Cut buns into 1-in. cubes; place half in a 13x9-in. baking dish coated with cooking spray. Layer with cream cheese, bananas and remaining cubed buns.
2. In a large bowl, whisk eggs, milk, sugar, syrup and cinnamon; pour over top. Refrigerate, covered, 8 hours or overnight.
3. Remove from refrigerator; let stand 30 minutes. Bake, covered, 30 minutes. Uncover; bake until a knife inserted near the comes out clean, 25-30 minutes longer. Let stand 10 minutes before serving.
Per 1 piece: 341 cal., 12g fat (6g sat. fat), 181mg chol., 379mg sod., 47g carb. (28g sugars, 4g fiber), 15g pro.

S **M**

ALMOND-CHAI GRANOLA

My crunchy granola is great with milk or yogurt—or to snack on by the handful!
—Rachel Preus, Marshall, MI

Prep: 20 min.
Bake: 1 hour 20 min.
Makes: 8 cups

- 2 chai tea bags
- ¼ cup boiling water
- 3 cups quick-cooking oats
- 2 cups almonds, coarsely chopped
- 1 cup sweetened shredded coconut
- ½ cup honey
- ¼ cup olive oil
- ⅓ cup sugar
- 2 teaspoons vanilla extract
- ¾ teaspoon salt
- ¾ teaspoon ground cinnamon
- ¾ teaspoon ground nutmeg
- ¼ teaspoon ground cardamom

1. Preheat oven to 250°. Steep tea bags in boiling water 5 minutes. Meanwhile, combine oats, almonds and coconut. Discard tea bags; stir remaining ingredients into tea. Pour tea mixture over oat mixture; mix well to coat.
2. Spread evenly in a greased 15x10-in. rimmed pan. Bake until golden brown, stirring every 20 minutes, about 1¼ hours. Cool completely without stirring; store in an airtight container.
Per ½ cup: 272 cal., 16g fat (3g sat. fat), 0 chol., 130mg sod., 29g carb. (16g sugars, 4g fiber), 6g pro.
Diabetic exchanges: 3 fat, 2 starch.

CRISP CHOCOLATE CHIP WAFFLES

This variation on classic waffles is a great choice when you're in a rush. The recipe makes a big batch, so I freeze what I don't eat.
—Lauren Reiff, East Earl, PA

Prep: 15 min.
Cook: 5 min./batch
Makes: 12 waffles

1¼ cups all-purpose flour
¾ cup whole wheat flour
¼ cup quick-cooking oats
2 teaspoons baking powder
1 teaspoon sugar
¼ teaspoon salt
2 large eggs
1⅓ cups fat-free milk
2 tablespoons olive oil
1 tablespoon butter, melted
1 tablespoon honey
½ cup miniature semisweet chocolate chips

1. In a large bowl, whisk the first six ingredients. In another bowl, whisk eggs, milk, oil, butter and honey until blended. Add to the dry ingredients; stir just until moistened. Stir in chocolate chips.
2. Bake in a preheated waffle iron according to manufacturer's directions until golden brown.
Per 2 waffles: 339 cal., 13g fat (5g sat. fat), 77mg chol., 361mg sod., 49g carb. (15g sugars, 4g fiber), 10g pro.

TEST KITCHEN TIP
For fast homemade freezer waffles, bake and cool on a wire rack; freeze in a single layer on a baking sheet. When frozen, store in heavy-duty freezer bags. When ready to use, pop into the toaster or toaster oven to defrost and reheat.

CHICKEN BRUNCH BAKE

When my son was in high school, he told me this casserole was his favorite hot lunch meal. I serve it for brunch, but it can be enjoyed any time of day. Tender chunks of chicken give it a stick-to-your-ribs goodness that can't be beat.
—DeLee Jochum, Dubuque, IA

Prep: 10 min.
Bake: 1 hour
Makes: 8 servings

9 slices day-old bread, cubed
3 cups chicken broth
4 cups cubed cooked chicken
½ cup uncooked instant rice
½ cup diced pimientos
2 tablespoons minced fresh parsley
½ teaspoon salt, optional
4 large eggs, beaten

1. In a large bowl, toss bread cubes and broth. Add the chicken, rice, pimientos, parsley and, if desired, salt; mix well. Transfer mixture to a greased 13x9-in. baking dish. Pour eggs over all.
2. Bake, uncovered, at 325° for 1 hour or until a knife inserted near the center comes out clean.
Per serving: 233 cal., 6g fat (2g sat. fat), 62mg chol., 458mg sod., 18g carb. (2g sugars, 3g fiber), 27g pro.
Diabetic exchanges: 3 lean meat, 1 starch.

2. Meanwhile, in a large nonstick skillet coated with cooking spray, cook sausage and mushrooms over medium heat 4-6 minutes or until sausage is no longer pink and mushrooms are tender, breaking up sausage into crumbles. Drain and remove sausage mixture. Add hash browns, garlic salt and pepper to the same skillet; cook and stir until browned.

3. Sprinkle sausage mixture over prepared crust; layer with potatoes, green onions, red pepper and cheese. Carefully pour egg substitute over top. Bake 10-12 minutes or until egg is set and cheese is melted.

Per serving: 1 slice: 241 cal., 10g fat (2g sat. fat), 24mg chol., 744mg sod., 22g carb. (5g sugars, 1g fiber), 16g pro.
Diabetic exchanges: 2 lean meat, 1½ starch, ½ fat.

★ ★ ★ ★ ★ **READER REVIEW**

"Had to substitute Italian sausage so calories went up, but we loved the pizza. Made it also to take to a friend's get-together and everyone raved. Must take two next time."

GRANNYTWOSHOES
TASTEOFHOME.COM

FAST FIX ▶
SAUSAGE & EGG PIZZA

I love breakfast pizza, but not all the fat and calories that go with it. My lighter version gives you a big energy boost. It's just as good for lunch or dinner, too.
—Vicki Meyers, Castalia, OH

Start to Finish: 30 min.
Makes: 6 slices

- 1 tube (8 ounces) refrigerated reduced-fat crescent rolls
- ½ pound Italian turkey sausage links, casings removed
- 1¾ cups sliced fresh mushrooms
- 1¼ cups frozen shredded hash brown potatoes
- ¼ teaspoon garlic salt
- ¼ teaspoon pepper
- 2 green onions, chopped
- 2 tablespoons finely chopped sweet red pepper
- ½ cup shredded fat-free cheddar cheese
- ¾ cup egg substitute

1. Preheat oven to 375°. Unroll the crescent dough and separate into eight triangles; arrange triangles in a single layer on a greased 12-in. pizza pan. Press dough onto pan to form a crust and seal seams; pinch edge to form a rim. Bake crust for 8 minutes.

LEMON CHIA SEED PARFAITS

These bright and tangy parfaits start the day on a healthy note, but they're also sweet enough to double as a dessert.
—Crystal Schlueter, Northglenn, CO

Start to Finish: 15 min.
Makes: 4 servings

- 2 cups reduced-fat plain Greek yogurt
- ¼ cup agave nectar or honey
- 2 tablespoons lemon juice
- 2 teaspoons grated lemon peel
- 2 tablespoons chia seeds or ground flaxseed
- 1 teaspoon vanilla extract
- 1 cup fresh raspberries
- 1 cup fresh blueberries

Combine the first six ingredients. Layer half of the yogurt mixture into 4 small parfait glasses or custard cups. Top with half of the berries. Repeat layers.

HEALTH TIP Chia seeds are antioxidant-rich edible seeds high in omega-3 fatty acids, protein, fiber, calcium, vitamins and minerals. Their health benefits include supporting the heart and digestive system, building stronger bones and muscles, and reducing the risk of obesity and diabetes. Sprinkle them over cereal, yogurt, vegetable dishes and salads, or mix into smoothies, beverages or baked goods.

Per serving: 214 cal., 4g fat (2g sat. fat), 7mg chol., 48mg sod., 33g carb. (26g sugars, 5g fiber), 13g pro.
Diabetic exchanges: 1½ starch, ½ fruit, ½ reduced-fat milk.

VANILLA FRENCH TOAST

We discovered this recipe in Mexico. We couldn't figure out what made the French toast so delicious until we learned the secret was vanilla—one of Mexico's most popular flavorings. Since then, we've added a touch of vanilla to all our waffle and pancake recipes, and it makes all the difference.
—Joe and Bobbi Schott Castroville, TX

Start to Finish: 15 min.
Makes: 6 servings

- 4 large eggs, lightly beaten
- 1 cup 2% milk
- 2 tablespoons sugar
- 2 teaspoons vanilla extract
- ⅛ teaspoon salt
- 12 slices day-old sandwich bread
  Optional toppings: butter, maple syrup, fresh berries and confectioners' sugar

1. In a shallow dish, whisk together first five ingredients. Preheat a greased griddle over medium heat.
2. Dip bread in egg mixture, allowing to soak 30 seconds on each side. Cook on griddle until golden brown on both sides. Serve with toppings as desired.
Per 2 slices: 218 cal., 6g fat (3g sat. fat), 127mg chol., 376mg sod., 30g carb. (9g sugars, 1g fiber), 10g pro.
Diabetic exchanges: 2 starch, 1 medium-fat meat.

SAUSAGE-SWEET POTATO HASH & EGGS

When I first began making this dish for breakfast I served it with fried eggs on top. Now I sometimes make it for supper and serve it without eggs. It's great when I want a dish I can make quickly, with minimal clean-up.
—Nancy Murphy, Mount Dora, FL

Start to Finish: 25 min.
Makes: 4 servings

½ **pound Italian turkey sausage links, casings removed**

2 **medium sweet potatoes, peeled and cut into ¼-inch cubes**
2 **medium Granny Smith apples, chopped**
¼ **cup dried cranberries**
¼ **cup chopped pecans**
¼ **teaspoon salt**
4 **green onions, sliced**
4 **large eggs**

1. In a large nonstick skillet coated with cooking spray, cook sausage and sweet potatoes over medium-high heat 8-10 minutes or until sausage is no longer pink, breaking up sausage into crumbles.

2. Add apples, cranberries, pecans and salt; cook and stir 4-6 minutes longer or until potatoes are tender. Remove from pan; sprinkle with green onions. Keep warm.

3. Wipe skillet clean and coat with cooking spray; place skillet over medium-high heat. Break eggs, one at a time, into pan. Reduce heat to low. Cook to desired doneness, turning after whites are set if desired. Serve with hash.

Per serving: 338 cal., 14g fat (3g sat. fat), 207mg chol., 465mg sod., 42g carb. (23g sugars, 6g fiber), 15g pro.
Diabetic exchanges: 2 starch, 2 medium-fat meat, ½ fruit.

C SUNDAY BRUNCH EGG CASSEROLE

My favorite brunch dish got a makeover with egg substitute and low-fat cheese. The lightened-up version still tastes delicious, but it won't weigh you down!
—Alice Hofmann, Sussex, WI

Prep: 20 min.
Bake: 30 min.
Makes: 8 servings

- 6 bacon strips, chopped
- 1 teaspoon canola oil
- 1 small green pepper, chopped
- 1 small onion, chopped
- 4 large eggs
- 2 cartons (8 ounces each) egg substitute
- 1 cup fat-free milk
- ¾ teaspoon salt
- ½ teaspoon pepper
- ¼ teaspoon dill weed
- 4 cups frozen shredded hash brown potatoes, thawed
- 1 cup shredded reduced-fat cheddar cheese

1. Preheat oven to 350°. In a large skillet, cook the bacon over medium heat until crisp, stirring occasionally. Remove with a slotted spoon; drain on paper towels. Discard drippings.
2. In same skillet, heat oil over medium-high heat. Add pepper and onion; cook and stir until tender. Remove from heat.
3. In a large bowl, whisk eggs, egg substitute, milk and seasonings until blended. Stir in potatoes, cheese, bacon and pepper mixture.
4. Transfer mixture to a 13x9-in. baking dish coated with cooking spray. Bake 30-35 minutes or until a knife inserted near the center comes out clean.

Per 1 piece: 181 cal., 8g fat (3g sat. fat), 122mg chol., 591mg sod., 11g carb. (4g sugars, 1g fiber), 16g pro. **Diabetic exchanges:** 2 lean meat, 1 starch.

★ ★ ★ ★ ★ **READER REVIEW**

"My husband is diabetic, but he hates knowing he's eating like it. He loved this casserole!"

VALERIEMS
TASTEOFHOME.COM

Place half of each of the following in a blender: Greek yogurt, honey, melon, cucumber and, if desired, mint. Cover; process until blended. Add 1 cup ice; cover and process until smooth. Pour mixture into three glasses; repeat with the remaining ingredients.

Per 1 cup: 155 cal., 2g fat (1g sat. fat), 4mg chol., 48mg sod., 28g carb. (26g sugars, 2g fiber), 9g pro.

M **FAST FIX**
PEANUT BUTTER OATMEAL

My son and I eat this every day for breakfast. It's a hearty, healthy breakfast to jump-start our day.
—Elisabeth Reitenbach
Terryville, CT

Start to Finish: 15 min.
Makes: 2 servings

1¾ cups water
⅛ teaspoon salt
1 cup old-fashioned oats
2 tablespoons creamy peanut butter
2 tablespoons honey
2 teaspoons ground flaxseed
½ to 1 teaspoon ground cinnamon
Chopped apple, optional

In a small saucepan, bring water and salt to a boil. Stir in the oats; cook 5 minutes over medium heat, stirring occasionally. Transfer the oatmeal to individual bowls; stir in peanut butter, honey, flaxseed, cinnamon and, if desired, apple. Serve immediately.

Per ¾ cup: 323 cal., 12g fat (2g sat. fat), 0 chol., 226mg sod., 49g carb. (19g sugars, 6g fiber), 11g pro.

FAST FIX
SAUSAGE & SALSA BREAKFAST BURRITOS

My favorite breakfast foods are wrapped inside a whole wheat tortilla for a hand-held feast that makes a delish meal on the go.
—Michelle Burnett, Eden, UT

Start to Finish: 20 min.
Makes: 6 servings

5 breakfast turkey sausage links
2 cartons (8 ounces each) egg substitute
½ cup salsa
¼ teaspoon pepper
6 whole wheat tortilla (8 inches), warmed
½ cup shredded reduced-fat cheddar cheese

1. Cook sausage links according to the package directions. Meanwhile, in a large bowl, whisk the egg substitute, salsa and pepper. Pour into a large nonstick skillet coated with cooking spray. Cook and stir over medium heat until eggs are nearly set. Chop the sausage links. Add to egg mixture; cook and stir until completely set.
2. Spoon ⅓ cup egg mixture off center on each tortilla and sprinkle with 4 teaspoons cheese. Fold sides and ends over filling and roll up.

Per 1 burrito: 265 cal., 10g fat (3g sat. fat), 25mg chol., 602mg sod., 25g carb. (3g sugars, 2g fiber), 18g pro.
Diabetic exchanges: 2 lean meat, 1½ starch, 1 fat.

F **S** **M** **FAST FIX**
CUCUMBER MELON SMOOTHIES

A five-ingredient smoothie is the perfect thing for busy mornings. I sometimes add an avocado for extra creaminess.
—Crystal Schlueter
Northglenn, CO

Start to Finish: 15 min.
Makes: 6 servings

2 cups reduced-fat plain Greek yogurt
⅓ cup honey
3 cups chopped honeydew melon
2 medium cucumbers, peeled, seeded and chopped
1 to 2 tablespoons fresh mint leaves, optional
2 cups crushed ice cubes

GARDEN VEGGIE EGG BAKE

C M

PICTURED ON PAGE 22

Children will actually enjoy eating their veggies when they're baked into this cheesy, nutrition-packed egg dish.
—JoAnne Wilson, Roselle Park, NJ

Prep: 20 min.
Bake: 45 min. + standing
Makes: 6 servings

- 5 large eggs
- 2 cups egg substitute
- ½ cup 2% cottage cheese
- ⅓ cup shredded pepper jack cheese
- ⅓ cup shredded cheddar cheese
- ¼ cup grated Romano cheese
- ¼ teaspoon pepper
- ¼ teaspoon hot pepper sauce
- 1 medium zucchini, chopped
- 2 cups fresh broccoli florets
- 2 cups coarsely chopped fresh spinach
- ½ cup shredded carrots
- ½ cup cherry tomatoes, quartered

1. Preheat oven to 350°. In a large bowl, whisk eggs, egg substitute, cheeses, pepper and pepper sauce. Stir in the vegetables. Transfer to an 11x7-in. baking dish coated with cooking spray.
2. Bake, uncovered, 45-50 minutes or until a knife inserted near center comes out clean. Let stand 10 minutes before cutting.
Per 1 piece: 202 cal., 10g fat (5g sat. fat), 197mg chol., 478mg sod., 7g carb. (4g sugars, 2g fiber), 22g pro.
Diabetic exchanges: 3 lean meat, 1 vegetable, ½ fat.

NUTTY APPLE BUTTER

F S C M

I was born and raised in New England, and picking apples is one of my favorite pastimes. My love for the fruit—and peanut butter—inspired me to make this creamy PB&J riff. Use it as a dip for sliced fruit or graham crackers or spread it on toast.
—Brandie Cranshaw, Rapid City, SD

Prep: 20 min. • **Cook:** 8 hours
Makes: 5 cups

- 4 pounds apples (about 8 large), peeled and chopped
- ¾ to 1 cup sugar
- ¼ cup water
- 3 teaspoons ground cinnamon
- ¼ teaspoon ground nutmeg
- ¼ teaspoon ground cloves
- ¼ teaspoon ground allspice
- ¼ cup creamy peanut butter

1. In a greased 5-qt. slow cooker, combine the first seven ingredients. Cook, covered, on low 8-10 hours or until apples are tender.
2. Whisk in peanut butter until mixture is smooth. Cool to room temperature. Store in an airtight container in the refrigerator.
Per 2 tablespoons: 43 cal., 1g fat (0 sat. fat), 0 chol., 7mg sod., 9g carb. (8g sugars, 1g fiber), 0 pro.
Diabetic exchanges: ½ starch.

FAST FIX
CHORIZO & GRITS BREAKFAST BOWLS

Growing up, I bonded with Dad over breakfasts of chorizo and eggs. My fresh take on the dish includes grits and black beans. Add a spoonful of pico de gallo for extra flavor if desired.
—Jenn Tidwell, Fair Oaks, CA

Start to Finish: 30 min.
Makes: 6 servings

- 2 teaspoons olive oil
- 1 package (12 ounces) fully cooked chorizo chicken sausages or flavor of choice, sliced
- 1 large zucchini, chopped
- 3 cups water
- ¾ cup quick-cooking grits
- 1 can (15 ounces) black beans, rinsed and drained
- ½ cup shredded cheddar cheese
- 6 large eggs
  Pico de gallo and chopped fresh cilantro, optional

1. In a large nonstick skillet, heat oil over medium heat. Add sausage; cook and stir 2-3 minutes or until lightly browned. Add zucchini; cook and stir 4-5 minutes longer or until tender. Remove from the pan; keep warm.
2. Meanwhile, in a large saucepan, bring water to a boil. Slowly stir in the grits. Reduce heat to medium-low; cook grits, covered, about 5 minutes or until thickened, stirring occasionally. Stir in beans and cheese until blended. Remove from heat.
3. Wipe skillet clean; coat with cooking spray and place over medium heat. In batches, break eggs, one at a time, into pan. Immediately reduce heat to low; cook until whites are completely set and yolks begin to thicken but are not hard, about 5 minutes.
4. To serve, divide grits mixture among six bowls. Top with chorizo mixture, eggs and, if desired, pico de gallo and cilantro.

Note: Pulses like black beans are part of the legume family and a rich source of iron, which helps transport oxygen to muscles.
Per serving: 344 cal., 14g fat (5g sat. fat), 239mg chol., 636mg sod., 30g carb. (4g sugars, 4g fiber), 24g pro.
Diabetic exchanges: 3 medium-fat meat, 2 starch.

F S M FAST FIX
PEACH SMOOTHIE

Whip up this creamy concoction for a refreshing and nutritious snack. Frozen peaches work with equally good results.
—Martha Polasek, Markham, TX

Start to Finish: 5 min.
Makes: 2 servings

- ½ cup peach or apricot nectar
- ½ cup sliced fresh or frozen peaches
- ¼ cup fat-free vanilla yogurt
- 2 ice cubes

In a blender, combine all the ingredients. Cover and process until blended. Pour into chilled glasses; serve immediately.
Per ¾ cup: 68 cal., 0 fat (0 sat. fat), 1mg chol., 4mg sod., 16g carb. (14g sugars, 1g fiber), 2g pro.
Diabetic exchanges: 1 starch.

2. Spread evenly in a 15x10x1-in. baking pan coated with cooking spray. Bake 30-40 minutes or until golden brown, stirring every 10 minutes. Cool completely on a wire rack. Stir in cranberries and raisins. Store in an airtight container.

Per ½ cup: 255 cal., 10g fat (1g sat. fat), 0 chol., 84mg sod., 40g carb. (15g sugars, 5g fiber), 7g pro.

S M FAST FIX ▶

CREAMY BERRY SMOOTHIES

No one will know there's protein-packed tofu in these thick, silky smoothies. The blend of berries and pomegranate juice is a welcome delight.
—Sonya Labbe, West Hollywood, CA

Start to Finish: 10 min.
Makes: 2 servings

- ½ cup pomegranate juice
- 1 tablespoon agave syrup or honey
- 3 ounces silken firm tofu (about ½ cup)
- 1 cup frozen unsweetened mixed berries
- 1 cup frozen unsweetened strawberries

Place all ingredients in a blender; cover and process until blended. Serve immediately.

Per 1 cup: 157 cal., 1g fat (0 sat. fat), 0 chol., 24mg sod., 35g carb. (29g sugars, 3g fiber), 4g pro.

S M

GET-UP-AND-GO GRANOLA

My family loves this soul-warming granola as an energizing treat before hiking, biking or even when camping. It smells delicious while baking, and you can easily make it in large batches for special occasions or to send in gift packages to family and friends.
—Sabrina Olson, Otsego, MN

Prep: 15 min.
Bake: 30 min. + cooling
Makes: 7½ cups

- 6 cups old-fashioned oats
- ½ cup unblanched almonds, coarsely chopped
- ¼ cup packed brown sugar
- ¼ cup flaxseed
- ¼ cup canola oil
- ¼ cup honey
- 1 tablespoon maple syrup
- 1 teaspoon apple pie spice
- ½ teaspoon salt
- ½ teaspoon vanilla extract
- ½ cup dried cranberries
- ½ cup raisins

1. Preheat oven to 300°. In a large bowl, combine oats, almonds, brown sugar and flax. In a microwave-safe dish, whisk oil, honey, maple syrup, pie spice and salt. Microwave on high for 30-45 seconds or until heated through, stirring once. Stir in vanilla. Pour over oat mixture; toss to coat.

BRUNCH BANANA SPLITS

We love fruit and granola for breakfast. One day I decided to top it all with yogurt, nuts and honey and call it a split. Now I serve this dish on both busy mornings and special occasions.

—Nancy Heishman, Las Vegas, NV

Start to Finish: 10 min.
Makes: 4 servings

- 4 small bananas, peeled and halved lengthwise
- 2 cups (16 ounces) fat-free vanilla Greek yogurt
- 2 small peaches, sliced
- 1 cup fresh raspberries
- ½ cup granola without raisins
- 2 tablespoons sliced almonds, toasted
- 2 tablespoons sunflower kernels
- 2 tablespoons honey

Divide bananas among four shallow dishes. Top with the remaining ingredients.

Note: The carbohydrates and protein in yogurt help give you long-lasting energy. Yogurt is also a rich source of phosphorous, which is vital to energy production and storage.

Per serving: 340 cal., 6g fat (1g sat. fat), 0 chol., 88mg sod., 61g carb. (38g sugars, 9g fiber), 17g pro.

M **FAST FIX**

UPSIDE-DOWN PEAR PANCAKE

The fragrant fruit from the pear tree in my yard inspires me to bake. This upside-down pancake is a favorite. It works best with a firm, not fully ripe, pear.
—Helen Nelander, Boulder Creek, CA

Start to Finish: 30 min.
Makes: 2 servings

½ **cup all-purpose flour**
½ **teaspoon baking powder**
1 **large egg**
¼ **cup 2% milk**
1 **tablespoon butter**
1 **teaspoon sugar**
1 **medium pear, peeled and thinly sliced lengthwise**
Confectioners' sugar

1. Preheat oven to 375°. Whisk flour and baking powder. In a separate bowl, whisk egg and milk until blended. Add to the dry ingredients, stirring just until combined.

2. Meanwhile, in a small ovenproof skillet, melt butter over medium-low heat. Sprinkle with sugar. Add pear slices in a single layer; cook 5 minutes. Spread prepared batter over pears. Cover and cook until top is set, about 5 minutes.

3. Transfer pan to oven; bake until the edges are lightly brown, 8-10 minutes. Invert onto a serving plate. Sprinkle with confectioners' sugar. Serve warm.

Per ½ pancake: 274 cal., 9g fat (5g sat. fat), 111mg chol., 197mg sod., 41g carb. (12g sugars, 4g fiber), 8g pro.
Diabetic exchanges: 2 starch, 1½ fat, 1 medium-fat meat, ½ fruit.

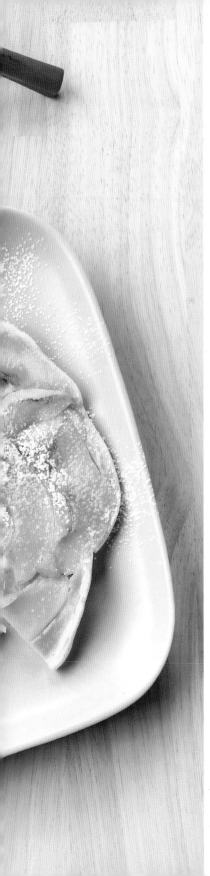

S **M**

RHUBARB COMPOTE WITH YOGURT & ALMONDS

My Grandma Dot used to make rhubarb compote and always had some in the freezer when I came to visit. This breakfast is a tribute to her. No two stalks of rhubarb are exactly alike, so make sure to taste your compote before you chill it. It should be tart, but sometimes needs a little extra sugar.
—Michael Hoffman, Brooklyn, NY

Prep: 10 min.
Cook: 15 min. + chilling
Makes: 6 servings

- 2 **cups finely chopped fresh rhubarb**
- ¼ **cup sugar**
- 2 **tablespoons water**
- 3 **cups reduced-fat plain Greek yogurt**
- 2 **tablespoons honey**
- ¾ **cup sliced almonds, toasted**

1. In a small saucepan, combine rhubarb, sugar and water. Bring to a boil. Reduce heat; simmer, uncovered, 10-15 minutes or until the rhubarb is tender, stirring occasionally. Transfer to a bowl; cool slightly. Refrigerate until cold.
2. In a small bowl, whisk yogurt and honey until blended. Spoon into serving dishes. Top with compote; sprinkle with almonds.
Note: To toast nuts, bake in a shallow pan in a 350° oven for 5-10 minutes or cook in a skillet over low heat until lightly browned, stirring occasionally.
Per ½ cup yogurt with about 2 tablespoons compote and 2 tablespoons almonds: 218 cal., 8g fat (2g sat. fat), 7mg chol., 49mg sod., 23g carb. (20g sugars, 2g fiber), 14g pro.
Diabetic exchanges: 1 starch, 1 reduced-fat milk, 1 fat.

Southwest Flank Steak
page 49

MEATY MAINSTAYS

Time to dig in to a hearty dinner! Whether you're following a special diet or not, these meaty entrees are sure to rise to the top of your list of most-requested meals.

G GREAT-GRANDMA'S ITALIAN MEATBALLS

A classic Italian dish isn't complete without homemade meatballs. This versatile recipe can be used in other dishes starring meatballs, too.
—Audrey Colantino, Winchester, MA

....

Prep: 30 min.
Bake: 20 min.
Makes: 8 servings

- 2 teaspoons olive oil
- 1 medium onion, chopped
- 3 garlic cloves, minced
- ¾ cup seasoned bread crumbs
- ½ cup grated Parmesan cheese
- 2 large eggs, lightly beaten
- 1 teaspoon each dried basil, oregano and parsley flakes
- ¾ teaspoon salt
- 1 pound lean ground turkey
- 1 pound lean ground beef (90% lean)
  Hot cooked pasta and pasta sauce, optional

1. Preheat oven to 375°. In a small skillet, heat oil over medium-high heat. Add onion; cook and stir 3-4 minutes or until tender. Add garlic; cook 1 minute longer. Cool slightly.

2. In a large bowl, combine bread crumbs, cheese, eggs, seasonings and onion mixture. Add turkey and beef; mix lightly but thoroughly. Shape into 1½-in. balls.

3. Place meatballs on a rack coated with cooking spray in a 15x10x1-in. baking pan. Bake 18-22 minutes or until lightly browned and cooked through. If desired, serve with pasta and pasta sauce.

Per serving: 271 cal., 13g fat (5g sat. fat), 125mg chol., 569mg sod., 10g carb. (1g sugars, 1g fiber), 27g pro.
Diabetic exchanges: 4 lean meat, 1 fat, ½ starch.

C
SALISBURY STEAK SUPREME

One night I was running late and wasn't sure what I could put on the table fast. Then a go-to recipe of my mom's popped into my head. It was a success, and now it's one of my husband's favorites.
—Patricia Swart, Galloway, NJ

....

Prep: 20 min.
Cook: 15 min.
Makes: 4 servings

2 medium red onions, divided
½ cup soft bread crumbs
¾ teaspoon salt-free seasoning blend
½ teaspoon pepper
   Dash ground nutmeg
1 pound lean ground beef (90% lean)
1 teaspoon cornstarch
1 teaspoon reduced-sodium beef bouillon granules
½ cup cold water
2 teaspoons butter
1½ cups sliced fresh mushrooms

1. Thinly slice 1½ onions; finely chop remaining onion half. In a large bowl, toss bread crumbs with chopped onion and seasonings. Add the beef; mix lightly but thoroughly. Shape meat mixture into four ½-in.-thick oval patties.
2. Place a large nonstick skillet coated with cooking spray over medium heat. Add patties; cook 5-6 minutes on each side or until a thermometer reads 160°. Remove from pan. Discard drippings from pan.
3. In a small bowl, mix cornstarch, bouillon and water until smooth. In same skillet, heat butter over medium-high heat. Add mushrooms and sliced onions; cook and stir 5-7 minutes or until onions are tender.
4. Stir in cornstarch mixture. Bring to a boil; cook and stir 1-2 minutes or until thickened. Return Salisbury steaks to pan, turning to coat with sauce; heat through.

Note: To make soft bread crumbs, tear bread into pieces and place in a food processor or blender. Cover and pulse until crumbs form. One slice of bread yields ½ to ¾ cup crumbs.
Per serving: 244 cal., 12g fat (5g sat. fat), 76mg chol., 192mg sod., 10g carb. (3g sugars, 1g fiber), 24g pro.
Diabetic exchanges: 3 lean meat, 1 starch, ½ fat.

FAST FIX ▶

HEARTY BEEF RAVIOLI

In this fun family-friendly supper, we add our favorite taco toppings to beef ravioli. It's easy for kids to customize their fixings for a no-fuss meal.
—*Taste of Home* Test Kitchen

Start to Finish: 25 min.
Makes: 6 servings

- 1   package (25 ounces) frozen beef ravioli
- ½   pound extra-lean ground beef (95% lean)
- 1   medium green pepper, chopped
- 1   can (14½ ounces) no-salt-added diced tomatoes, undrained
- 1   can (8 ounces) no-salt-added tomato sauce
- 2   tablespoons reduced-sodium taco seasoning
- ¾   cup shredded reduced-fat cheddar cheese
- 1   can (2¼ ounces) sliced ripe olives, drained

1. Cook ravioli according to package directions; drain.
2. Meanwhile, in a large nonstick skillet, cook beef and pepper over medium heat 4-6 minutes or until beef is no longer pink, breaking up beef into crumbles. Stir in tomatoes, tomato sauce and taco seasoning. Bring to a boil. Reduce heat; simmer, uncovered, until slightly thickened, 5-7 minutes.
3. Serve with ravioli. Top with cheese and olives.
Per serving: 375 cal., 10g fat (5g sat. fat), 44mg chol., 695mg sod., 49g carb. (7g sugars, 4g fiber), 21g pro.

PEPPER STEAK WITH SQUASH

My family loves this colorful stir-fry with savory strips of flank steak, colorful veggies and hot rice. It's a satisfying supper that's on the table in less than half an hour. If you like, add ginger, sesame oil or a touch of hoisin sauce to spice it up.
—Gayle Lewis, Yucaipa, CA

....

Start to Finish: 30 min.
Makes: 6 servings

- 1 can (14½ ounces) reduced-sodium beef broth
- 2 tablespoons reduced-sodium soy sauce
- 3 tablespoons cornstarch
- 2 tablespoons canola oil, divided
- 1 beef flank steak (1 pound), cut into thin strips
- 1 medium green pepper, cut into thin strips
- 1 medium sweet red pepper, cut into thin strips
- 2 medium zucchini, cut into thin strips
- 1 small onion, cut into thin strips
- 3 garlic cloves, minced
- 1 cup fresh snow peas
- 1 cup sliced fresh mushrooms
- 1 can (8 ounces) sliced water chestnuts, drained
  Hot cooked rice

1. Mix broth and soy sauce with cornstarch until smooth. Set aside.
2. In a large skillet or wok, heat 1 tablespoon oil over medium-high heat. Add beef; stir-fry until no longer pink, 2-3 minutes. Remove from pan.
3. In same skillet, heat remaining oil. Stir-fry peppers about 2 minutes. Add the zucchini, onion and garlic; cook and stir 2 minutes longer. Add snow peas, mushrooms and water chestnuts. Stir-fry until crisp-tender, about 2 minutes more.
4. Stir cornstarch mixture and add to pan. Bring to a boil; cook and stir until the sauce is thickened, 1-2 minutes. Return beef to skillet; heat through. Serve stir-fry with hot cooked rice.

Per 1½ cups stir-fry without rice: 229 cal., 11g fat (3g sat. fat), 37mg chol., 381mg sod., 16g carb. (5g sugars, 3g fiber), 18g pro.
Diabetic exchanges: 2 lean meat, 1 vegetable, ½ starch.

★ ★ ★ ★ ★ **READER REVIEW**

"Loved the beef with vegetables! We added ginger and sesame oil and that was a great flavor addition. I appreciate that it's healthy and comes together quickly."

CURLYLIS85 TASTEOFHOME.COM

SAUCY BEEF WITH BROCCOLI

I turn to this beef and broccoli stir-fry when I'm looking for a fast entree. It features a tantalizing sauce made with garlic and ginger.
—Rosa Evans, Odessa, MO

Start to Finish: 30 min.
Makes: 2 servings

- 1 tablespoon cornstarch
- ½ cup reduced-sodium beef broth
- ¼ cup sherry or additional beef broth
- 2 tablespoons reduced-sodium soy sauce
- 1 tablespoon brown sugar
- 1 garlic clove, minced
- 1 teaspoon minced fresh gingerroot
- 2 teaspoons canola oil, divided
- ½ pound beef top sirloin steak, cut into ¼-inch-thick strips
- 2 cups fresh small broccoli florets
- 8 green onions, cut into 1-inch pieces

1. Mix the first seven ingredients. In a large nonstick skillet, heat 1 teaspoon oil over medium-high heat; stir-fry beef until browned, 1-3 minutes. Remove from pan.

2. Stir-fry broccoli in remaining oil until crisp-tender, 3-5 minutes. Add the green onions; cook just until tender, 1-2 minutes. Stir cornstarch mixture and add to pan. Bring to a boil; cook and stir until sauce is thickened, 2-3 minutes. Add beef and heat through.

Per 1¼ cups: 313 cal., 11g fat (3g sat. fat), 68mg chol., 816mg sod., 20g carb. (11g sugars, 4g fiber), 29g pro.
Diabetic exchanges: 3 lean meat, 1 starch, 1 vegetable, 1 fat.

CHILI TORTILLA BAKE

A zesty Tex-Mex casserole is all it takes to gather the whole family around the dinner table. With its popular flavors and bubbly cheese topping, there is never a need to worry about leftovers.
—Celine Weldy, Cave Creek, AZ

Prep: 20 min. • **Bake:** 25 min.
Makes: 6 servings

- 1 **pound extra-lean ground beef (95% lean)**
- 2 **cans (8 ounces each) no-salt-added tomato sauce**
- 1 **can (15 ounces) black beans, rinsed and drained**
- 1 **cup frozen corn**
- 1 **can (4 ounces) chopped green chilies**
- 2 **tablespoons dried minced onion**
- 2 **tablespoons chili powder**
- 1 **teaspoon ground cumin**
- ½ **teaspoon garlic powder**
- ½ **teaspoon dried oregano**
- 6 **whole wheat tortillas (8 inches)**
- 1 **cup shredded reduced-fat cheddar cheese**

1. In a large skillet, cook beef over medium heat until no longer pink. Stir in the tomato sauce, beans, corn, green chilies, onion, chili powder, cumin, garlic powder and oregano; heat through.
2. In an 11x7-in. baking dish coated with cooking spray, layer half of the tortillas, beef mixture and cheese. Repeat layers. Bake, uncovered, at 350° for 25-30 minutes or until bubbly.
Freeze option: Cool unbaked casserole; cover and freeze. To use, partially thaw in refrigerator overnight. Remove from refrigerator 30 minutes before baking. Preheat oven to 350°. Bake casserole as directed, increasing time as necessary to heat through and for a thermometer inserted in center to read 165°.
Per 1 piece: 413 cal., 11g fat (4g sat. fat), 56mg chol., 590mg sod., 47g carb. (8g sugars, 8g fiber), 28g pro.

S C FAST FIX
SOUTHWEST FLANK STEAK
PICTURED ON PAGE 42

Marinades are great, but they can be time-consuming when you've got a hungry crowd to feed. The perfectly balanced rub in this dish imparts deep flavors without all the fuss.
—Kenny Fisher, Circleville, OH

Start to Finish: 25 min.
Makes: 6 servings

- 3 **tablespoons brown sugar**
- 3 **tablespoons chili powder**
- 4½ **teaspoons ground cumin**
- 1 **tablespoon garlic powder**
- 1 **tablespoon cider vinegar**
- 1½ **teaspoons Worcestershire sauce**
- ½ **teaspoon cayenne pepper**
- 1 **beef flank steak (1½ pounds)**

1. In a small bowl, combine the first seven ingredients; rub over steak.
2. On a greased grill rack, grill steak, covered, over medium heat or broil 4 in. from the heat until meat reaches desired doneness (for medium-rare, a thermometer should read 135°; medium, 140°; medium-well, 145°), 6-8 minutes on each side.
3. Let stand for 5 minutes. To serve, thinly slice across the grain.
Per 3 ounces cooked beef: 219 cal., 9g fat (4g sat. fat), 54mg chol., 127mg sod., 11g carb. (7g sugars, 2g fiber), 23g pro.
Diabetic exchanges: 3 lean meat, 1 starch.

SPINACH DIP BURGERS

Every Friday night is burger night at our house. The tomatoes add fresh flavor and the cool spinach dip brings it all together. We often skip the buns and serve these over a bed of grilled cabbage.
—Courtney Stultz, Weir, KS

Start to Finish: 20 min.
Makes: 4 servings

- 1 large egg, lightly beaten
- 2 tablespoons fat-free milk
- ½ cup soft bread crumbs
- 1 teaspoon dried basil
- ½ teaspoon salt
- ¼ teaspoon pepper
- 1 pound lean ground beef (90% lean)
- 4 whole wheat hamburger buns, split
- ¼ cup spinach dip
- ¼ cup julienned soft sun-dried tomatoes (not packed in oil)
  Lettuce leaves

1. Combine first six ingredients. Add the beef; mix lightly but thoroughly. Shape meat into four ½-in.-thick patties.
2. Place burgers on an oiled grill rack or in a greased 15x1x1-in. pan. Grill, covered, over medium heat or broil 4-5 in. from the heat until a thermometer reads 160°, 4-5 minutes per side. Grill buns, cut side down, over medium heat until toasted. Serve burgers on the buns; top with spinach dip, tomatoes and lettuce.

Per 1 burger: 389 cal., 17g fat (6g sat. fat), 125mg chol., 737mg sod., 29g carb. (7g sugars, 4g fiber), 29g pro.
Diabetic exchanges: 3 lean meat, 2 starch, 1½ fat.

SESAME BEEF SKEWERS

A bottle of sesame-ginger dressing makes this amazing dish doable on any weeknight. My pineapple-y salad easily caps off dinner. You can broil the beef, too, but we live in the South so we have the advantage of being able to grill outdoors all year long.
—Janice Elder, Charlotte, NC

Start to Finish: 30 min.
Makes: 4 servings

- 1 pound beef top sirloin steak, cut into 1-inch cubes
- 6 tablespoons sesame ginger salad dressing, divided
- 1 tablespoon reduced-sodium soy sauce
- 2 cups chopped fresh pineapple
- 2 medium apples, chopped
- 1 tablespoon sweet chili sauce
- 1 tablespoon lime juice
- ¼ teaspoon pepper
- 1 tablespoon sesame seeds, toasted

1. In a bowl, toss beef cubes with 3 tablespoons dressing and the soy sauce; let stand 10 minutes. Meanwhile, in a large bowl, combine pineapple, apples, chili sauce, lime juice and pepper; toss to combine.
2. Thread beef onto four metal or soaked wooden skewers; discard remaining marinade. Grill kabobs, covered, over medium heat or broil 4 in. from heat until desired doneness, 7-9 minutes, turning occasionally; brush generously with the remaining dressing during the last 3 minutes. Sprinkle with sesame seeds. Serve with the pineapple mixture.

Per 1 kabob with 1 cup salad: 311 cal., 11g fat (3g sat. fat), 46mg chol., 357mg sod., 28g carb. (21g sugars, 3g fiber), 25g pro.
Diabetic exchanges: 3 lean meat, 1 starch, 1 fruit, ½ fat.

¾ cup shredded reduced-fat cheddar cheese
5 tablespoons fat-free sour cream

1. In a large nonstick skillet coated with cooking spray, cook beef and peppers over medium heat for 6-8 minutes or until beef is no longer pink and vegetables are tender, breaking up beef into crumbles; drain. Stir in salsa, corn and water; bring to a boil.

2. Stir in tortilla strips. Reduce heat; simmer, covered, 10-15 minutes or until tortillas are softened. Sprinkle with cheese; cook, covered, 2-3 minutes longer or until cheese is melted. Serve with sour cream.

Freeze option: Freeze cooled meat mixture in freezer containers. To use, partially thaw in refrigerator overnight. Heat through in a saucepan, stirring occasionally and adding a little water if necessary. Serve with sour cream.

Per serving: 1 cup meat mixture with 1 tablespoon sour cream: 329 cal., 11g fat (5g sat. fat), 59mg chol., 679mg sod., 28g carb. (6g sugars, 6g fiber), 25g pro.

Diabetic exchanges: 3 lean meat, 1½ starch, 1 vegetable, ½ fat.

FAST FIX

SKILLET BEEF TAMALES

My southwestern skillet dinner is so cheesy and delicious that no one will guess it's light. It's sure to become a much-requested recipe.
—Deborah Williams, Peoria, AZ

Start to Finish: 30 min.
Makes: 5 servings

1 pound lean ground beef (90% lean)
⅓ cup chopped sweet red pepper
⅓ cup chopped green pepper
2 cups salsa
¾ cup frozen corn
2 tablespoons water
6 corn tortillas (6 inches), halved and cut into ½-inch strips

FAST FIX ▶
ONE-POT SAUCY BEEF ROTINI

My husband loves pasta, but I cringe over the messy dishes. On Spaghetti Day, as he calls it, I make a one-pot saucy rotini that keeps everyone happy.
—Lorraine Caland, Shuniah, ON

Start to Finish: 30 min.
Makes: 4 servings

- ¾ pound lean ground beef (90% lean)
- 2 cups sliced fresh mushrooms
- 1 medium onion, chopped
- 3 garlic cloves, minced
- ¾ teaspoon Italian seasoning
- 2 cups tomato basil pasta sauce
- ¼ teaspoon salt
- 2½ cups water
- 3 cups uncooked whole wheat rotini (about 8 ounces)
- ¼ cup grated Parmesan cheese

1. In a 6-qt. stockpot, cook the first five ingredients over medium-high heat 6-8 minutes or until beef is no longer pink, breaking up beef into crumbles; drain.

2. Add pasta sauce, salt and water; bring to a boil. Stir in rotini; return to a boil. Reduce heat; simmer, covered, 8-10 minutes or until pasta is al dente, stirring occasionally. Serve with cheese.

Per 1½ cups: 414 cal., 11g fat (4g sat. fat), 57mg chol., 806mg sod., 49g carb. (12g sugars, 8g fiber), 28g pro.

FAST FIX ▶
TEXAS TACOS

I created these tasty tacos by combining a variety of my family's favorite ingredients. I keep the beef mixture warm in a slow cooker so my kids can quickly stuff it into taco shells after an afternoon of rigorous soccer practice.
—Susan Scully, Mason, OH

Start to Finish: 30 min.
Makes: 10 servings

- 1½ pounds lean ground beef (90% lean)
- 1 medium sweet red pepper, chopped
- 1 small onion, chopped
- 1 can (14½ ounces) diced tomatoes, drained
- 1⅓ cups frozen corn, thawed
- 1 can (8 ounces) tomato sauce
- 2 tablespoons chili powder
- ½ teaspoon salt
- 1 package (8.8 ounces) ready-to-serve brown rice
- 20 taco shells, warmed
  Optional toppings: shredded lettuce, chopped fresh tomatoes and reduced-fat sour cream

1. In a Dutch oven, cook beef, red pepper and onion over medium heat 8-10 minutes or until beef is no longer pink and vegetables are tender, breaking up beef into crumbles. Drain.

2. Stir in tomatoes, corn, tomato sauce, chili powder and salt; bring to a boil. Add rice; heat through. Serve in taco shells with toppings of your choice.

Per 2 tacos: 294 cal., 11g fat (4g sat. fat), 42mg chol., 420mg sod., 30g carb. (3g sugars, 3g fiber), 17g pro.
Diabetic exchanges: 2 starch, 2 lean meat.

ASIAN BEEF & NOODLES

I created this dish on a whim to feed my kids one night when they were hungry teenagers. It has since become a dinnertime staple.
—Judy Batson, Tampa, FL

Start to Finish: 25 min.
Makes: 4 servings

- 1 beef top sirloin steak (1 pound), cut into ¼-inch-thick strips
- 6 tablespoons reduced-sodium teriyaki sauce, divided
- 8 ounces uncooked whole grain thin spaghetti
- 2 tablespoons canola oil, divided
- 3 cups broccoli coleslaw mix
- 1 medium onion, halved and thinly sliced
  Chopped fresh cilantro, optional

1. Toss beef with 2 tablespoons teriyaki sauce. Cook spaghetti noodles according to the package directions; drain.
2. In a skillet, heat 1 tablespoon oil over medium-high heat; stir-fry beef until browned, 1-3 minutes. Remove from pan.
3. In same skillet, heat remaining oil over medium-high heat; stir-fry coleslaw mix and onion until crisp-tender, 3-5 minutes. Add spaghetti and remaining teriyaki sauce; toss and heat through. Stir in beef strips. If desired, sprinkle with cilantro.
Per 2 cups: 462 cal., 13g fat (2g sat. fat), 46mg chol., 546mg sod., 52g carb., 8g fiber, 35g pro.

C ZIPPY SIRLOIN STEAK

The homemade rub on this steak packs a punch, and it's easy to mix together. If you have leftover steak, add slices to mixed greens for a tasty next-day salad.
—Lisa Finnegan, Forked River, NJ

Prep: 15 min. + marinating
Grill: 20 min.
Makes: 6 servings

- 1 tablespoon paprika
- 2 teaspoons pepper
- 1½ teaspoons kosher salt
- 1½ teaspoons brown sugar
- 1½ teaspoons ground cumin
- 1½ teaspoons chili powder
- 1 teaspoon sugar
- ¼ teaspoon cayenne pepper
- 1 beef sirloin tip steak (1½ pounds)

1. In a small bowl, combine the first eight ingredients. Rub over both sides of beef. Cover and refrigerate for 2 hours.
2. Grill beef, covered, over medium heat on an oiled rack or broil 4 in. from the heat for 8-10 minutes on each side or until meat reaches desired doneness (for medium-rare, a thermometer should read 135°; medium, 140°; medium-well, 145°). Let stand for 5 minutes before slicing.
Per 3 ounces cooked beef: 160 cal., 6g fat (2g sat. fat), 73mg chol., 512mg sod., 3g carb. (2g sugars, 1g fiber), 23g pro.
Diabetic exchanges: 3 lean meat.

MEXICAN FIESTA STEAK STIR-FRY

The best part of throwing a weeknight party is being able to enjoy time with family. With this flavorful stir-fry on the menu, you'll be out of the kitchen with time to spare!
—Patricia Swart, Galloway, NJ

Start to Finish: 30 min.
Makes: 4 servings

- 1 pound boneless beef top loin steak, trimmed and cut into thin strips
- 3 garlic cloves, minced
- 1 to 2 tablespoons canola oil
- 1 package (14 ounces) frozen pepper strips, thawed
- 1⅓ cups chopped sweet onion
- 2 plum tomatoes, chopped
- 1 can (4 ounces) chopped green chilies
- ½ teaspoon salt
- ½ teaspoon dried oregano
- ¼ teaspoon pepper
  Hot cooked rice

1. In a large skillet or wok, stir-fry beef and garlic in oil until meat is no longer pink. Remove from pan and keep warm.
2. Add peppers and onion to pan; stir-fry until tender. Stir in the tomatoes, chilies, salt, oregano, pepper and beef; heat through. Serve with rice.
Per 1½ cups without rice: 247 cal., 9g fat (2g sat. fat), 50mg chol., 473mg sod., 13g carb. (7g sugars, 3g fiber), 26g pro.
Diabetic exchanges: 3 lean meat, 2 vegetable, 1 fat.

BRUSCHETTA STEAK

My husband and I love bruschetta, especially in the summertime with fresh tomatoes and herbs from our garden.
—Kristy Still, Broken Arrow, OK

Start to Finish: 25 min.
Makes: 4 servings

- 3 medium tomatoes, chopped
- 3 tablespoons minced fresh basil
- 3 tablespoons chopped fresh parsley
- 2 tablespoons olive oil
- 1 teaspoon minced fresh oregano or ½ teaspoon dried oregano
- 1 garlic clove, minced
- ¾ teaspoon salt, divided
- 1 beef flat iron or top sirloin steak (1 pound), cut into four portions
- ¼ teaspoon pepper
  Grated Parmesan cheese, optional

1. Combine first six ingredients; stir in ¼ teaspoon salt.
2. Sprinkle beef with pepper and remaining salt. Grill, covered, over medium heat or broil 4 in. from heat until meat reaches desired doneness (for medium-rare, a thermometer should read 135°; medium, 140°), 4-6 minutes per side. Top with tomato mixture. If desired, sprinkle with cheese.
Per 1 steak with ½ cup tomato mixture: 280 cal., 19g fat (6g sat. fat), 73mg chol., 519mg sod., 4g carb. (2g sugars, 1g fiber), 23g pro.
Diabetic exchanges: 3 lean meat, 1½ fat, 1 vegetable.

MAKEOVER BEEF STROGANOFF

I trimmed the calories, fat and sodium in a classic Stroganoff, and my comfy, cozy version still tastes like a culinary masterpiece.
—Candace Clark, Kelso, WA

Start to Finish: 30 min.
Makes: 6 servings

- ½ cup plus 1 tablespoon all-purpose flour, divided
- ½ teaspoon pepper, divided
- 1 beef top round steak (1½ pounds), cut into thin strips
- 2 tablespoons canola oil
- 1 cup sliced fresh mushrooms
- 1 small onion, chopped
- 1 garlic clove, minced
- 1 can (14½ ounces) reduced-sodium beef broth
- ½ teaspoon salt
- 1 cup (8 ounces) reduced-fat sour cream
  Chopped fresh parsley, optional
  Coarsely ground pepper, optional
- 3 cups cooked yolk-free noodles

1. Combine ½ cup flour and ¼ teaspoon pepper in a large resealable plastic bag. Add the beef, a few pieces at a time, and shake to coat.

2. In a large nonstick skillet, heat oil over medium-high heat. Cook beef in batches until no longer pink. Remove and keep warm. In same skillet, saute mushrooms and onion in drippings until tender. Add garlic; cook 1 minute longer.

3. Whisk the remaining flour with broth until smooth; stir into skillet. Bring to a boil; cook and stir until thickened, about 2 minutes. Add beef, salt and remaining pepper. Stir in sour cream; heat through (do not boil). If desired, sprinkle with parsley and coarsely ground pepper. Serve with noodles.

Per 1 cup beef stroganoff with ½ cup noodles: 349 cal., 12g fat (4g sat. fat), 78mg chol., 393mg sod., 25g carb. (5g sugars, 2g fiber), 33g pro. **Diabetic exchanges:** 3 lean meat, 2 fat, 1½ starch.

8   ounces uncooked
    whole wheat spaghetti,
    broken in half
¼   cup grated Parmesan
    cheese
    Additional chopped parsley

1. In a 6-qt. stockpot, cook and crumble beef with garlic over medium heat until no longer pink, 5-7 minutes. Stir in sugar and seasonings. Add tomatoes, tomato sauce, water and ¼ cup parsley; bring to a boil. Reduce heat; simmer, covered, 5 minutes.
2. Stir in spaghetti, a little at a time; return to a boil. Reduce heat to medium-low; cook, uncovered, until spaghetti is al dente, 8-10 minutes, stirring occasionally. Stir in cheese. Sprinkle with additional chopped parsley.
Per 1⅓ cups: 292 cal., 6g fat (2g sat. fat), 46mg chol., 737mg sod., 40g carb. (6g sugars, 8g fiber), 24g pro.
Diabetic exchanges: 3 starch, 2 lean meat.

TEST KITCHEN TIP
To prevent spaghetti from sticking together when cooking, use a large kettle or Dutch oven and 3 quarts of water for every 8 ounces of pasta you plan to cook. Then add 1 tablespoon olive or vegetable oil to the water. (This will also help prevent it from boiling over.) Be sure the water has come to a full rolling boil before stirring in the pasta. Then stir several times while the pasta is cooking to separate the strands.

FAST FIX
ONE-POT MEATY SPAGHETTI

I used to help my mom make this pasta when I was growing up, and the recipe stuck.
It was a beloved comfort food at college, and is now a weeknight staple for my fiance and me.
—Kristin Michalenko, Seattle, WA

Start to Finish: 30 min.
Makes: 6 servings

1   pound extra-lean ground
    beef (95% lean)
2   garlic cloves, minced
1   teaspoon sugar
1   teaspoon dried basil
½   teaspoon dried oregano
¼   teaspoon salt
¼   teaspoon paprika
¼   teaspoon pepper
1   can (28 ounces) diced
    tomatoes, undrained
1   can (15 ounces)
    tomato sauce
2   cups water
¼   cup chopped fresh parsley

POTATO-TOPPED GROUND BEEF SKILLET

The depth of flavor in this recipe is amazing. I never have leftovers when I take it to potlucks. I love recipes that I can cook and serve in the same skillet.

—Fay Moreland, Wichita Falls, TX

Prep: 25 min. • **Cook:** 45 min.
Makes: 8 servings

- 2 pounds lean ground beef (90% lean)
- ½ teaspoon salt
- ¼ teaspoon pepper
- 1 tablespoon olive oil
- 1 large onion, chopped
- 4 medium carrots, sliced
- 8 ounces sliced fresh mushrooms
- 4 garlic cloves, minced
- 2 tablespoons all-purpose flour
- 2 teaspoons herbes de Provence
- 1¼ cups dry red wine or reduced-sodium beef broth
- 1 can (14½ ounces) reduced-sodium beef broth

TOPPING
- 1¼ pounds red potatoes (about 4 medium), cut into ¼-inch slices
- 1 tablespoon olive oil
- ¼ teaspoon salt
- ⅛ teaspoon pepper
- ⅓ cup shredded Parmesan cheese
  Minced fresh parsley, optional

1. In a broiler-safe 12-in. skillet, cook and crumble the beef over medium-high heat until no longer pink, 6-8 minutes. Stir in salt and pepper; remove from pan.

2. In same pan, heat the oil over medium-high heat; saute the onion, carrots, mushrooms and garlic until onion is tender, 4-6 minutes. Stir in flour and herbs; cook for 1 minute. Stir in the wine; bring to a boil. Cook 1 minute, stirring to loosen the browned bits from pan. Add beef and broth; return to a boil. Reduce heat; simmer, covered, until flavors are blended, about 30 minutes, stirring occasionally. Remove pan from heat.

3. Meanwhile, place potatoes in a large saucepan; add water to cover. Bring to a boil. Reduce heat; cook, uncovered, until tender, 10-12 minutes. Drain; cool slightly.

4. Preheat broiler. Arrange potatoes over stew, overlapping slightly; brush lightly with oil. Sprinkle with salt and pepper, then cheese. Broil 5-6 in. from heat until potatoes are lightly browned, 6-8 minutes. Let stand 5 minutes. If desired, sprinkle with parsley.

Per 1¼ cups: 313 cal., 14g fat (5g sat. fat), 74mg chol., 459mg sod., 18g carb. (4g sugars, 3g fiber), 26g pro.
Diabetic exchanges: 3 lean meat, ½ starch, 1 vegetable, ½ fat.

resealable plastic bag; refrigerate 6 hours or overnight, turning occasionally.

2. Grill steaks, covered, over medium heat or broil 4 in. from heat until meat reaches desired doneness (for medium-rare, a thermometer should read 135°; medium, 140°; medium-well, 145°), 6-9 minutes on each side.

3. Let steaks stand 5 minutes. Thinly slice across the grain.

Per 3 ounces cooked beef: 187 cal., 10g fat (4g sat. fat), 54mg chol., 259mg sod., 2g carb. (0 sugars, 0 fiber), 22g pro.

Diabetic exchanges: 3 lean meat, 1 fat.

SOUTHWEST STEAK

My husband and I make an easy marinade that bumps our grilled steak up to a whole new level. Lime juice tenderizes the meat while garlic, chili powder and red pepper flakes kick up the flavor.
—Caroline Shively, New York, NY

Prep: 15 min. + marinating
Grill: 15 min.
Makes: 8 servings

- ¼ cup lime juice
- 6 garlic cloves, minced
- 4 teaspoons chili powder
- 4 teaspoons canola oil
- 1 teaspoon salt
- 1 teaspoon crushed red pepper flakes
- 1 teaspoon pepper
- 2 beef flank steaks (1 pound each)

1. In a small bowl, mix the first seven ingredients; spread over both sides of steaks. Place in a large

SPAGHETTI SQUASH MEATBALL CASSEROLE

One of our favorite comfort foods is spaghetti and meatballs. We love this light, healthy version that features a bounty of veggies and fewer carbs.
—Courtney Stultz, Weir, KS

Prep: 35 min.
Bake: 30 min.
Makes: 6 servings

- 1 medium spaghetti squash (about 4 pounds)
- ½ teaspoon salt, divided
- ½ teaspoon fennel seed
- ¼ teaspoon ground coriander
- ¼ teaspoon dried basil
- ¼ teaspoon dried oregano
- 1 pound lean ground beef (90% lean)
- 2 teaspoons olive oil
- 1 medium onion, chopped
- 1 garlic clove, minced
- 2 cups chopped collard greens

- 1 cup chopped fresh spinach
- 1 cup reduced-fat ricotta cheese
- 2 plum tomatoes, chopped
- 1 cup pasta sauce
- 1 cup shredded part-skim mozzarella cheese

1. Cut squash lengthwise in half; discard seeds. Place halves on a microwave-safe plate, cut side down. Microwave, uncovered, on high until tender, 15-20 minutes. Cool slightly.

2. Preheat oven to 350°. Mix ¼ teaspoon salt with remaining seasonings; add to beef, mixing lightly but thoroughly. Shape into 1½-in. balls. In a large skillet, brown meatballs over medium heat; remove from pan.

3. In same pan, heat oil over medium heat; saute onion until tender, 3-4 minutes. Add garlic; cook and stir 1 minute. Stir in collard greens, spinach, ricotta cheese and remaining salt; remove from heat.

4. Using a fork, separate strands of spaghetti squash; stir into greens mixture. Transfer to a greased 13x9-in. baking dish. Top with tomatoes, meatballs, sauce and cheese. Bake, uncovered, until meatballs are cooked through, 30-35 minutes.

Per serving: 362 cal., 16g fat (6g sat. fat), 69mg chol., 618mg sod., 32g carb. (7g sugars, 7g fiber), 26g pro.

Diabetic exchanges: 3 lean meat, 2 starch, 1 fat.

1 cup dry red wine or reduced-sodium beef broth
2 tablespoons red currant jelly
2 bay leaves
2 fresh oregano sprigs
1 can (15 ounces) white kidney or cannellini beans, rinsed and drained
Minced fresh parsley, optional

1. Preheat oven to 350°. Toss beef with flour and steak seasoning.
2. In an ovenproof Dutch oven, heat 1 tablespoon oil over medium heat. Brown beef in batches; remove with a slotted spoon.
3. In same pan, heat remaining oil over medium heat. Add onion, celery, parsnips and carrots; cook and stir until onion is tender. Add garlic; cook 1 minute longer. Stir in tomatoes, wine, jelly, bay leaves, oregano and beef; bring to a boil.
4. Bake, covered, 1½ hours. Stir in the beans; bake, covered, until beef and vegetables are tender, 30-40 minutes longer. Remove bay leaves and oregano sprigs. If desired, sprinkle with parsley.

Freeze option Freeze cooled stew in freezer containers. To use, partially thaw in refrigerator overnight. Heat through in a saucepan, stirring occasionally and adding a little broth or water if necessary.

Per 1 cup: 310 cal., 9g fat (3g sat. fat), 64mg chol., 373mg sod., 26g carb. (8g sugars, 5g fiber), 25g pro.
Diabetic exchanges: 3 lean meat, 1 starch, 1 vegetable, 1 fat.

WINTERTIME BRAISED BEEF STEW

This wonderful beef stew makes an easy Sunday meal. It's even better a day or two later, so we make a double batch for leftovers.
—Michaela Rosenthal, Woodland Hills, CA

Prep: 40 min. • **Bake:** 2 hours
Makes: 8 servings (2 quarts)

2 pounds boneless beef sirloin steak or chuck roast, cut into 1-inch pieces
2 tablespoons all-purpose flour
2 teaspoons Montreal steak seasoning
2 tablespoons olive oil, divided
1 large onion, chopped
2 celery ribs, chopped
2 medium parsnips, peeled and cut into 1½-inch pieces
2 medium carrots, peeled and cut into 1½-inch pieces
2 garlic cloves, minced
1 can (14½ ounces) diced tomatoes, undrained

RICH BAKED SPAGHETTI

Baked spaghetti takes a bit longer to make than stovetop pasta, but the difference in taste, texture and richness is well worth the time. I serve this lasagna-style dish with a tossed green salad and breadsticks for a hearty meal.
—Betty Rabe, Mahtomedi, MN

....

Prep: 20 min.
Bake: 30 min. + standing
Makes: 6 servings

- 8 **ounces uncooked spaghetti, broken into thirds**
- 1 **large egg**
- ½ **cup fat-free milk**
- ½ **pound lean ground beef (90% lean)**
- ½ **pound Italian turkey sausage links, casings removed**
- 1 **small onion, chopped**
- ¼ **cup chopped green pepper**
- 1 **jar (14 ounces) meatless spaghetti sauce**
- 1 **can (8 ounces) no-salt-added tomato sauce**
- ½ **cup shredded part-skim mozzarella cheese**

1. Cook spaghetti according to package directions; drain. In a large bowl, beat egg and milk. Add the spaghetti; toss to coat. Transfer to a 13x9-in. baking dish coated with cooking spray.

2. In a large skillet, cook the beef, sausage, onion and green pepper over medium heat until meat is no longer pink; drain. Stir in spaghetti sauce and tomato sauce. Spoon over the spaghetti mixture.

3. Bake, uncovered, at 350° for 20 minutes. Sprinkle with the cheese. Bake 10 minutes longer or until cheese is melted. Let stand for 10 minutes before cutting.

Per serving: 343 cal., 10g fat (3g sat. fat), 87mg chol., 616mg sod., 39g carb. (9g sugars, 3g fiber), 23g pro.
Diabetic exchanges: 2 starch, 2 medium-fat meat, 1 vegetable.

CHEESEBURGER MACARONI SKILLET

This is the ultimate satisfying skillet. It's convenient, too, because it calls for items I typically have on hand in my pantry. And since everything is cooked in one pan, cleanup is a snap!
—Juli Meyers, Hinesville, GA

Start to Finish: 30 min.
Makes: 6 servings

- 1 pound lean ground beef (90% lean)
- 8 ounces uncooked whole wheat elbow macaroni
- 3 cups reduced-sodium beef broth
- ¾ cup fat-free milk
- 3 tablespoons ketchup
- 2 teaspoons Montreal steak seasoning
- 1 teaspoon prepared mustard
- ¼ teaspoon onion powder
- 1 cup (4 ounces) shredded reduced-fat cheddar cheese
  Minced chives

1. In a large skillet, cook beef over medium heat 6-8 minutes or until no longer pink, breaking into crumbles; drain.
2. Stir in macaroni, broth, milk, ketchup, steak seasoning, mustard and onion powder; bring to a boil. Reduce heat; simmer, uncovered, 10-15 minutes or until macaroni is tender. Stir in cheese until melted. Sprinkle with chives.
Per 1 cup: 338 cal., 11g fat (5g sat. fat), 64mg chol., 611mg sod., 32g carb. (5g sugars, 4g fiber), 27g pro.

SAUCY BEEF & CABBAGE SUPPER

My beef and cabbage supper began as a way to enjoy all the flavors of a Reuben sandwich minus the gluten. It's also great with smoked sausage.
—Courtney Stultz, Weir, KS

Prep: 15 min.
Cook: 20 min.
Makes: 6 servings

- 1 pound lean ground beef (90% lean)
- 1 medium onion, chopped
- 2 large garlic cloves, minced
- 1 small head cabbage, chopped (about 8 cups)
- 5 medium carrots, peeled and diced
- 3 tablespoons olive oil, divided
- 1 teaspoon salt
- 1 teaspoon pepper
- ½ teaspoon caraway seeds
- ¼ teaspoon ground allspice
- ⅛ teaspoon ground cloves
- ½ cup ketchup
- 2 teaspoons cider vinegar

1. In a 6-qt. stockpot, cook and crumble beef with onion and garlic over medium-high heat until no longer pink, 5-7 minutes. Stir in cabbage, carrots, 2 tablespoons oil and seasonings; cook and stir until vegetables are slightly softened, 7-11 minutes.
2. Stir in ketchup, vinegar and remaining oil. Cook, uncovered, 5 minutes, stirring occasionally.
Per 1¼ cups: 260 cal., 13g fat (3g sat. fat), 47mg chol., 671mg sod., 20g carb. (12g sugars, 5g fiber), 17g pro.
Diabetic exchanges: 2 lean meat, 2 vegetable, 1½ fat, ½ starch.

Spicy Apricot-Glazed
Chicken *page 71*

CHICKEN & TURKEY DINNERS

Chicken and turkey are great lean protein choices that everyone enjoys. Tonight, shake up your usual dinner routine with these flavorful poultry options.

GINGER VEGGIE BROWN RICE PASTA

Once I discovered brown rice pasta, I never looked back. Tossed with ginger, veggies and rotisserie chicken, this dish tastes like a deconstructed egg roll! It's great for anyone who is on a gluten-free diet.
—Tiffany Ihle, Bronx, NY

....

Start to Finish: 30 min.
Makes: 8 servings

- 2 cups uncooked brown rice elbow pasta
- 1 tablespoon coconut oil
- ½ small red onion, sliced
- 2 teaspoons ginger paste
- 2 teaspoons garlic paste
- 1½ cups chopped fresh Brussels sprouts
- ½ cup chopped red cabbage
- ½ cup shredded carrots
- ½ medium sweet red pepper, chopped
- ½ teaspoon salt
- ¼ teaspoon ground ancho chili pepper
- ¼ teaspoon coarsely ground pepper
- 1 shredded rotisserie chicken, skin removed
- 2 green onions, chopped

1. In a Dutch oven, cook pasta according to package directions.

2. Meanwhile, in a large skillet, heat coconut oil over medium heat. Add red onion, ginger paste and garlic paste; saute 2 minutes. Stir in the next seven ingredients; cook until the vegetables are crisp-tender, 4-6 minutes. Add the chicken; heat through.

3. Drain the pasta, reserving 1 cup pasta water. Return the pasta to the Dutch oven. Add the vegetable mixture; toss to coat, adding enough reserved pasta water to moisten pasta. Sprinkle with green onions before serving.

Per 1 cup: 270 cal., 7g fat (3g sat. fat), 55mg chol., 257mg sod., 29g carb. (2g sugars, 2g fiber), 21g pro.
Diabetic exchanges: 3 lean meat, 2 starch, 1 fat.

SAUSAGE-STUFFED BUTTERNUT SQUASH

I fill butternut squash shells with an Italian turkey sausage and squash mixture for a quick and easy meal. The squash is sweet when roasted in the oven. Even better, it's loaded with nutrients and low in calories.
—Katia Slinger, West Jordan, UT

....

Start to Finish: 30 min.
Makes: 4 servings

- 1 medium butternut squash (about 3 pounds)
- 1 pound Italian turkey sausage links, casings removed
- 1 medium onion, finely chopped
- 4 garlic cloves, minced
- ½ cup shredded Italian cheese blend
  Crushed red pepper flakes, optional

1. Preheat broiler. Cut squash lengthwise in half; discard seeds. Place squash in a large microwave-safe dish, cut side down; add ½ in. of water. Microwave, covered, on high until soft, 20-25 minutes. Let squash cool slightly.

2. Meanwhile, in a large nonstick skillet, cook and crumble sausage with onion over medium-high heat until no longer pink, 5-7 minutes. Add garlic; cook and stir 1 minute.

3. Leaving ½-in.-thick shells, scoop pulp from squash and stir into sausage mixture. Place squash shells on a baking sheet; fill each shell with sausage mixture. Sprinkle with cheese.

4. Broil 4-5 in. from heat until the cheese is melted, 1-2 minutes. If desired, sprinkle with pepper flakes. To serve, cut each squash half into two portions.

HEALTH TIP Butternut squash is an excellent source of vitamin A in the form of beta carotene, which is important for normal vision and a healthy immune system.

Note: This recipe was tested in a 1,100-watt microwave.

Per serving: 325 cal., 10g fat (4g sat. fat), 52mg chol., 587mg sod., 44g carb. (10g sugars, 12g fiber), 19g pro.
Diabetic exchanges: 3 starch, 3 lean meat.

TEST KITCHEN TIP
Butternut squash, a winter squash variety, has a hardy outer shell with flavorful flesh on the inside. Winter squash are harvested in the fall but can be stored for use throughout the winter, hence their name. Look for squash that feel heavy for their size and have hard, deep-colored rinds that are free of blemishes. Unwashed winter squash can be stored in a dry, cool, well-ventilated place for up to 1 month.

½ cup grated Parmesan cheese
½ cup finely chopped walnuts
1 teaspoon lemon-pepper seasoning
1 package (20 ounces) turkey breast tenderloins
¼ teaspoon salt
¼ teaspoon pepper
3 tablespoons olive oil, divided
Additional fresh basil

1. Whisk together the first five ingredients. Stir in green pepper, celery, onion and basil. Cut the tomatoes into wedges; cut wedges in half. Stir into pepper mixture.
2. In a shallow bowl, whisk together the egg and lemon juice. In another shallow bowl, toss bread crumbs with cheese, walnuts and lemon pepper.
3. Cut tenderloins crosswise into 1-in. slices; flatten slices with a meat mallet to ½-in. thickness. Sprinkle with salt and pepper. Dip in egg mixture, then in crumb mixture, patting to adhere.
4. In a skillet, heat 1 tablespoon oil over medium-high heat. Add a third of the turkey tenderloins; cook until golden brown, 2-3 minutes per side. Repeat twice with remaining oil and turkey. Serve with tomato mixture; sprinkle with basil.

HEALTH TIP At just 13 grams of carbohydrates, this is a hearty option for anyone looking to cut carbs.

Per serving: 351 cal., 21g fat (3g sat. fat), 68mg chol., 458mg sod., 13g carb. (4g sugars, 2g fiber), 29g pro.

C

TURKEY MEDALLIONS WITH TOMATO SALAD

This is a quick-to-cook meal using turkey tenderloins coated with crispy bread crumbs. The turkey is enhanced by the bright flavor of a simple tomato salad.
—Gilda Lester, Millsboro, DE

Prep: 30 min. • **Cook:** 15 min.
Makes: 6 servings

2 tablespoons olive oil
1 tablespoon red wine vinegar
½ teaspoon sugar
¼ teaspoon dried oregano
¼ teaspoon salt
1 medium green pepper, coarsely chopped
1 celery rib, coarsely chopped
¼ cup chopped red onion
1 tablespoon thinly sliced fresh basil
3 medium tomatoes
TURKEY MEDALLIONS
1 large egg
2 tablespoons lemon juice
1 cup panko (Japanese) bread crumbs

SPICY APRICOT-GLAZED CHICKEN

F **FAST FIX**

PICTURED ON PAGE 66

Before you make a grocery run for dinner tonight, check your fridge. Plain chicken turns sweet and hot when you pull out the chili sauce, mustard and apricot preserves.
—Sonya Labbe
West Hollywood, CA

Start to Finish: 20 min.
Makes: 4 servings

- ⅓ cup apricot preserves
- ¼ cup chili sauce
- 1 tablespoon hot mustard
- ¼ teaspoon salt
- ⅛ teaspoon pepper
- 4 boneless skinless chicken breast halves (4 ounces each)

1. Preheat the broiler. In a small saucepan, combine the first five ingredients; cook and stir over medium heat until heated through.
2. Place chicken in a 15x10x1-in. baking pan coated with cooking spray. Broil 3-4 in. from heat 6-8 minutes on each side or until a thermometer reads 165°. Brush chicken occasionally with preserves mixture during the last 5 minutes of cooking.
Per 1 chicken breast half: 209 cal., 3g fat (1g sat. fat), 63mg chol., 476mg sod., 23g carb. (13g sugars, 0 fiber), 23g pro.

FAST FIX

BALSAMIC CHICKEN & PEARS

Pears and dried cherries taste amazingly good with chicken and balsamic vinegar. We use them to make an attractive and tasty meal for date nights.
—Marcia Whitney, Gainesville, FL

Start to Finish: 30 min.
Makes: 4 servings

- 4 boneless skinless chicken breast halves (6 ounces each)
- ¾ teaspoon salt
- ½ teaspoon pepper
- 1 tablespoon canola oil
- 1 cup reduced-sodium chicken broth
- 3 tablespoons white balsamic vinegar
- ½ teaspoon minced fresh rosemary
- 2 teaspoons cornstarch
- 1½ teaspoons sugar
- 2 medium unpeeled pears, each cut into 8 wedges
- ⅓ cup dried cherries or dried cranberries

1. Sprinkle the chicken breasts with salt and pepper. In a large nonstick skillet, heat the oil over medium-high heat. Add the chicken; cook until a thermometer reads 165°, 8-10 minutes. Remove.
2. Meanwhile, stir together next five ingredients until blended. Pour into skillet; add pears and dried cherries. Bring to a boil over medium-high heat; reduce the heat and simmer, covered, until the pears are tender, about 5 minutes. Return chicken to skillet; simmer, uncovered, until heated through, 3-5 minutes. If desired, sprinkle with additional minced rosemary.
Per 1 chicken breast half with ⅓ cup sauce and 4 pear wedges: 335 cal., 8g fat (1g sat. fat), 94mg chol., 670mg sod., 30g carb. (22g sugars, 3g fiber), 36g pro.
Diabetic exchanges: 3 lean meat, 1½ starch, ½ fruit.

SOUTHWEST TURKEY LETTUCE WRAPS

If you're tired of the same old taco routine, give these zippy wraps a try. I tweaked a friend's recipe to suit our tastes and my family's loved it since. It's healthy and low maintenance.
—Ally Billhorn, Wilton, IA

Start to Finish: 25 min.
Makes: 6 servings

- 2 pounds extra-lean ground turkey
- 1 small onion, finely chopped
- 2 tablespoons chili powder
- ¾ teaspoon ground cumin
- ½ teaspoon salt
- ½ teaspoon pepper
- 1 can (15 ounces) tomato sauce
- 18 Bibb or iceberg lettuce leaves
- ¾ cup shredded cheddar cheese
  Optional toppings: sour cream, salsa and guacamole

1. In a large skillet, cook and crumble turkey with onion over medium-high heat until no longer pink, 8-10 minutes.
2. Stir in seasonings and tomato sauce; bring to a boil. Reduce heat; simmer, covered, until flavors are blended, about 10 minutes. Serve in lettuce with cheese and toppings as desired.
To freeze: Freeze the cooled meat mixture in freezer containers. To use, partially thaw in refrigerator overnight. Heat through in a saucepan, stirring occasionally and adding a little water if necessary.
Per 3 filled lettuce wraps: 251 cal., 7g fat (3g sat. fat), 75mg chol., 806mg sod., 7g carb. (2g sugars, 2g fiber), 43g pro.
Diabetic exchanges: 5 lean meat, 1 vegetable.

TURKEY ASPARAGUS STIR-FRY

Twenty minutes is all you'll need to make this quick stir-fry. Turkey and veggies make it nutritious, too.
—Darlene Kennedy, Galion, OH

Start to Finish: 20 min.
Makes: 5 servings

- 1 tablespoon olive oil
- 1 pound boneless skinless turkey breast halves, cut into strips
- 1 pound fresh asparagus, cut into 1-inch pieces
- 4 ounces fresh mushrooms, sliced
- 2 medium carrots, quartered lengthwise and cut into 1-inch pieces
- 4 green onions, cut into 1-inch pieces
- 2 garlic cloves, minced
- ½ teaspoon ground ginger
- ⅔ cup water
- 2 tablespoons reduced-sodium soy sauce
- 4 teaspoons cornstarch
- 1 can (8 ounces) sliced water chestnuts, drained
- 3½ cups hot cooked white or brown rice
- 1 medium tomato, cut into wedges

1. In a large skillet or wok, heat oil over medium-high heat. Add the turkey; stir-fry until it is no longer pink, about 5 minutes. Remove and keep warm.
2. Add next six ingredients to pan; stir-fry until the vegetables are crisp-tender, about 5 minutes. Combine water, soy sauce and cornstarch; add to skillet with water chestnuts. Bring to a boil; cook and stir 1-2 minutes or until sauce is thickened. Return turkey to skillet and heat through. Serve with rice and tomato wedges.
Per 1 cup with ¾ cup rice: 343 cal., 5g fat (1g sat. fat), 52mg chol., 363mg sod., 47g carb. (4g sugars, 4g fiber), 28g pro.
Diabetic exchanges: 3 starch, 3 lean meat, 1 vegetable, ½ fat.

PECAN-CRUSTED CHICKEN NUGGETS

I enjoyed chicken nuggets as a child. The baked version here is healthier than the original, and it's a great meal for kids.
—Haili Carroll, Valencia, CA

Start to Finish: 30 min.
Makes: 6 servings

- 1½ cups cornflakes
- 1 tablespoon dried parsley flakes
- 1 teaspoon salt
- ½ teaspoon garlic powder
- ½ teaspoon pepper
- ½ cup panko (Japanese) bread crumbs
- ½ cup finely chopped pecans
- 3 tablespoons 2% milk
- 1½ pounds boneless skinless chicken breasts, cut into 1-inch pieces
  Cooking spray

1. Preheat oven to 400°. Place cornflakes, parsley, salt, garlic powder and pepper in a blender; cover and pulse until finely ground. Transfer to a shallow bowl; stir in bread crumbs and pecans. Place milk in another shallow bowl. Dip chicken in milk, then roll in crumb mixture to coat.
2. Place on a greased baking sheet; spritz chicken with cooking spray. Bake 12-16 minutes or until chicken is no longer pink, turning once halfway through cooking.
Per 3 ounces cooked chicken:
206 cal., 9g fat (1g sat. fat), 63mg chol., 290mg sod., 6g carb. (1g sugars, 1g fiber), 24g pro.
Diabetic exchanges: 3 lean meat, 1 fat, ½ starch.

HONEY CHICKEN STIR-FRY

I'm a new mom, and my schedule is dependent upon my young son. So I like meals that can be ready in as little time as possible. This all-in-one stir-fry with a hint of sweetness from honey is a big time-saver.
—Caroline Sperry, Allentown, MI

Start to Finish: 30 min.
Makes: 4 servings

- 2 teaspoons cornstarch
- 1 tablespoon cold water
- 3 teaspoons olive oil, divided
- 1 pound boneless skinless chicken breasts, cut into 1-inch pieces
- 1 garlic clove, minced
- 3 tablespoons honey
- 2 tablespoons reduced-sodium soy sauce
- ⅛ teaspoon salt
- ⅛ teaspoon pepper
- 1 package (16 ounces) frozen broccoli stir-fry vegetable blend
  Hot cooked rice

1. Mix cornstarch and water until smooth. In a large nonstick skillet, heat 2 teaspoons oil over medium-high heat; stir-fry chicken and garlic 1 minute. Add honey, soy sauce, salt and pepper; cook and stir until chicken is no longer pink, 2-3 minutes. Remove from pan.
2. In same pan, stir-fry vegetable blend in remaining oil just until tender, 4-5 minutes. Return chicken to pan. Stir cornstarch mixture and add to pan; bring to a boil. Cook and stir until thickened, about 1 minute. Serve with rice.
Per 1 cup without rice: 249 cal., 6g fat (1g sat. fat), 63mg chol., 455mg sod., 21g carb. (15g sugars, 3g fiber), 25g pro.
Diabetic exchanges: 3 lean meat, 2 vegetable, ½ starch.

TURKEY SALSA BOWLS WITH TORTILLA WEDGES

I used this recipe when I taught Junior Chef classes at my church. The kids loved designing their own salsa bowls using whole grains, colorful veggies and lean protein. It was a great way to teach them that food can be both delicious and nutritious!

—Jean Gottfried
Upper Sandusky, OH

....

Prep: 15 min.
Cook: 25 min.
Makes: 8 servings

- 1 pound lean ground turkey
- ½ cup chopped sweet pepper
- ¼ cup thinly sliced celery
- 2 green onions, chopped
- 1 jar (16 ounces) medium salsa
- 1 can (16 ounces) kidney beans, rinsed and drained
- 1 cup uncooked instant brown rice
- 1 cup water
- 4 whole wheat tortillas (8 inches)
- 1 tablespoon canola oil
- 8 cups torn romaine (about 1 head)
  Optional toppings: chopped tomatoes, sliced ripe olives, cubed avocado, shredded cheddar cheese and chopped green onions

1. Preheat oven to 400°. In a large skillet, cook and crumble turkey with pepper, celery and green onions over medium-high heat until no longer pink, 5-7 minutes. Stir in salsa, beans, rice and water; bring to a boil. Reduce heat; simmer, covered, until liquid is absorbed, about 15 minutes.

2. Brush both sides of tortillas with oil; cut each into eight wedges. Arrange in a single layer on a baking sheet. Bake until lightly browned, 8-10 minutes.

3. To serve, divide lettuce among eight bowls; top with the turkey mixture. Serve with tortilla wedges and toppings as desired.

Per serving: 279 cal., 8g fat (1g sat. fat), 39mg chol., 423mg sod., 36g carb. (4g sugars, 6g fiber), 18g pro.
Diabetic exchanges: 2 lean meat, 1 vegetable, 2 starch.

GRILLED ASIAN CHICKEN PASTA SALAD

This cold noodle salad has lots of pleasing contrasts in color, taste and texture. It makes a great dinner or potluck contribution.
—Sharon Tipton, Casselberry, FL

Prep: 25 min. + marinating
Grill: 10 min.
Makes: 6 servings

- ¾ cup lime juice
- 3 tablespoons olive oil
- 3 tablespoons sesame oil
- 3 tablespoons reduced-sodium soy sauce
- 2 tablespoons minced fresh gingerroot
- 3 garlic cloves, minced
- 1 tablespoon sugar
- 1½ pounds boneless skinless chicken breasts
- 12 ounces uncooked angel hair pasta, broken
- 1 large sweet yellow pepper, chopped
- 1 large sweet red pepper, chopped
- 1 medium cucumber, peeled and chopped
- ¼ cup minced fresh parsley
- 2 green onions, sliced
- ¼ teaspoon crushed red pepper flakes

1. Combine first seven ingredients. Pour ¼ cup of the marinade into a shallow dish, reserving remainder. Add the chicken and turn to coat. Refrigerate 30 minutes.
2. Drain chicken; discard marinade. Grill chicken, covered, on an oiled grill rack over medium heat (or broil 4 in. from heat) 5-7 minutes on each side, until a thermometer reads 165°.
3. Meanwhile, cook pasta according to package directions; drain and rinse in cold water. Combine the remaining ingredients with reserved marinade. Cut chicken into 1-in. slices. Add pasta and chicken to vegetable mixture; toss to coat. Refrigerate until serving.
Per 1⅓ cups: 478 cal., 16g fat (3g sat. fat), 63mg chol., 321mg sod., 51g carb. (6g sugars, 3g fiber), 32g pro.

SAVORY TURKEY POTPIES

These ramekin-style potpies will perk you up on a cold, rainy day. I serve them with a green salad or cranberry sauce on the side.
—Judy Wilson, Sun City West, AZ

Prep: 25 min. • **Bake:** 20 min.
Makes: 8 servings

- 1 small onion, chopped
- ¼ cup all-purpose flour
- 3 cups chicken stock
- 3 cups cubed cooked turkey breast
- 1 package (16 ounces) frozen peas and carrots
- 2 medium red potatoes, cooked and cubed
- 3 tablespoons minced fresh parsley
- 1 tablespoon minced fresh thyme
- ¼ teaspoon pepper
- 1 sheet refrigerated pie pastry
  Additional fresh parsley or thyme leaves, optional
- 1 large egg
- 1 teaspoon water
- ½ teaspoon kosher salt

1. In a Dutch oven coated with cooking spray, saute onion until tender. In a small bowl, whisk flour and stock until smooth; gradually stir into Dutch oven. Bring to a boil; cook and stir 2 minutes or until thickened. Remove from the heat. Add the turkey, peas and carrots, potatoes, parsley, thyme and pepper; stir gently.
2. Preheat oven to 425°. Divide turkey mixture among eight 10-oz. ramekins. On a lightly floured surface, unroll pastry. Cut out eight 3-in. circles. Gently press parsley into pastry if desired. Place over turkey mixture. Beat egg and water; brush over tops. Sprinkle with salt.
3. Place ramekins on a baking sheet. Bake 20-25 minutes or until crusts are golden brown.
To freeze: Securely wrap baked and cooled potpies in plastic wrap and foil; freeze. To use, partially thaw in the refrigerator overnight. Remove from refrigerator 30 minutes before baking. Preheat oven to 425°. Unwrap potpies; bake in oven until heated through and a thermometer inserted in center reads 165°. Cover top with foil to prevent overbrowning if necessary.
Per 1 potpie: 279 cal., 9g fat (3g sat. fat), 77mg chol., 495mg sod., 28g carb. (5g sugars, 3g fiber), 22g pro.
Diabetic exchanges: 2 starch, 2 lean meat, ½ fat.

PARMESAN CHICKEN WITH LEMON RICE

I like the challenge of inventing recipes using ingredients I already have on hand. This easy meal is a winner.
—Colleen Doucette, Truro, NS

Start to Finish: 30 min.
Makes: 4 servings

- 2 cups reduced-sodium chicken broth
- 2 tablespoons lemon juice
- 1 cup uncooked long grain rice
- ½ cup chopped onion
- 1 large egg
- 2 tablespoons fat-free milk
- ¾ cup panko (Japanese) bread crumbs
- ⅔ cup grated Parmesan cheese, divided
- 1 teaspoon dried oregano
- 1 pound boneless skinless chicken breasts
- 2 tablespoons olive oil
- 1 cup frozen peas (about 4 ounces), thawed
- ¼ teaspoon grated lemon peel
  Freshly ground pepper, optional

1. In a saucepan, bring broth and lemon juice to a boil. Stir in rice and onion; return to a boil. Reduce heat; simmer, covered, until liquid is almost absorbed and rice is tender, 15-20 minutes.

2. Meanwhile, in a shallow bowl, whisk together egg and milk. In another bowl, toss bread crumbs with ⅓ cup cheese and oregano. Pound chicken breasts with a meat mallet to ¼-in. thickness. Dip in egg mixture, then in crumb mixture to coat both sides.

3. In a large skillet, heat oil over medium heat. Cook chicken until golden brown and chicken is no longer pink, 2-3 minutes per side.

4. When rice is cooked, gently stir in peas; cook, covered, until heated through, 1-2 minutes. Stir in lemon peel and remaining cheese. Cut chicken into slices; serve with rice. If desired, sprinkle with pepper.

Per 3 ounces cooked chicken with ¾ cup rice: 500 cal., 14g fat (4g sat. fat), 96mg chol., 623mg sod., 55g carb. (4g sugars, 3g fiber), 36g pro.

BUFFALO CHICKEN TENDERS

These chicken tenders get a spicy kick thanks to homemade Buffalo sauce. They taste like they're from a restaurant, but are so easy to make at home. Blue cheese salad dressing takes them over the top.
—Dahlia Abrams, Detroit, MI

Start to Finish: 20 min.
Makes: 4 servings

- 1 pound chicken tenderloins
- 2 tablespoons all-purpose flour
- ¼ teaspoon pepper
- 2 tablespoons butter, divided
- ⅓ cup Louisiana-style hot sauce
- 1¼ teaspoons Worcestershire sauce
- 1 teaspoon minced fresh oregano
- ½ teaspoon garlic powder
  Blue cheese salad dressing, optional

1. Toss chicken with flour and pepper. In a large skillet, heat 1 tablespoon butter over medium heat. Add chicken; cook until no longer pink, 4-6 minutes per side. Remove from pan.

2. Mix hot sauce, Worcestershire sauce, oregano and garlic powder. In same skillet, melt remaining butter; stir in sauce mixture. Add chicken; heat through, turning to coat. If desired, serve with blue cheese dressing.

Per serving: 184 cal., 7g fat (4g sat. fat), 71mg chol., 801mg sod., 5g carb. (1g sugars, 0 fiber), 27g pro.
Diabetic exchanges: 3 lean meat, 1½ fat.

SMOTHERED TURKEY CUTLETS

Why enjoy turkey only on holidays? This easy recipe makes it feel like Thanksgiving or Christmas any day of the week.
—Lisa Keys, Kennett Square, PA

....

Prep: 30 min. • **Bake:** 5 min
Makes: 4 servings

1 cup mild chunky salsa
¼ cup dried cranberries
1 tablespoon chopped fresh cilantro
1 cup orange sections, cut into 1-inch pieces
2 tablespoons all-purpose flour
1 teaspoon ground cumin
1 large egg
1 tablespoon water
1 cup panko (Japanese) bread crumbs
¼ cup grated Parmesan cheese
4 turkey breast cutlets (2½ ounces each)
½ teaspoon pepper
⅛ teaspoon salt
2 tablespoons olive oil, divided
½ cup shredded sharp cheddar cheese
½ medium ripe avocado, cubed
Additional chopped cilantro
Reduced-fat sour cream, optional

1. Preheat oven to 350°. Mix salsa, cranberries and cilantro; gently stir in oranges. In a shallow bowl, mix flour and cumin. In another shallow bowl, whisk together the egg and water. In a third bowl, toss bread crumbs with Parmesan cheese.

2. Sprinkle cutlets with pepper and salt; coat lightly with flour mixture, shaking off excess. Dip in the egg mixture, then in crumb mixture, patting firmly.

3. In a big skillet, heat 1 tablespoon oil over medium heat; add 2 turkey cutlets and cook them until golden brown, 1-2 minutes per side. Transfer the cutlets to a foil-lined baking sheet. Repeat with the remaining oil and turkey.

4. Sprinkle cutlets with cheddar cheese; bake until cheese is melted and turkey is no longer pink, 4-6 minutes. Top with avocado, salsa mixture, additional cilantro and, if desired, sour cream.

Per serving: 401 cal., 19g fat (5g sat. fat), 106mg chol., 638mg sod., 31g carb. (12g sugars, 4g fiber), 26g pro.

1. Preheat oven to 375°. Cut each slice of bread into 12 cubes; scatter over a 15x10-in. pan. Bake until toasted, 8-10 minutes, stirring halfway. Cool 5 minutes.

2. Meanwhile, combine next six ingredients in a jar with a tight-fitting lid. Shake until blended. In a large nonstick skillet, cook sausage over medium heat until browned and heated through, 2-3 minutes per side.

3. Divide salad greens among four dinner-size plates; add sausage to each plate. Top with pear slices, walnuts, cherries and croutons. Shake dressing again; spoon over salad and serve immediately.

Note: To toast nuts, bake in a shallow pan in a 350° oven for 5-10 minutes or cook in a skillet over low heat until lightly browned, stirring occasionally.

Per serving: 404 cal., 23g fat (4g sat. fat), 40mg chol., 441mg sod., 39g carb. (23g sugars, 5g fiber), 14g pro.

TEST KITCHEN TIP
Chicken sausage, which is lower in fat than pork sausage, is sold in most supermarkets. A number of different brands are available in a wide variety of flavors. You'll find products for every preference, including hot and spicy, organic, gluten-free and mild-flavored sausages.

APPLE SAUSAGE SALAD WITH CINNAMON VINAIGRETTE

Making croutons with cinnamon raisin bread is sweet genius. Toss together the rest of the salad while they toast.

—Kim Van Dunk, Caldwell, NJ

Prep: 25 min.
Bake: 10 min.
Makes: 6 servings

- 4 slices cinnamon-raisin bread
- ⅓ cup olive oil
- 3 tablespoons cider vinegar
- 2 teaspoons honey
- ½ teaspoon ground cinnamon
- ⅛ teaspoon sea salt
  Dash pepper
- 1 package (12 ounces) fully cooked apple chicken sausage links, cut diagonally in ½-inch thick slices
- 2 packages (5 ounces each) spring mix salad greens
- 2 cups fresh Bartlett pears, sliced vertically
- ½ cup chopped walnuts, toasted
- ½ cup dried sweet cherries

GRECIAN CHICKEN

The caper, tomato and olive flavors whisk you away to the Greek Isles in this easy skillet dish that's perfect for busy weeknights.
—Jan Marler, Murchison, TX

....

Start to Finish: 30 min.
Makes: 4 servings

3 **teaspoons olive oil, divided**
1 **pound chicken tenderloins**
2 **medium tomatoes, sliced**
1 **cup sliced fresh mushrooms**
½ **cup chopped onion**
1 **tablespoon capers, drained**
1 **tablespoon lemon-pepper seasoning**
1 **tablespoon salt-free Greek seasoning**
1 **medium garlic clove, minced**
½ **cup water**
2 **tablespoons chopped ripe olives**
   Hot cooked orzo pasta, optional

1. In a large skillet, heat 2 teaspoons oil over medium heat. Add chicken; saute until no longer pink, 7-9 minutes. Remove and keep warm.
2. In same skillet, heat remaining oil; add next six ingredients. Cook and stir until the onion is translucent, 2-3 minutes. Stir in garlic; cook 1 minute more. Add water; bring to a boil. Reduce heat; simmer, uncovered, until vegetables are tender, 3-4 minutes. Return chicken to skillet; add the olives. Simmer, uncovered, until chicken is heated through, 2-3 minutes. If desired, serve with orzo.

Per serving: 172 cal., 5g fat (1g sat. fat), 56mg chol., 393mg sod., 6g carb. (3g sugars, 2g fiber), 28g pro.
Diabetic exchanges: 3 lean meat, 1 vegetable, 1 fat.

CALIFORNIA BURGER BOWLS

Skip the fries, chips and bun—you won't need them with these loaded veggie and fruit burgers.
—Courtney Stultz, Weir, KS

Start to Finish: 25 min.
Makes: 4 servings

- 3 tablespoons fat-free milk
- 2 tablespoons quick-cooking oats
- ¾ teaspoon salt
- ½ teaspoon ground cumin
- ½ teaspoon chili powder
- ½ teaspoon pepper
- 1 pound lean ground turkey
- 4 cups baby kale salad blend
- 1½ cups cubed fresh pineapple (½ inch)
- 1 medium mango, peeled and thinly sliced
- 1 medium ripe avocado, peeled and thinly sliced
- 1 medium sweet red pepper, cut into strips
- 4 tomatillos, husks removed, thinly sliced
- ¼ cup reduced-fat chipotle mayonnaise

1. In a bowl, mix milk, oats and seasonings. Add turkey; mix. Shape into four ½-in.-thick patties.
2. Grill burgers over medium heat, covered, until a thermometer reads 165°, 4-5 minutes per side. Serve over the salad blend, along with remaining ingredients.
Per serving: 390 cal., 23g fat (4g sat. fat), 83mg chol., 666mg sod., 33g carb. (22g sugars, 7 fiber), 26g pro.
Diabetic exchanges: 3 lean meat, 1 fruit, 2 vegetable, 2.5 fat.

OVEN BARBECUED CHICKEN

A friend made this moist chicken for us after we had our first child. I pared down the recipe to make it lower in fat and calories, but it tastes just as good.
—Marge Wagner, Roselle, IL

Prep: 20 min.
Bake: 35 min.
Makes: 6 servings

- 6 bone-in chicken breast halves (8 ounces each)
- ⅓ cup chopped onion
- ¾ cup ketchup
- ½ cup water
- ⅓ cup white vinegar
- 3 tablespoons brown sugar
- 1 tablespoon Worcestershire sauce
- 1 teaspoon ground mustard
- ¼ teaspoon salt
- ⅛ teaspoon pepper

1. Preheat the oven to 350°. In a nonstick skillet coated with cooking spray, brown chicken over medium heat. Transfer to a 13x9-in. baking dish coated with cooking spray.
2. Recoat skillet with cooking spray. Add onion; cook and stir over medium heat until tender. Stir in remaining ingredients; bring to a boil. Reduce the heat; simmer, uncovered, 15 minutes. Pour the sauce over chicken.
3. Bake chicken, uncovered, until a thermometer inserted in it reads 170°, 35-45 minutes.
Per 1 chicken breast half: 324 cal., 10g fat (3g sat. fat), 111mg chol., 602mg sod., 16g carb. (15g sugars, 0 fiber), 39g pro.
Diabetic exchanges: 5 lean meat, 1 starch.

C

ENCHILADA CHICKEN

We enjoy southwestern flavors, and this six-ingredient recipe never gets boring. The chicken sizzles in the skillet before getting baked and comes out tender and juicy every time.
—Nancy Sousley, Lafayette, IN

....

Prep: 15 min.
Bake: 20 min.
Makes: 4 servings

- **4 boneless skinless chicken breast halves (6 ounces each)**
- **2 teaspoons salt-free Southwest chipotle seasoning blend**
- **1 tablespoon olive oil**
- **¼ cup enchilada sauce**
- **½ cup shredded sharp cheddar cheese**
- **2 tablespoons minced fresh cilantro**

Sprinkle chicken with seasoning blend. In an ovenproof skillet, brown chicken in oil. Top with enchilada sauce, cheese and cilantro. Bake at 350° for 18-20 minutes or until a thermometer reads 170°.

Per 1 chicken breast half : 265 cal., 11g fat (5g sat. fat), 109mg chol., 252mg sod., 2g carb. (0 sugars, 0 fiber), 38g pro.
Diabetic exchanges: 5 lean meat, 1 fat.

GRILLED KIWI-CHICKEN KABOBS WITH HONEY-CHIPOTLE GLAZE

When guests bite into these juicy grilled kabobs, their eyes widen with satisfaction. Our four kids are crazy about the spicy-sweet sauce.
—Joni Hilton, Rocklin, CA

Prep: 20 min. + marinating
Grill: 10 min.
Makes: 8 kabobs

- 6 garlic cloves, minced
- 2 tablespoons lime juice
- 1 tablespoon olive oil
- 1 teaspoon salt
- 1 pound boneless skinless chicken breasts, cut into 1-inch cubes
- 8 medium kiwifruit, peeled and halved
- 3 tablespoons honey
- 1 tablespoon minced chipotle peppers in adobo sauce

1. In a large resealable plastic bag, combine garlic, lime juice, oil and salt. Add chicken and kiwi; seal bag and turn to coat. Refrigerate up to 30 minutes.
2. Mix honey and chipotle peppers. Drain chicken and kiwi, discarding marinade. On eight metal or soaked wooden skewers, alternately thread chicken and kiwi.
3. Grill, covered, on an oiled rack over medium heat, turning occasionally, until juices run clear, about 10-12 minutes. During the last 4 minutes, baste frequently with honey-chipotle mixture.
Per 2 kabob: 284 cal., 5g fat (1g sat. fat), 63mg chol., 380mg sod., 37g carb. (27g sugars, 5g fiber), 25g pro.

FAST FIX ▶

SPICY TURKEY QUESADILLAS

Make use of leftover Thanksgiving Day turkey and cranberries by including them in quesadillas. The bold flavor of the chillies and hot sauce adds extra zip.
—*Taste of Home* Test Kitchen

Start to Finish: 25 min.
Makes: 2 servings

- 3 ounces fat-free cream cheese
- ¼ cup chopped fresh or frozen cranberries, thawed
- 1 tablespoon canned chopped green chilies
- 1½ teaspoons honey
- 1 teaspoon Louisiana-style hot sauce
- 4 flour tortillas (6 inches)
- 1 cup diced cooked turkey breast

1. Mix the first five ingredients until blended; spread over each tortilla. Place turkey on two tortillas; top with remaining tortillas, pressing down lightly.
2. Cook in a large nonstick skillet over medium heat until lightly browned, 2-3 minutes per side.
Per 1 quesadilla: 391 cal., 9g fat (3g sat. fat), 61mg chol., 870mg sod., 43g carb. (8g sugars, 4g fiber), 33g pro.
Diabetic exchanges: 3 lean meat, 2 starch, 1 fat.

FAST FIX ▶

CARIBBEAN CHICKEN STIR-FRY

Fruit cocktail in stir-fry? You might be surprised how much you like the flavor combination in this dish. It's a promising go-to option when time's tight.
—Jeanne Holt
Mendota Heights, MN

Start to Finish: 25 min.
Makes: 4 servings

- 2 teaspoons cornstarch
- ¼ cup water
- 1 pound boneless skinless chicken breasts, cut into ½-inch strips
- 2 teaspoons Caribbean jerk seasoning
- 1 can (15 ounces) mixed tropical fruit, drained and coarsely chopped
- 2 packages (8.8 ounces each) ready-to-serve brown rice

1. In a small bowl, mix cornstarch and water until smooth.
2. Coat a large skillet with cooking spray; heat over medium-high heat. Add chicken; sprinkle with jerk seasoning. Stir-fry 3-5 minutes or until no longer pink. Stir cornstarch mixture and add to pan with fruit. Bring to a boil; cook and stir 1-2 minutes or until sauce is thickened.
3. Meanwhile, heat rice according to the package directions. Serve with chicken.

Per ½ cup stir-fry with ½ cup rice:
432 cal., 5g fat (1g sat. fat), 63mg chol., 210mg sod., 60g carb. (0 sugars, 3g fiber), 28g pro.

C

CHICKEN PESTO ROLL-UPS

One night I looked in the fridge and thought, "What can I make with chicken, cheese, mushrooms and pesto?" This pretty dish was my answer!
—Melissa Nordmann, Mobile, AL

Prep: 15 min. • **Bake:** 30 min.
Makes: 4 servings

- 4 boneless skinless chicken breast halves (6 ounces each)
- ½ cup prepared pesto, divided
- 1 pound medium fresh mushrooms, sliced
- 4 slices reduced-fat provolone cheese, halved

1. Preheat oven to 350°. Pound chicken breasts with a meat mallet to ¼-in. thickness. Spread ¼ cup pesto over chicken breasts.
2. Coarsely chop half of the sliced mushrooms; scatter remaining sliced mushrooms in a 15x10x1-in. baking pan coated with cooking spray. Top each chicken breast with a fourth of the chopped mushroom pieces and a halved cheese slice. Roll up chicken from a short side; secure with toothpicks. Place the chicken seam side down on top of the sliced mushrooms.
3. Bake, covered, until chicken is no longer pink, 25-30 minutes. Preheat broiler; top chicken with remaining pesto and remaining cheese. Broil until the cheese is melted and browned, 3-5 minutes longer. Discard the toothpicks.

Per 1 stuffed chicken breast half:
374 cal., 17g fat (5g sat. fat), 104mg chol., 582mg sod., 7g carb. (1g sugars, 1g fiber), 44g pro.
Diabetic exchanges: 5 lean meat, 2 fat.

CHICKEN & SPANISH CAULIFLOWER RICE

I learned about the paleo diet from some friends who tried it with success. Since then, I've changed my eating habits, too. Everyone from my dad to my young nephew loves this riced cauliflower.
—Megan Schmoldt
Westminster, CO

Start to Finish: 30 min.
Makes: 4 servings

1 **large head cauliflower**
1 **pound boneless skinless chicken breasts, cut into ½-inch cubes**
½ **teaspoon salt**
½ **teaspoon pepper**
1 **tablespoon canola oil**
1 **medium green pepper, chopped**
1 **small onion, chopped**
1 **garlic clove, minced**
½ **cup tomato juice**
¼ **teaspoon ground cumin**
¼ **cup chopped fresh cilantro**
1 **tablespoon lime juice**

1. Core and cut cauliflower into 1-in. pieces. In batches, pulse cauliflower pieces in a food processor until it resembles rice (do not overprocess).
2. Toss chicken with salt and pepper. In a large skillet, heat oil over medium-high heat; saute chicken until lightly browned, about 5 minutes. Add green pepper, onion and garlic; cook and stir 3 minutes.
3. Stir in tomato juice and cumin; bring to a boil. Add cauliflower; cook, covered, over medium heat until cauliflower is tender, 7-10 minutes, stirring occasionally. Stir in cilantro and lime juice.

Per 1½ cups: 227 cal., 7g fat (1g sat. fat), 63mg chol., 492mg sod., 15g carb. (6g sugars, 5g fiber), 28g pro.
Diabetic exchanges: 3 lean meat, 1 starch, ½ fat.

FAST FIX ▶

ZINGY BAKED CHICKEN NUGGETS

These crispy chicken nuggets have just the right amount of spice. Yogurt makes them extra tender.
—Lee Evans, Queen Creek, AZ

....

Start to Finish: 30 min.
Makes: 6 servings

¼ cup plain yogurt
1 tablespoon lemon juice
1½ teaspoons seasoned salt
1 teaspoon garlic powder
1 teaspoon ground coriander
½ to ¾ teaspoon cayenne pepper
1½ pounds boneless skinless chicken breasts, cut into 1½-inch pieces
2 cups whole wheat or regular panko (Japanese) bread crumbs
Honey mustard, optional

1. Preheat oven to 400°. Mix first six ingredients; stir in chicken to coat.
2. Place bread crumbs in a shallow bowl; add chicken, one piece at a time, and toss to coat. Place 1 in. apart on a greased baking sheet.
3. Bake until lightly browned and chicken is no longer pink, 18-20 minutes. If desired, serve with honey mustard.
Per serving: 222 cal., 4g fat (1g sat. fat), 64mg chol., 481mg sod., 19g carb. (2g sugars, 2g fiber), 26g pro.
Diabetic exchanges: 3 lean meat, 1 starch.

FAST FIX ▶

SAUSAGE & VEGETABLE SKILLET DINNER

I threw this together one night when I wanted to use up the last of my produce before going out of town. Who knew it was going to be such a hit? Now it's a mainstay when I'm pressed for time.
—Elizabeth Kelley, Chicago, IL

....

Start to Finish: 30 min.
Makes: 4 servings

1 tablespoon olive oil
1 package (12 ounces) fully cooked Italian chicken sausage links, cut into 1-inch pieces
1 large onion, chopped
3 garlic cloves, minced
¼ teaspoon crushed red pepper flakes
1½ pounds red potatoes (about 5 medium), thinly sliced
1 package (10 ounces) frozen corn
¼ teaspoon pepper
1¼ cups vegetable broth
2 cups fresh baby spinach

1. In a 12-in. skillet, heat oil over medium-high heat; saute sausage and onion until onion is tender. Add garlic and pepper flakes; cook and stir 1 minute.
2. Add potatoes, corn, pepper and broth; bring to a boil. Reduce heat to medium; cook, covered, until potatoes are tender, 15-20 minutes. Stir in spinach until wilted.
HEALTH TIP Italian chicken sausage has less than half the fat of regular. It's lean, but adds a lot of flavor.
Per 2 cups: 413 cal., 11g fat (3g sat. fat), 65mg chol., 804mg sod., 58g carb. (6g sugars, 7g fiber), 22g pro.

Mediterranean
Pork & Orzo
page 97

PORK CLASSICS

Sink your teeth into something special tonight! From lean cuts of pork tenderloin to smoky ham, these dishes let you enjoy a hearty dinner without feeling weighed down.

C
SPICE-RUBBED HAM
Now this is a ham—it's sweet and smoky, with just the right amount of cloves and ginger.
—Sharon Tipton, Casselberry, FL

Prep: 15 min.
Bake: 3¼ hours + standing
Makes: 24 servings

- 1 **fully cooked semi-boneless ham (8 to 10 pounds)**
- ½ **cup spicy brown mustard**
- ¼ **cup packed brown sugar**
- ¼ **teaspoon ground ginger**
- ¼ **teaspoon ground cinnamon**
  Whole cloves

1. Place ham on a rack in a shallow roasting pan. Score the surface of the ham, making diamond shapes ½ in. deep. Combine the mustard, brown sugar, ginger and cinnamon; rub over surface of ham. Insert a clove in each diamond.
2. Bake, uncovered, at 325° for 1½ hours. Cover and bake 1¾ to 2 hours longer or until a meat thermometer reads 140°. Cover loosely with foil if ham browns too quickly. Discard cloves. Let stand for 10 minutes before slicing.
Per 3 ounces cooked ham: 139 cal., 4g fat (1g sat. fat), 66mg chol., 858mg sod., 3g carb. (3g sugars, 0 fiber), 22g pro.
Diabetic exchanges: 3 lean meat.

FAST FIX ▶
PORK & MANGO STIR-FRY
A recipe is special when everyone in your family raves about it. My finicky eaters give thumbs up for this hearty, nutty stir-fry.
—Kathy Specht, Clinton, MT

Start to Finish: 25 min.
Makes: 4 servings

- 1 **pork tenderloin (1 pound)**
- 1 **tablespoon plus 2 teaspoons canola oil, divided**
- ¼ **teaspoon salt**
- ½ **teaspoon crushed red pepper flakes, optional**
- 6 **ounces uncooked multigrain angel hair pasta**
- 1 **package (8 ounces) fresh sugar snap peas**
- 1 **medium sweet red pepper, cut into thin strips**
- ⅓ **cup reduced-sugar orange marmalade**
- ¼ **cup reduced-sodium teriyaki sauce**
- 1 **tablespoon packed brown sugar**
- 2 **garlic cloves, minced**
- 1 **cup chopped peeled mango**
- ¼ **cup lightly salted cashews, coarsely chopped**

1. Cut tenderloin lengthwise in half; cut each half crosswise into thin slices. Toss pork with 1 tablespoon oil, salt and, if desired, pepper flakes. Cook pasta according to package directions.
2. Place a large nonstick skillet over medium-high heat. Add half of the pork; stir-fry 2-3 minutes or just until browned. Remove from pan; repeat with remaining pork.
3. Stir-fry snap peas and red pepper in the remaining oil 2-3 minutes or just until crisp-tender. Stir in the marmalade, teriyaki sauce, brown sugar and garlic; cook 1-2 minutes longer. Return the pork to the pan and add mango and cashews; heat it through, stirring to combine. Serve with pasta.
Per 1½ cups pork mixture with ¾ cup pasta: 515 cal., 16g fat (3g sat. fat), 64mg chol., 553mg sod., 58g carb. (23g sugars, 6g fiber), 36g pro.

MOLASSES-GLAZED PORK CHOPS

How can you go wrong with these savory chops that call for only a handful of ingredients? Best of all, they are impressive enough to serve to guests.

—Angela Spengler, Tampa, FL

Start to Finish: 30 min.
Makes: 4 servings

- ¼ cup molasses
- 1 tablespoon Worcestershire sauce
- 1½ teaspoons brown sugar
- 4 boneless pork loin chops (¾ inch thick and 5 ounces each)

1. Using a small bowl, combine the molasses, Worcestershire sauce and brown sugar. Reserve 3 tablespoons sauce for serving.
2. Grill the pork, covered, over medium heat or broil 4 in. from heat 4-5 minutes on each side or until a thermometer reads 145°, brushing with remaining sauce during last 3 minutes of cooking. Let stand 5 minutes before serving. Serve with reserved sauce.
Per 1 pork chop with about 2 teaspoons sauce: 256 cal., 8g fat (3g sat. fat), 68mg chol., 89mg sod., 17g carb. (13g sugars, 0 fiber), 27g pro.
Diabetic exchanges: 4 lean meat, 1 starch.

JUST PEACHY PORK TENDERLOIN

I decided to combine ripe peaches with a pork tenderloin. The result was irresistible! It's a fresh entree that tastes like summer.

—Julia Gosliga, Addison, VT

Start to Finish: 20 min.
Makes: 4 servings

- 1 pound pork tenderloin, cut into 12 slices
- ½ teaspoon salt
- ¼ teaspoon pepper
- 2 teaspoons olive oil
- 4 medium peaches, peeled and sliced
- 1 tablespoon lemon juice
- ¼ cup peach preserves

1. Flatten each tenderloin slice to ¼-in. thickness. Sprinkle with salt and pepper. In a large nonstick skillet over medium heat, cook the pork in oil until tender. Remove and keep warm.
2. Add the peaches and lemon juice, stirring to loosen the browned bits from the pan. Cook and stir the blend for 3-4 minutes or until the peaches are tender. Stir in the pork and preserves; heat through.
Per serving: 241 cal., 6g fat (2g sat. fat), 63mg chol., 340mg sod., 23g carb. (20g sugars, 2g fiber), 23g pro.
Diabetic exchanges: 3 lean meat, 1 fruit, ½ starch, ½ fat.

S FAST FIX
APRICOT PORK MEDALLIONS

There's nothing we love more than a great pork dish for supper in our house, and this recipe is up there with the best of them. I find that apricot preserves give the pork just the right amount of sweetness without being overwhelming.
—Crystal Jo Bruns, Iliff, CO

Start to Finish: 20 min.
Makes: 4 servings

- 1 pork tenderloin (1 pound), cut into eight slices
- 1 tablespoon plus 1 teaspoon butter, divided
- ½ cup apricot preserves
- 2 green onions, sliced
- 1 tablespoon cider vinegar
- ¼ teaspoon ground mustard

1. Pound pork slices with a meat mallet to ½-in. thickness. In a large skillet, heat 1 tablespoon butter over medium heat. Brown pork on each side. Remove pork from pan, reserving drippings.

2. Add preserves, green onions, vinegar, mustard and remaining butter to pan; bring just to a boil, stirring to loosen browned bits from pan. Reduce heat; simmer, covered, 3-4 minutes to allow flavors to blend.

3. Return pork to pan; cook until pork is tender. Let stand 5 minutes before serving.

Per 3 ounces cooked pork with 1 tablespoon sauce: 266 cal., 8g fat (4g sat. fat), 73mg chol., 89mg sod., 26g carb. (15g sugars, 0 fiber), 23g pro.

FAST FIX
ASPARAGUS HAM DINNER

I've been making this light meal for my family for years now, and it's always well received. With asparagus, tomato, pasta and chunks of ham, it's a tempting blend of tastes and textures.
—Rhonda Zavodny, David City, NE

Start to Finish: 25 min.
Makes: 6 servings

- 2 cups uncooked corkscrew or spiral pasta
- ¾ pound fresh asparagus, cut into 1-inch pieces
- 1 medium sweet yellow pepper, julienned
- 1 tablespoon olive oil
- 6 medium tomatoes, diced
- 6 ounces boneless fully cooked ham, cubed
- ¼ cup minced fresh parsley
- ½ teaspoon salt
- ½ teaspoon dried oregano
- ½ teaspoon dried basil
- ⅛ to ¼ teaspoon cayenne pepper
- ¼ cup shredded Parmesan cheese

Cook pasta according to package directions. Meanwhile, in a large nonstick skillet, saute asparagus and yellow pepper in oil until crisp-tender. Add tomatoes and ham; heat through. Drain pasta; add to vegetable mixture. Stir in parsley and seasonings. Sprinkle with cheese.

Per 1⅓ cups: 204 cal., 5g fat (1g sat. fat), 17mg chol., 561mg sod., 29g carb. (5g sugars, 3g fiber), 12g pro. **Diabetic exchanges:** 1½ starch, 1 lean meat, 1 vegetable, ½ fat.

APPLE CIDER PORK CHOPS

These pork chops are a must for family dinners when fall arrives. I serve them with buttered egg noodles to soak up more of the delicious cider gravy. This recipe is easily doubled to serve company.
—Debiana Casterline
Egg Harbor Township, NJ

Start to Finish: 25 min.
Makes: 6 servings

- 2 tablespoons olive oil
- 6 boneless pork loin chops (6 to 8 ounces each), about ¾ inch thick
- 1 garlic clove, minced
- 1 tablespoon Dijon mustard
- 1 teaspoon honey
- ½ teaspoon apple pie spice
- ½ teaspoon coarsely ground pepper
- ¼ teaspoon dried thyme
- ¼ teaspoon salt
- 1 cup apple cider
- 1 tablespoon plus 1 teaspoon cornstarch
- 2 tablespoons water
  Minced fresh parsley

1. In a large skillet, heat olive oil over medium heat. Brown pork chops on both sides.
2. Meanwhile, in a small bowl, combine next seven ingredients; stir in apple cider. Pour over pork chops. Reduce heat to medium-low; cook, covered, until a thermometer inserted into chops reads 145°, about 4-5 minutes. Remove chops from skillet; let stand for 5 minutes.
3. In a small bowl, mix cornstarch and water until smooth; stir into cider mixture in skillet. Return to a boil, stirring constantly; cook and stir until thickened, 1-2 minutes. Pour over the chops; sprinkle with fresh parsley.
Per 1 pork chop: 301 cal., 14g fat (4g sat. fat), 82mg chol., 210mg sod., 8g carb. (5g sugars, 0 fiber), 33g pro.
Diabetic exchanges: 4 lean meat, 1 fat, ½ starch.

LINGUINE WITH HAM & SWISS CHEESE

This version of a classic linguine casserole eliminates nearly half of the saturated fat from the original recipe without losing the creamy texture or distinctive Swiss cheese flavor.
—Mike Tchou, Pepper Pike, OH

Prep: 15 min. • **Bake:** 45 min.
Makes: 8 servings

- 8 ounces uncooked whole wheat linguine, broken in half
- 2 cups cubed fully cooked ham
- 1¾ cups shredded Swiss cheese, divided
- 1 can (10¾ ounces) reduced-fat reduced-sodium condensed cream of mushroom soup, undiluted
- 1 cup (8 ounces) reduced-fat sour cream
- 1 medium onion, chopped
- 1 small green pepper, finely chopped

1. Cook linguine according to package directions. Meanwhile, in a large bowl, combine the ham, 1½ cups cheese, soup, sour cream, onion and green pepper. Drain pasta; add to ham mixture and stir to coat.
2. Transfer to a 13x9-in. baking dish coated with cooking spray. Cover and bake at 350° for 35 minutes. Uncover; sprinkle with remaining cheese. Bake 10-15 minutes longer or until cheese is melted.
Per 1 cup: 293 cal., 12g fat (7g sat. fat), 47mg chol., 665mg sod., 29g carb. (5g sugars, 4g fiber), 19g pro.
Diabetic exchanges: 2 starch, 2 lean meat, 1 fat.

MEDITERRANEAN PORK & ORZO

PICTURED ON PAGE 90

This meal-in-a-bowl is one of my top picks on a really busy day. It's quick to put together, leaving me a lot more time to relax at the table.
—Mary Relyea, Canastota, NY

Start to Finish: 30 min.
Makes: 6 servings

- 1½ pounds pork tenderloin
- 1 teaspoon coarsely ground pepper
- 2 tablespoons olive oil
- 3 quarts water
- 1¼ cups uncooked orzo pasta
- ¼ teaspoon salt
- 1 package (6 ounces) fresh baby spinach
- 1 cup grape tomatoes, halved
- ¾ cup crumbled feta cheese

1. Rub pork with pepper; cut into 1-in. cubes. In a large nonstick skillet, heat oil over medium heat. Add pork; cook and stir 8-10 minutes or until no longer pink.
2. Meanwhile, in a Dutch oven, bring water to a boil. Stir in the orzo and salt; cook, uncovered, 8 minutes. Stir in the spinach; cook 45-60 seconds longer or until the orzo is tender and the spinach is wilted. Drain.
3. Add tomatoes to the pork; heat through. Stir in the orzo mixture and cheese.

Per 1⅓ cups: 372 cal., 11g fat (4g sat. fat), 71mg chol., 306mg sod., 34g carb. (2g sugars, 3g fiber), 31g pro.
Diabetic exchanges: 3 lean meat, 2 starch, 1 vegetable, 1 fat.

BERNIE'S PORK CHOP SANDWICHES

My aunt worked in Butte, MT, and whenever we visited we had pork chop sandwiches. This recipe is a fun take on that sandwich.
—Jeanette Kotecki, Helena, MT

Start to Finish: 25 min.
Makes: 4 servings

- ¾ cup cornmeal
- 1 cup all-purpose flour
- ½ teaspoon onion powder
- ½ teaspoon garlic powder
- ½ teaspoon dry mustard
- ½ teaspoon paprika
- 1 cup fat-free milk
- 4 boneless pork loin chops (3 ounces each)
- ½ teaspoon salt
- ¼ teaspoon pepper
- 2 tablespoons canola oil
- 4 whole wheat hamburger buns, split and warmed

Thinly sliced onion, optional
Pickle slices, optional
Prepared mustard, optional

1. Place cornmeal in a shallow bowl. In another bowl, mix flour and spices; add milk, stirring just until dry ingredients are moistened. Pound chops with a meat mallet to ¼-in. thickness; season with salt and pepper.
2. In two batches, heat oil in a large skillet over medium heat. Lightly coat chops with cornmeal. Dip in batter, allowing excess to drip off; place in skillet. Cook until golden brown, 2-4 minutes per side. Drain on paper towels. Serve in buns, topping with remaining ingredients if desired.

Per 1 sandwich: 476 cal., 15g fat (3g sat. fat), 42mg chol., 564mg sod., 60g carb. (6g sugars, 5g fiber), 26g pro.

CURRIED SQUASH & SAUSAGE

This stovetop supper is simple to make, and it charms my whole clan of curry lovers. My kids even ask for it cold to have in their school lunches.
—Colette Lower, York, PA

Prep: 15 min. • **Cook:** 20 min.
Makes: 8 servings

- 1   pound mild bulk Italian sausage
- 1   tablespoon olive oil
- 1   medium onion, chopped
- 1   medium green pepper, chopped
- 1   large acorn squash or 6 cups butternut squash, seeded, peeled and cubed (½-in.)
- 1   large unpeeled apple, cubed (½-in.)
- 2   to 3 teaspoons curry powder
- 1   teaspoon salt
- 3   cups cooked small pasta shells
- ¼   cup water

1. In a stockpot, cook and crumble sausage over medium heat until no longer pink, 5-6 minutes; remove.
2. In same pan, heat oil; cook and stir onion and pepper 3 minutes. Add squash; cook 5 minutes. Stir in the apple, curry powder and salt until vegetables are crisp-tender, 3-4 minutes.
3. Return sausage to pan; add pasta and water. Heat through.
Per 1⅓ cups: 385 cal., 18g fat (5g sat. fat), 38mg chol., 735mg sod., 44g carb. (7g sugars, 4g fiber), 14g pro.

APRICOT-ROSEMARY PORK MEDALLIONS

I needed to use a pork tenderloin in my fridge before it expired, but I didn't have time to wait for it to roast. I tried this recipe, and it was not only quick but my family loved it. Try it with any flavor preserves.
—Lynn Caruso, Gilroy, CA

Prep: 10 min. • **Cook:** 30 min.
Makes: 8 servings

- 2   pork tenderloins (1 pound each)
- ½   cup seasoned bread crumbs
- 2   tablespoons olive oil
- 6   cups fresh broccoli florets
- ⅔   cup apricot preserves
- ¼   cup white wine or chicken broth
- 2   teaspoons minced fresh rosemary or ½ teaspoon dried rosemary, crushed
- ½   teaspoon salt
- ⅛   teaspoon pepper
- 5⅓   cups hot cooked brown rice

1. Cut each tenderloin crosswise into eight 1-in. slices. Place bread crumbs in a shallow bowl. Dip pork slices in crumbs, patting to help coating adhere. In a large nonstick skillet, heat oil over medium heat. Add pork in batches; cook 3-4 minutes on each side or until a thermometer reads 145°.
2. Meanwhile, in a large saucepan, place the steamer basket over 1 in. of water. Place the broccoli in the basket. Bring the water to a boil. Reduce the heat to maintain a simmer; steam it, covered, for 4-6 minutes or until tender.
3. In a small saucepan, mix the preserves, wine, rosemary, salt and pepper. Cook and stir over medium-low heat 3-5 minutes or until preserves are melted. Serve with pork, broccoli and rice.
Per serving: 404 cal., 9g fat (2g sat. fat), 64mg chol., 321mg sod., 53g carb. (12g sugars, 4g fiber), 28g pro.

3 tablespoons sugar
3 tablespoons Worcestershire sauce
2 tablespoons prepared mustard
½ teaspoon salt
½ teaspoon pepper
¼ teaspoon liquid smoke, optional

1. Place ribs in an 11x7-in. baking dish coated with cooking spray. Sprinkle with liquid smoke if desired and salt. Add water to pan. Cover and bake at 350° for 1 hour.
2. Meanwhile, in a saucepan, saute onion in oil until tender. Add the remaining sauce ingredients; bring to a boil. Reduce heat; simmer, uncovered, for 15 minutes or until slightly thickened.
3. Drain ribs; top with half of the barbecue sauce. Cover and bake 1 hour longer or until meat is tender, basting every 20 minutes. Serve with remaining sauce.
Freeze option: Place cooled meat mixture in freezer containers. To use, partially thaw in refrigerator overnight. Microwave, covered, on high in a microwave-safe dish until heated through, gently stirring and adding a little water if necessary.
Per 4 ounces: 292 cal., 14g fat (4g sat. fat), 91mg chol., 668mg sod., 14g carb. (0 sugars, 1g fiber), 28g pro.

BBQ COUNTRY RIBS

I created this sauce for ribs many years ago when I adapted a recipe I saw in a magazine. I often triple the sauce and keep some in my freezer to use on chicken, beef or pork.
—Barbara Gerriets, Topeka, KS

Prep: 25 min. • **Bake:** 2 hours
Makes: 8 servings

2½ pounds boneless country-style pork ribs
2 teaspoons liquid smoke, optional
½ teaspoon salt
1 cup water
BARBECUE SAUCE
⅔ cup chopped onion
1 tablespoon canola oil
¾ cup each water and ketchup
⅓ cup lemon juice

SKILLET PORK CHOPS WITH APPLES

My family loves apples, so I often include them in savory dishes for a fresh, fruity flavor. After experimenting with a few pork chop and apple recipes to find the perfect pairing, we all agreed this skillet sensation was our favorite.

—Amanda Jobe, Olathe, KS

Prep: 15 min.
Cook: 20 min.
Makes: 4 servings

4   **boneless pork loin chops (4 ounces each and ¾ inch thick)**
1   **teaspoon dried oregano, divided**
½   **teaspoon salt**
¼   **teaspoon coarsely ground pepper**
1½ **teaspoons canola oil**
2   **small apples, cut into ½-inch slices**
1   **cup sliced sweet onion (¼ inch thick)**
⅓   **cup unsweetened applesauce**
¼   **cup cider vinegar**

1. Sprinkle the pork chops with ½ teaspoon oregano, salt and pepper. Place a large nonstick skillet coated with cooking spray over medium-high heat. Brown chops, about 3 minutes per side; remove from pan.

2. In the same pan, heat the oil over medium-high heat. Add the apples, onion and remaining oregano; cook and stir 6-8 minutes or until apples are tender.

3. Reduce heat to medium; stir in applesauce and vinegar. Return chops to the pan; cook, covered, 4-6 minutes or until pork is tender. Let stand 5 minutes before serving.

Per 1 pork chop with ½ cup apple mixture: 215 cal., 8g fat (2g sat. fat), 55mg chol., 329mg sod., 12g carb. (8g sugars, 2g fiber), 22g pro.
Diabetic exchanges: 3 lean meat, ½ fruit, ½ fat.

C
ORANGE-GLAZED PORK LOIN

This crazy-good tenderloin sprinkled with thyme and ginger is one of the best pork recipes I've ever tried. Guests always ask for the recipe.
—Lynnette Miete, Alna, ME

Prep: 10 min.
Bake: 1 hour 20 min. + standing
Makes: 16 servings

- 1   teaspoon salt
- 1   garlic clove, minced
- ¼   teaspoon dried thyme
- ¼   teaspoon ground ginger
- ¼   teaspoon pepper
- 1   boneless pork loin roast (5 pounds)

GLAZE
- 1   cup orange juice
- ¼   cup packed brown sugar
- 1   tablespoon Dijon mustard
- ⅓   cup water
- 1   tablespoon cornstarch

1. Preheat oven to 350°. Combine the first five ingredients; rub over roast. Place fat side up on a rack in a shallow roasting pan. Bake, uncovered, for 1 hour.
2. Meanwhile, in a saucepan over medium heat, combine orange juice, brown sugar and mustard. In a small bowl, mix water and cornstarch until smooth. Add to orange juice mixture. Bring to a boil; cook and stir 2 minutes. Reserve 1 cup glaze for serving; brush half of the remaining glaze over the roast.
3. Bake until a thermometer reads 145°, about 20-40 minutes longer, brushing the meat occasionally with the remaining glaze. Let stand for 10 minutes before slicing. Reheat reserved glaze; serve with roast.
Per 4 ounces: 199 cal., 7g fat (2g sat. fat), 71mg chol., 212mg sod., 6g carb. (5g sugars, 0 fiber), 28g pro.
Diabetic exchanges: 4 lean meat, ½ starch.

FAST FIX ▶
SKEWERLESS STOVETOP KABOBS

My family loves this quick and easy recipe so much, we never have any leftovers. It's also great on the grill.
—Jennifer Mitchell, Altoona, PA

Start to Finish: 30 min.
Makes: 4 servings

- 1   pork tenderloin (1 pound), cut into ¾-inch cubes
- ¾   cup fat-free Italian salad dressing, divided
- 2   large green peppers, cut into ¾-inch pieces
- 2   small zucchini, cut into ½-inch slices
- 1   large sweet onion, cut into wedges
- ½   pound medium fresh mushrooms, halved
- 1   cup cherry tomatoes
- ¼   teaspoon pepper
- ⅛   teaspoon seasoned salt

1. In a large nonstick skillet, cook pork over medium-high heat in ¼ cup salad dressing until no longer pink. Remove from pan.
2. In same pan, cook peppers, zucchini, onion, mushrooms, tomatoes, pepper and seasoned salt in remaining salad dressing until vegetables are tender. Return pork to skillet; heat through.
Per 2 cups: 236 cal., 5g fat (2g sat. fat), 65mg chol., 757mg sod., 22g carb. (12g sugars, 4g fiber), 27g pro.
Diabetic exchanges: 3 lean meat, 2 starch.

C
GREEK PORK CHOPS

My in-laws taught me a lot about cooking, so whenever I stumble upon a new recipe, I make it for them. They gave these seasoned grilled chops a big thumbs-up!
—Geri Lipczynski, Oak Lawn, IL

Prep: 15 min. + marinating
Grill: 10 min.
Makes: 4 servings

- 2 tablespoons olive oil
- 4 teaspoons lemon juice
- 1 tablespoon Worcestershire sauce
- 2 teaspoons dried oregano
- 1 teaspoon salt
- 1 teaspoon onion powder
- 1 teaspoon garlic powder
- 1 teaspoon pepper
- ½ teaspoon ground mustard
- 4 boneless pork loin chops (¾ inch thick and 4 ounces each)

1. In a large resealable plastic bag, mix first nine ingredients. Add pork chops; seal bag and turn to coat. Refrigerate 8 hours or overnight.
2. Drain pork, discarding marinade. Grill chops, covered, over medium heat or broil 4 in. from heat until a thermometer reads 145°, about 4-5 minutes per side. Let stand 5 minutes before serving.
Freeze option: Freeze chops with marinade in a resealable plastic freezer bag. To use, thaw in refrigerator overnight. Drain pork, discarding marinade. Grill as directed.
Per 1 pork chop: 193 cal., 10g fat (3g sat. fat), 55mg chol., 348mg sod., 2g carb. (1g sugars, 1g fiber), 22g pro.
Diabetic exchanges: 3 lean meat, ½ fat.

HAM & SPINACH COUSCOUS

This foolproof dish makes a tasty one-pot meal when time is tight.
—Lisa Shannon, Cullman, AL

Start to Finish: 20 min.
Makes: 4 servings

- 2 cups water
- 1 cup chopped fully cooked ham
- 1 cup chopped fresh spinach
- ½ teaspoon garlic salt
- 1 cup uncooked couscous
- ¼ cup shredded cheddar cheese

In a large saucepan, combine the water, ham, spinach and garlic salt. Bring to a boil. Stir in couscous. Remove from the heat; cover and let stand for 5-10 minutes or until water is absorbed. Fluff with a fork. Sprinkle with cheese.
Per 1 cup: 248 cal., 6g fat (3g sat. fat), 26mg chol., 727mg sod., 36g carb. (1g sugars, 2g fiber), 14g pro.
Diabetic exchanges: 2 starch, 1 lean meat, 1 fat.

★ ★ ★ ★ ★ **READER REVIEW**

"Very good and insanely quick and simple to make with only six ingredients. Great for a busy weeknight and easily adaptable to many different tastes."

CONNIEK TASTEOFHOME.COM

CUBAN-STYLE PORK CHOPS

These chops taste just like a Cuban sandwich without the bread. I like the fact they're a bit more elegant. Let your family customize their own with pickles, mustard and other condiments.
—Erica Allen, Tuckerton, NJ

Prep: 15 min. + marinating
Grill: 10 min.
Makes: 4 servings

- 1 tablespoon Dijon mustard
- 1 tablespoon lime juice
- 1 teaspoon adobo seasoning
- 4 boneless pork loin chops (4 ounces each)
- 4 slices deli ham (about 3 ounces)
- 4 slices Swiss cheese
- 2 tablespoons chopped fresh cilantro
  Optional ingredients: mayonnaise, additional Dijon mustard and thinly sliced dill pickles

1. Mix mustard, lime juice and adobo seasoning. Lightly pound pork chops with a meat mallet to ½-in. thickness; spread both sides with mustard mixture. Refrigerate, covered, 3-4 hours.
2. Grill pork, covered, over medium heat 3 minutes. Turn pork and top with ham; grill 2 minutes longer. Top with cheese and cilantro; grill, covered, 30-60 seconds longer or until the cheese is melted and a thermometer inserted in chops reads 145°. Let stand 5 minutes before serving. If desired, serve pork chops with mayonnaise, mustard and pickles.

Per serving: 247 cal., 12g fat (5g sat. fat), 84mg chol., 700mg sod., 2g carb. (1g sugars, 0 fiber), 31g pro.
Diabetic exchanges: 4 lean meat, ½ fat.

F FAST FIX▶
OPEN-FACED HAM & APPLE MELTS

Whether you enjoy them as a light lunch or a late-night snack, you're sure to love these yummy melts that mix hearty ham with a sweet apple crunch.
—Sally Maloney, Dallas, GA

Start to Finish: 15 min.
Makes: 4 servings

- 2 whole wheat English muffins, split
- 2 teaspoons Dijon mustard
- 4 slices deli ham
- ½ medium apple, thinly sliced
- 2 slices reduced-fat Swiss cheese, halved

1. Place the English muffin halves cut side up on a baking sheet. Broil 4-6 in. from heat for 2-3 minutes or until golden brown.
2. Spread with mustard. Top with ham, apple slices and cheese. Broil 3-4 minutes longer or until cheese is melted.

Per 1 muffin half: 130 cal., 3g fat (1g sat. fat), 14mg chol., 429mg sod., 17g carb. (5g sugars, 3g fiber), 10g pro.

APPLE ROASTED PORK WITH CHERRY BALSAMIC GLAZE

I added roasted apples, cherries and onions to turn ordinary pork into a break-away dish and I have not turned back since. There's a short time frame between perfectly caramelized onions and burned ones, so be sure to pay attention once they start cooking.
—Josh Downey, McHenry, IL

Prep: 30 min.
Bake: 50 min.+ standing
Makes: 8 servings

- 1 boneless pork loin roast (3 pounds)
- 1½ teaspoons salt, divided
- ¾ teaspoon pepper, divided
- ¼ cup olive oil, divided
- 3 medium apples, sliced
- 1½ cups unsweetened apple juice
- 6 medium onions, sliced (about 5 cups)
- 3 tablespoons balsamic vinegar
- 1½ cups frozen pitted dark sweet cherries
- ½ cup cherry juice

1. Preheat oven to 350°. Sprinkle roast with 1 teaspoon salt and ½ teaspoon pepper. In an ovenproof Dutch oven, heat 2 tablespoons oil over medium-high heat; brown roast on all sides. Add apples and apple juice to pan. Bake the roast, uncovered, 50-60 minutes or until a thermometer inserted in pork reads 145°, basting occasionally with pan juices.

2. Meanwhile, in a large skillet, heat remaining oil over medium heat. Add the onions and the remaining salt and pepper; cook and stir 8-10 minutes or until softened. Reduce heat to medium-low; cook 35-40 minutes or until deep golden brown, stirring occasionally. Keep onions warm.

3. Remove roast and apples to a serving plate; tent with foil. Let stand 10 minutes before slicing.

4. Skim fat from pork pan juices. Place over medium-high heat; add vinegar and cook 1 minute, stirring to loosen browned bits from pan. Stir in cherries and cherry juice. Bring to a boil; cook 10-15 minutes or until mixture is reduced to about 1 cup. Serve pork, apples and onions with cherry glaze.

Per serving: 387 cal., 15g fat (4g sat. fat), 85mg chol., 498mg sod., 29g carb. (20g sugars, 3g fiber), 34g pro.

PORK CHOPS WITH HONEY-GARLIC SAUCE

The honey-garlic sauce in this recipe is so good, I often double it so there's extra for dipping.
—Michelle Smith, Eldersburg, MD

Start to Finish: 25 min.
Makes: 4 servings

- 4 **bone-in pork loin chops (6 ounces each)**
- ¼ **cup lemon juice**
- ¼ **cup honey**
- 2 **tablespoons reduced-sodium soy sauce**
- 1 **garlic clove, minced**

In a large nonstick skillet coated with cooking spray, cook the pork chops over medium heat until a thermometer reads 145°, about 5-6 minutes on each side. Remove; let chops stand 5 minutes. Combine remaining ingredients; add to pan. Cook the sauce over medium heat 3-4 minutes, stirring occasionally. Serve with chops.

Per 1 pork chop with 2 tablespoons sauce: 249 cal., 7g fat (3g sat. fat), 74mg chol., 342mg sod., 19g carb. (18g sugars, 0 fiber), 27g pro.
Diabetic exchanges: 4 lean meat, 1 starch.

★ ★ ★ ★ ★ **READER REVIEW**

"This is my husband's all-time favorite. He requests it all the time. I used boneless center-cut chops instead."

BNELSON1972
TASTEOFHOME.COM

FAST FIX

PEPPERED PORK PITAS

It may be hard to believe, but cracked black pepper and garlic are all I need to give my pork loin chops some pop. Then I stuff the meat inside pitas along with roasted sweet red peppers and garlic mayo. With these tasty hand-helds, any weeknight meal is awesome!
—Kathy White, Henderson, NV

Start to Finish: 20 min.
Makes: 4 servings

- 1 **pound boneless pork loin chops, cut into thin strips**
- 1 **tablespoon olive oil**
- 2 **teaspoons coarsely ground pepper**
- 2 **garlic cloves, minced**
- 1 **jar (12 ounces) roasted sweet red peppers, drained and julienned**
- 4 **whole pita breads, warmed Garlic mayonnaise and torn leaf lettuce, optional**

In a small bowl, combine pork, oil, pepper and garlic; toss to coat. Place a large skillet over medium-high heat. Add pork mixture; cook and stir until no longer pink. Stir in red peppers; heat through. Serve on pita breads. Top the pitas with mayonnaise and lettuce if desired.
Per 1 sandwich: 380 cal., 11g fat (3g sat. fat), 55mg chol., 665mg sod., 37g carb. (4g sugars, 2g fiber), 27g pro.
Diabetic exchanges: 3 lean meat, 2 starch, 1 fat.

ITALIAN HERB-CRUSTED PORK LOIN

When it comes to meals, I like to change things up. This herb-rubbed roasted pork loin dazzles my family, whether it be a special occasion or a weeknight dinner.
—Kim Palmer, Kingston, GA

Prep: 15 min. + chilling
Bake: 50 min. + standing
Makes: 8 servings

- 3 tablespoons olive oil
- 5 garlic cloves, minced
- 1 teaspoon salt
- 1 teaspoon each dried basil, thyme and rosemary, crushed
- ½ teaspoon Italian seasoning
- ½ teaspoon pepper
- 1 boneless pork loin roast (3 to 4 pounds)
- 8 medium carrots, halved lengthwise
- 2 medium onions, quartered

1. In a small bowl, mix oil, garlic and seasonings; rub over roast. Arrange carrots and onions on the bottom of a 13x9-in. baking pan. Place the roast over vegetables, fat side up. Refrigerate, covered, 1 hour.
2. Preheat oven to 475°. Roast the pork for 20 minutes.
3. Reduce oven setting to 425°. Roast 30-40 minutes longer or until a thermometer reads 145° and vegetables are tender. Remove roast from oven; tent with foil. Let stand 20 minutes before slicing.
Per serving: 295 cal., 13g fat (4g sat. fat), 85mg chol., 388mg sod., 9g carb. (4g sugars, 2g fiber), 34g pro.
Diabetic exchanges: 5 lean meat, 1 vegetable, 1 fat.

GLAZED PORK ON SWEET POTATO BEDS

When solving the "What's for dinner?" puzzle, this maple-glazed pork tenderloin is often our top choice. Add sweet potatoes for a comfy side.
—Jessie Grearson-Sapat Falmouth, ME

Prep: 20 min. • **Cook:** 30 min.
Makes: 6 servings

- 1½ pounds sweet potatoes, peeled and cubed
- 1 medium apple, peeled and cut into 8 pieces
- 2 tablespoons butter
- 1 tablespoon lemon juice
- 2 teaspoons minced fresh gingerroot
- ½ teaspoon salt
- ½ teaspoon pepper

PORK

- 1 teaspoon water
- ½ teaspoon cornstarch
- 3 tablespoons maple syrup
- 2 teaspoons wasabi mustard
- 2 teaspoons soy sauce
- ½ teaspoon pepper
- 2 pork tenderloins (¾ pound each), cut into 1-inch slices
- 1 tablespoon olive oil
- 2 garlic cloves, minced

1. Place sweet potatoes and apple in a large saucepan with water to cover. Bring it to a boil over high heat. Reduce the heat to medium; cover and cook just until tender, 10-12 minutes. Drain. Mash the potatoes and apple. Add the next five ingredients; keep warm.
2. Stir water into cornstarch until smooth; add syrup, mustard, soy sauce and pepper. Add the pork; stir to coat.
3. In a large skillet, heat oil over medium heat. Brown pork. Add garlic; cook until meat is no longer pink, 3-5 minutes longer. Serve with sweet potatoes and pan juices.
Per 3 ounces pork with ½ cup sweet potato and apple: 327 cal., 10g fat (4g sat. fat), 74mg chol., 473mg sod., 33g carb. (13g sugars, 4g fiber), 25g pro.
Diabetic exchanges: 3 lean meat, 2 starch, 1 fat.

Tilapia with Fiesta Rice
page 135

FISH & SEAFOOD FAVORITES

When it comes to eating healthy, fish and seafood are natural choices. Turn here to find a new and exciting catch-of-the-day recipe to wow your crowd.

THE ULTIMATE FISH TACOS

My twist on the marinade makes these fish tacos pop with flavor. I warm corn tortillas on the grill and add salsa, cilantro, purple cabbage and fresh-squeezed lime. Tapatio hot pepper sauce works well in these tacos.

—Yvonne Molina, Moreno Valley, CA

Prep: 20 min. + marinating
Grill: 10 min.
Makes: 6 servings

- ¼ cup olive oil
- 1 teaspoon ground cardamom
- 1 teaspoon paprika
- 1 teaspoon salt
- 1 teaspoon pepper
- 6 mahi mahi fillets (6 ounces each)
- 12 corn tortillas (6 inches)
- 2 cups chopped red cabbage
- 1 cup chopped fresh cilantro
  Salsa verde, optional
- 2 medium limes, cut into wedges
  Hot pepper sauce

1. In a 13x9-in. baking dish, whisk the first five ingredients. Add fillets; turn to coat. Refrigerate, covered, 30 minutes.

2. Drain fish and discard marinade. On an oiled grill rack, grill mahi mahi, covered, over medium-high heat (or broil 4 in. from heat) until it flakes easily with a fork, 4-5 minutes per side. Remove fish. Place tortillas on grill rack; heat through, 30-45 seconds. Keep warm.

3. To assemble, divide fish among the tortillas; layer with red cabbage, cilantro and, if desired, salsa verde. Squeeze a little lime juice and hot pepper sauce over fish mixture; fold sides of tortilla over mixture. Serve with lime wedges and additional pepper sauce.

Per 2 tacos: 284 cal., 5g fat (1g sat. fat), 124mg chol., 278mg sod., 26g carb. (2g sugars, 4g fiber), 35g pro. **Diabetic exchanges:** 5 lean meat, 1½ starch, ½ fat.

FAST FIX

GRILLED SALMON WITH NECTARINES

I served this to my family for dinner one night. They gave it the stamp of approval, so I made it again to take to a potluck the next day. Everyone raved about it there, too...even the non-fish lovers!

—Kerin Benjamin, Citrus Heights, CA

Start to Finish: 10 min.
Makes: 4 servings

- 4 salmon fillets (4 ounces each)
- ½ teaspoon salt, divided
- ⅛ teaspoon pepper
- 1 tablespoon honey
- 1 tablespoon lemon juice
- 1 tablespoon olive oil
- 3 medium nectarines, thinly sliced
- 1 tablespoon minced fresh basil

1. Sprinkle salmon with ¼ teaspoon salt and pepper. Place on an oiled grill, skin side down. Grill, covered, over medium heat 8-10 minutes or until fish just begins to flakes easily with a fork.

2. Meanwhile, in a bowl, mix honey, lemon juice, oil and remaining salt. Stir in nectarines and basil. Serve with salmon.

Per 1 fillet with ⅓ cup nectarines: 307 cal., 16g fat (3g sat. fat), 67mg chol., 507mg sod., 17g carb. (13g sugars, 2g fiber), 23g pro. **Diabetic exchanges:** 3 lean meat, 1½ fat, 1 fruit.

TEST KITCHEN TIP
The five most common species of Pacific salmon are chinook, coho, sockeye, pink and chum. Keep salmon in the coldest part of your fridge. Use it within a day or two.

begins to flake easily with a fork. Open foil carefully to allow steam to escape.

Per serving: 270 cal., 9g fat (2g sat. fat), 83mg chol., 443mg sod., 15g carb. (6g sugars, 3g fiber), 35g pro.

Diabetic exchanges: 5 lean meat, 1½ fat, 1 vegetable, ½ starch.

C **FAST FIX**

PECAN-ORANGE SALMON

This nutty, citrusy baked salmon is a favorite that I've prepared for family and guests many times.
—Kari Kelley, Plains, MT

Start to Finish: 25 min.
Makes: 4 servings

- 1 tablespoon grated orange peel
- ⅓ cup orange juice
- 1 tablespoon Dijon mustard
- 1 tablespoon honey
- 2 teaspoons olive oil
- ½ teaspoon salt
- ¼ teaspoon pepper
- 4 salmon fillets (5 ounces each)
- 2 tablespoons finely chopped pecans

1. Preheat oven to 425°. In a small bowl, whisk the first seven ingredients until blended.
2. Place salmon in a greased 11x7-in. baking dish. Pour sauce over the salmon; sprinkle with pecans. Bake, uncovered, 15-18 minutes or until fish just begins to flake easily with a fork.

Per 1 fillet: 297 cal., 18g fat (3g sat. fat), 71mg chol., 456mg sod., 8g carb. (6g sugars, 1g fiber), 24g pro.

Diabetic exchanges: 4 lean meat, 1½ fat, ½ starch.

C **FAST FIX**

TOMATO-HERB GRILLED TILAPIA

Trust me: This super tilapia with ginger and lemon takes dinner over the top with minimal prep. Grilling the fish in foil is about as easy as it gets.
—Trisha Kruse, Eagle, ID

Start to Finish: 30 min.
Makes: 4 servings

- 1 cup fresh cilantro leaves
- 1 cup fresh parsley leaves
- 2 tablespoons olive oil
- 2 teaspoons grated lemon peel
- 2 tablespoons lemon juice
- 1 tablespoon coarsely chopped fresh gingerroot
- ¾ teaspoon sea salt or kosher salt, divided
- 2 cups grape tomatoes, halved lengthwise
- 1½ cups fresh or frozen corn (about 8 ounces), thawed
- 4 tilapia fillets (6 ounces each)

1. Place the first six ingredients in a food processor; add ½ teaspoon salt. Pulse until mixture is finely chopped.
2. In a bowl, combine tomatoes and corn; stir in 1 tablespoon herb mixture and remaining salt.
3. Place each fillet on a piece of heavy-duty foil (about 12 in. square). Top with herb mixture; spoon tomato mixture alongside fish. Fold foil around fish and vegetables, sealing tightly.
4. Grill, covered, over medium-high heat 6-8 minutes or until fish just

C **FAST FIX**

CRUNCHY TUNA SALAD WITH TOMATOES

On a hot summer day, there's nothing more refreshing than my tuna salad. I grow a few tomato plants in my garden and the homegrown taste makes the recipe even more of a treat.
—Diane Selich, Vassar, MI

Start to Finish: 20 min.
Makes: 4 servings

- ⅔ cup reduced-fat mayonnaise
- ½ cup chopped sweet onion
- 1 celery rib, chopped
- 1 teaspoon minced fresh parsley or ¼ teaspoon dried parsley flakes
- ¾ teaspoon pepper
- 1 can (12 ounces) albacore white tuna in water, drained and flaked
- 4 medium tomatoes, cut into wedges

In a small bowl, combine the mayonnaise, onion, celery, parsley and pepper. Stir in tuna. Serve with tomato wedges.

Per ½ cup tuna salad with 1 tomato:
280 cal., 16g fat (3g sat. fat), 50mg chol., 656mg sod., 12g carb. (7g sugars, 2g fiber), 22g pro.
Diabetic exchanges: 3 lean meat, 2 fat, 1 vegetable.

SOUTHERN SEAFOOD GUMBO

A local restaurant serves a terrific gumbo, and I duplicated it pretty closely with this recipe. I did lighten it up a bit, but no one in my family seems to mind.
—Susan Wright, Champaign, IL

Prep: 25 min. • **Cook:** 35 min.
Makes: 12 servings

- 1 medium onion, chopped
- 2 celery ribs with leaves, chopped
- 1 medium green pepper, chopped
- 1 tablespoon olive oil
- 3 garlic cloves, minced
- 1 bottle (46 ounces) spicy hot V8 juice
- 1 can (14½ ounces) diced tomatoes, undrained
- ¼ teaspoon cayenne pepper
- 1 package (16 ounces) frozen sliced okra, thawed
- 1 pound catfish fillets, cut into ¾-inch cubes
- ¾ pound uncooked medium shrimp, peeled and deveined
- 3 cups cooked long grain rice

1. In a Dutch oven, saute the onion, celery and green pepper in oil until tender. Add garlic; cook 1 minute longer. Stir in V8 juice, tomatoes and cayenne pepper; bring to a boil. Reduce heat; cover and simmer for 10 minutes.

2. Stir in okra and catfish; cook 8 minutes longer. Add the shrimp; cook 7 minutes longer or until shrimp turn pink. Place rice in 12 individual serving bowls; top with gumbo.

Per 1 cup: 180 cal., 5g fat (1g sat. fat), 60mg chol., 512mg sod., 22g carb. (7g sugars, 3g fiber), 14g pro.
Diabetic exchanges: 2 lean meat, 2 vegetable, 1 starch.

GRILLED FISH SANDWICHES

I season these fish fillets with lime juice and lemon pepper before grilling them. A simple honey mustard-mayonnaise sauce puts the sandwiches ahead of the rest.
—Violet Beard, Marshall, IL

Start to Finish: 30 min.
Makes: 4 servings

       4   cod fillets (4 ounces each)
       1   tablespoon lime juice
       ½   teaspoon lemon-pepper
             seasoning
       ¼   cup fat-free mayonnaise
       2   teaspoons Dijon mustard
       1   teaspoon honey
       4   hamburger buns, split
       4   lettuce leaves
       4   tomato slices

1. Brush both sides of fillets with lime juice; sprinkle with lemon pepper. Grill fillets, covered, on an oiled rack over medium heat or broil 4 in. from the heat until fish flakes easily with a fork, 4-5 minutes on each side.
2. In a small bowl, combine the mayonnaise, mustard and honey. Spread over the bottom of each bun. Top with a fillet, lettuce and tomato; replace bun tops.
Per 1 sandwich: 241 cal., 3g fat (1g sat. fat), 49mg chol., 528mg sod., 28g carb. (0 sugars, 2g fiber), 24g pro.
Diabetic exchanges: 3 lean meat, 2 starch.

FISH TACOS WITH GUACAMOLE

Fish tacos with guacamole is my new favorite recipe—lighter than beef tacos smothered in cheese. Try hot sauce, onions, tomatoes or jalapenos on top.
—Deb Perry, Traverse City, MI

Prep: 25 min.
Cook: 10 min.
Makes: 4 servings

       2   cups angel hair coleslaw mix
     1½   teaspoons canola oil
     1½   teaspoons lime juice
   GUACAMOLE
       1   medium ripe avocado,
             peeled and quartered
       2   tablespoons fat-free
             sour cream
       1   tablespoon finely
             chopped onion
       1   tablespoon minced
             fresh cilantro
       ⅛   teaspoon salt
             Dash pepper
   TACOS
       1   pound tilapia fillets, cut
             into 1-inch pieces
       ¼   teaspoon salt
       ⅛   teaspoon pepper
       2   teaspoons canola oil
       8   corn tortillas
             (6 inches), warmed
             Optional toppings: hot
             pepper sauce and chopped
             tomatoes, green onions and
             jalapeno pepper

1. In a small bowl, toss coleslaw mix with oil and lime juice; refrigerate until serving. In another bowl, mash avocado with a fork; stir in sour cream, onion, cilantro, salt and pepper.
2. Sprinkle tilapia with salt and pepper. In a large nonstick skillet coated with cooking spray, heat oil over medium-high heat. Add tilapia; cook 3-4 minutes on each side or until fish just begins to flake easily with a fork. Serve in tortillas with coleslaw, guacamole and toppings as desired.
Per 2 tacos: 308 cal., 12g fat (2g sat. fat), 56mg chol., 299mg sod., 28g carb. (2g sugars, 6g fiber), 25g pro.
Diabetic exchanges: 3 lean meat, 2 starch, 2 fat.

SPICY SHRIMP & WATERMELON KABOBS

My three sons can polish off a juicy watermelon in one sitting. Before they dig in, I set aside a few slices to make these zesty shrimp kabobs.
—Jennifer Fisher, Austin, TX

Start to Finish: 30 min.
Makes: 4 servings

1   tablespoon reduced-sodium soy sauce
1   tablespoon Sriracha Asian hot chili sauce
1   tablespoon honey
1   garlic clove, minced
4   cups cubed seedless watermelon (1 inch), divided
1   pound uncooked shrimp (16-20 per pound), peeled and deveined
1   medium red onion, cut into 1-inch pieces
½   teaspoon sea salt
¼   teaspoon coarsely ground pepper
    Minced fresh cilantro

1. For glaze, place soy sauce, chili sauce, honey, garlic and 2 cups watermelon in a blender; cover and process until pureed. Transfer to a small saucepan; bring to a boil. Cook, uncovered, over medium-high heat until mixture is reduced by half, about 10 minutes. Reserve ¼ cup glaze for serving.
2. On four metal or soaked wooden skewers, alternately thread shrimp, onion and remaining watermelon. Sprinkle with salt and pepper.

3. Place kabobs on an oiled grill rack over medium heat. Grill, covered, 3-4 minutes on each side or until shrimp turns pink, brushing with remaining glaze during the last 2 minutes. Sprinkle with cilantro. Serve with reserved glaze.
Per 1 kabob with 1 tablespoon glaze: 172 cal., 2g fat (0 sat. fat), 138mg chol., 644mg sod., 23g carb. (19g sugars, 2g fiber), 20g pro.

Diabetic exchanges: 3 lean meat, 1 fruit, ½ starch.

TEST KITCHEN TIP
Fresh shrimp are available in different varieties and sizes. Uncooked shrimp will have shells that range in color from gray or brown to pink or red. They should have a firm texture with a mild odor.

DE-LIGHTFUL TUNA CASSEROLE

This lightened-up tuna casserole will satisfy your family's craving for comfort food without the unwanted calories and fat.
—Colleen Willey, Hamburg, NY

Prep: 15 min.
Bake: 25 min.
Makes: 5 servings

- 1 package (7 ounces) elbow macaroni
- 1 can (10¾ ounces) reduced-fat reduced-sodium condensed cream of mushroom soup, undiluted
- 1 cup sliced fresh mushrooms
- 1 cup shredded reduced-fat cheddar cheese
- 1 cup fat-free milk
- 1 can (5 ounces) light water-packed tuna, drained and flaked
- 2 tablespoons diced pimientos
- 3 teaspoons dried minced onion
- 1 teaspoon ground mustard
- ¼ teaspoon salt
- ⅓ cup crushed cornflakes

1. Cook macaroni according to package directions. Meanwhile, in a large bowl, combine the soup, mushrooms, cheese, milk, tuna, pimientos, onion, mustard and salt. Drain macaroni; add to tuna mixture and mix well.
2. Transfer to a 2-qt. baking dish coated with cooking spray. Sprinkle with cornflakes. Bake, uncovered, at 350° for 25-30 minutes or until bubbly.
Freeze option: Cool unbaked casserole before topping with cornflakes; cover and freeze. To use, partially thaw in refrigerator overnight. Remove from refrigerator 30 minutes before baking. Preheat oven to 350°. Top casserole with cornflakes and bake as directed; increase time as necessary to heat through and for a thermometer inserted in center to read 165°.
Per 1¼ cups: 329 cal., 8g fat (4g sat. fat), 32mg chol., 684mg sod., 43g carb. (7g sugars, 2g fiber), 23g pro.
Diabetic exchanges: 3 starch, 2 lean meat.

F **S** **FAST FIX**
PEPPERED TUNA KABOBS

When we host barbecues, we like to wow our guests, so dogs and burgers are out! We make tuna skewers topped with salsa—the perfect easy recipe. My five kids even like to help me put them together.
—Jennifer Ingersoll, Herndon, VA

Start to Finish: 30 min.
Makes: 4 servings

- ½ cup frozen corn, thawed
- 4 green onions, chopped
- 1 jalapeno pepper, seeded and chopped
- 2 tablespoons coarsely chopped fresh parsley
- 2 tablespoons lime juice
- 1 pound tuna steaks, cut into 1-inch cubes
- 1 teaspoon coarsely ground pepper
- 2 large sweet red peppers, cut into 2x1-inch pieces
- 1 medium mango, peeled and cut into 1-inch cubes

1. For salsa, in a small bowl, combine the first five ingredients; set aside.
2. Rub tuna with pepper. On four metal or soaked wooden skewers, alternately thread red peppers, tuna and mango.
3. Place skewers on greased grill rack. Cook, covered, over medium heat, turning occasionally, until tuna is slightly pink in center (medium-rare) and peppers are tender, 10-12 minutes. Serve with salsa.
Note: Wear disposable gloves when cutting hot peppers; the oils can burn skin. Avoid touching your face.
Per 1 kabob: 205 cal., 2g fat (0 sat. fat), 51mg chol., 50mg sod., 20g carb. (12g sugars, 4g fiber), 29g pro.
Diabetic exchanges: 3 lean meat, 1 starch.

CAJUN SHRIMP & CUCUMBER WRAPS

Balance the heat of spicy Cajun shrimp by wrapping them up with lettuce, cucumbers and parsley. This hand-held dinner is perfect for dining alfresco.
—Chantel Beauregard
Lake Arrowhead, CA

Start to Finish: 20 min.
Makes: 4 servings

- ¼ cup lemon juice
- 4 tablespoons olive oil, divided
- 1½ teaspoons Cajun seasoning, divided
- ⅛ teaspoon pepper
- 1 pound uncooked large shrimp, peeled and deveined (tails removed)
- 8 Bibb or Boston lettuce leaves
- 4 flatbread wraps
- 2 small cucumbers, cut lengthwise into quarters
- 4 thin slices red onion
- ¼ cup fresh parsley leaves

1. In a small bowl, whisk lemon juice, 3 tablespoons oil, 1 teaspoon Cajun seasoning and pepper. Set aside. Toss shrimp with remaining Cajun seasoning. In a large skillet, heat remaining oil over medium-high heat. Add shrimp mixture; cook and stir until shrimp turn pink.
2. Place lettuce on flatbread wraps; top with cucumbers, onion, parsley and shrimp. Drizzle with dressing; roll up and, if desired, secure with toothpicks.
Per 1 wrap: 365 cal., 17g fat (2g sat. fat), 138mg chol., 670mg sod., 29g carb. (3g sugars, 4g fiber), 26g pro.

ASIAN-STYLE SALMON PACKETS

My husband and I both love the blend of heat and citrus in this salmon. As an added bonus, the foil packet makes for easy cooking and cleanup.
—Roxanne Chan, Albany, CA

Start to Finish: 25 min.
Makes: 4 servings

- 4 slices sweet onion
- 4 salmon fillets (6 ounces each)
- 3 tablespoons chili sauce
- 1 tablespoon lime juice
- 1 tablespoon sesame oil
- 1 garlic clove, minced
- 1 teaspoon mustard seed
- 1 teaspoon minced fresh gingerroot
- ½ teaspoon black sesame seeds
  Chopped fresh mint
  Grated lime peel

1. Preheat oven to 400°. Place each onion slice on a double thickness of heavy-duty foil (about 12 in. square). Top with salmon. Combine next seven ingredients; spoon over fillets. Fold foil around mixture; crimp edges to seal.
2. Place on a baking sheet. Bake until fish flakes easily with a fork, 15-20 minutes. Be careful of escaping steam when opening packets. Serve with mint and lime peel.
Per 1 salmon fillet with 1 tablespoon sauce: 319 cal., 19g fat (4g sat. fat), 85mg chol., 259mg sod., 5g carb. (3g sugars, 0 fiber), 29g pro.
Diabetic exchanges: 4 lean meat, 1 fat.

QUICK SHRIMP CREOLE

My mom made shrimp Creole when I was growing up, so I've carried on the tradition. Add Louisiana hot sauce for extra kick.
—Gina Norton, Wonder Lake, IL

Start to Finish: 30 min.
Makes: 6 servings

- 3 **cups uncooked instant brown rice**
- 3 **tablespoons canola oil**
- 2 **medium onions, halved and sliced**
- 1 **medium sweet red pepper, coarsely chopped**
- 1 **medium green pepper, coarsely chopped**
- ½ **cup chopped celery**
- 2 **tablespoons all-purpose flour**
- 1 **teaspoon dried oregano**
- ¾ **teaspoon pepper**
- ½ **teaspoon salt**
- 1 **can (14½ ounces) diced tomatoes, undrained**
- 1 **can (8 ounces) tomato sauce**
- 1 **pound uncooked shrimp (31-40 per pound), peeled and deveined**
  Louisiana-style hot sauce, optional

1. Cook rice according to package directions. Meanwhile, in a large skillet, heat oil over medium-high heat. Add onions, peppers and celery; cook and stir 6-8 minutes or until tender.

2. Stir in flour, oregano, pepper and salt until blended. Stir in tomatoes and tomato sauce. Bring to a boil, stirring constantly; cook and stir until thickened. Reduce heat; simmer, covered, 5-8 minutes or until flavors are blended, stirring occasionally.

3. Add shrimp; cook, covered, 4-5 minutes longer or until shrimp turn pink, stirring occasionally. Serve with rice and, if desired, hot sauce.

Per 1 cup shrimp mixture with ⅔ cup rice: 356 cal., 10g fat (1g sat. fat), 92mg chol., 588mg sod., 48g carb. (6g sugars, 5g fiber), 19g pro.
Diabetic exchanges: 2½ starch, 2 lean meat, 1½ fat, 1 vegetable.

FISH & FRIES

Who doesn't love British pub fare? No need to cross the pond when you can make it in the comfort of your own kitchen. These oven-baked fish fillets have a fuss-free coating that's crunchy and golden. The lightly seasoned fries are baked, too, so the entire meal is a healthy alternative to traditional deep-fried fish and chips.
—Janice Mitchell, Aurora, CO

....

Prep: 10 min. • **Bake:** 35 min.
Makes: 4 servings

1 **pound potatoes (about 2 medium)**
2 **tablespoons olive oil**
¼ **teaspoon pepper**
FISH
⅓ **cup all-purpose flour**
¼ **teaspoon pepper**
1 **large egg**
2 **tablespoons water**
⅔ **cup crushed cornflakes**
1 **tablespoon grated Parmesan cheese**
⅛ **teaspoon cayenne pepper**
1 **pound haddock or cod fillets**
Tartar sauce, optional

1. Preheat oven to 425°. Peel and cut potatoes lengthwise into ½-in.-thick slices; cut slices into ½-in.-thick sticks.
2. In a large bowl, toss potatoes with oil and pepper. Transfer to a 15x10x1-in. baking pan coated with cooking spray. Bake, uncovered, 25-30 minutes or until golden brown and crisp, stirring once.
3. Meanwhile, in a shallow bowl, mix flour and pepper. In another shallow bowl, whisk egg with water. In a third bowl, toss cornflakes with cheese and cayenne. Dip fish in flour mixture to coat both sides; shake off excess. Dip in the egg mixture, then in cornflake mixture, patting to help coating adhere.
4. Place fish on a baking sheet coated with cooking spray. Bake 10-12 minutes or until fish just begins to flake easily with a fork.

Serve with potatoes and, if desired, tartar sauce.
Per serving: 376 cal., 9g fat (2g sat. fat), 120mg chol., 228mg sod., 44g carb. (3g sugars, 2g fiber), 28g pro.
Diabetic exchanges: 3 starch, 3 lean meat, 1½ fat.

1. Coarsely chop two plums; place in a small saucepan. Add water; bring to a boil. Reduce heat; simmer, uncovered, 10-15 minutes or until plums are softened and liquid is almost evaporated. Cool slightly. Transfer mixture to a food processor; add ketchup, chipotle, sugar and oil. Process until pureed. Reserve ¾ cup sauce for serving.
2. Sprinkle salmon with salt; place on a greased grill rack, skin side up. Grill, covered, over medium heat until fish just begins to flake easily with a fork, about 10 minutes. Brush with remaining sauce during last 3 minutes. Slice remaining plums. Serve salmon with plum slices and reserved sauce.

HEALTH TIP Plums are a good source of vitamins C, K and A. They're usually small, so try two for a healthy snack.

Per 1 fillet with ½ plum and 2 tablespoons sauce: 325 cal., 18g fat (3g sat. fat), 85mg chol., 460mg sod., 10g carb. (9g sugars, 1g fiber), 29g pro.
Diabetic exchanges: 5 lean meat, 1 fruit, ½ fat.

C **FAST FIX**
PEPPERED SOLE
My daughter isn't a big fan of fish, but she enjoys sole cooked with mushrooms and seasoned with lemon pepper and cayenne. It's good for her, so we're both happy.
—Jeannette Baye, Agassiz, BC

....

Start to Finish: 25 min.
Makes: 4 servings

  2 **tablespoons butter**
  2 **cups sliced fresh mushrooms**
  2 **garlic cloves, minced**
  4 **sole fillets (4 ounces each)**
  ¼ **teaspoon paprika**
  ¼ **teaspoon lemon-pepper seasoning**
  ⅛ **teaspoon cayenne pepper**
  1 **medium tomato, chopped**
  2 **green onions, thinly sliced**

1. In a large skillet, heat butter over medium-high heat. Add the mushrooms; cook and stir until tender. Add garlic; cook 1 minute longer. Place the sole fillets over mushrooms. Sprinkle with paprika, lemon pepper and cayenne.
2. Cook, covered, over medium heat 5-10 minutes or until fish just begins to flake easily with a fork. Sprinkle sole with tomato and green onions.

Per serving: 174 cal., 7g fat (4g sat. fat), 69mg chol., 166mg sod., 4g carb. (2g sugars, 1g fiber), 23g pro.
Diabetic exchanges: 3 lean meat, 1½ fat, 1 vegetable.

C
SPICY PLUM SALMON
I created this sweet and spicy salmon after being challenged to use healthier ingredients. The fresh plum sauce complements the smoky grilled fish.
—Cheryl Hochstettler
Richmond, TX

....

Prep: 25 min. • **Grill:** 10 min.
Makes: 6 servings

  5 **medium plums, divided**
  ½ **cup water**
  2 **tablespoons ketchup**
  1 **chipotle pepper in adobo sauce, finely chopped**
  1 **tablespoon sugar**
  1 **tablespoon olive oil**
  6 **salmon fillets (6 ounces each)**
  ¾ **teaspoon salt**

ORZO-TUNA SALAD WITH TOMATOES

Stuffed tomatoes provide endless options when you add cheese, veggies, rice or, in this case, orzo.
—Jenni Dise, Lakeside, AZ

Start to Finish: 25 min.
Makes: 4 servings

- ¾ cup uncooked whole wheat orzo pasta
- 4 large tomatoes, sliced
- 16 small fresh basil leaves
- 1 pouch (11 ounces) light tuna in water
- 1 cup cubed part-skim mozzarella cheese
- 3 tablespoons minced fresh basil
- 2 tablespoons olive oil
- 2 tablespoons balsamic vinegar
- ⅛ teaspoon salt
- ⅛ teaspoon pepper

1. Cook pasta according to package directions. Arrange sliced tomatoes on a serving plate; top with whole basil leaves.
2. Drain pasta; rinse with cold water and place in a large bowl. Add tuna, cheese and minced basil. In a small bowl, whisk oil, vinegar, salt and pepper; drizzle over pasta mixture and toss to combine. Spoon over the tomatoes.
Per serving: 392 cal., 15g fat (5g sat. fat), 41mg chol., 523mg sod., 31g carb. (6g sugars, 7g fiber), 34g pro.
Diabetic exchanges: 4 lean meat, 1½ starch, 1½ fat, 1 vegetable.

SOFT FISH TACOS

My husband, Bill, and I were cooking together in the kitchen one day and we came up with these tasty fish tacos. The combination of tilapia, cabbage and a hint of cumin is delicious. After one bite, everyone's hooked!
—Carrie Billups, Florence, OR

Start to Finish: 25 min.
Makes: 5 servings

- 4 cups coleslaw mix
- ½ cup fat-free tartar sauce
- ½ teaspoon salt
- ½ teaspoon ground cumin
- ¼ teaspoon pepper
- 1½ pounds tilapia fillets
- 2 tablespoons olive oil
- 1 tablespoon lemon juice
- 10 corn tortillas (6 inches), warmed
- Shredded cheddar cheese, chopped tomato and sliced avocado, optional

1. In a large bowl, toss the coleslaw mix, tartar sauce, salt, cumin and pepper; set aside. In a large nonstick skillet coated with cooking spray, cook tilapia in oil and lemon juice over medium heat for 4-5 minutes on each side or until fish flakes easily with a fork.
2. Place tilapia on tortillas; top with coleslaw mixture. Serve tacos with cheese, tomato and avocado if desired.
Per 2 tacos: 310 cal., 8g fat (2g sat. fat), 66mg chol., 542mg sod., 31g carb. (5g sugars, 4g fiber), 29g pro.
Diabetic exchanges: 4 lean meat, 2 starch, 1 fat.

LEMON-PARSLEY TILAPIA

I like to include seafood in our weekly dinner rotation but don't want to bother with anything complicated. My other challenge is making sure my family likes it. This herbed fish does the trick.
—Trisha Kruse, Eagle, ID

Start to Finish: 20 min.
Makes: 4 servings

- 4 tilapia fillets (about 4 ounces each)
- 2 tablespoons lemon juice
- 1 tablespoon butter, melted
- 2 tablespoons minced fresh parsley
- 2 garlic cloves, minced
- 2 teaspoons grated lemon peel
- ½ teaspoon salt
- ¼ teaspoon pepper

1. Preheat oven to 375°. Place tilapia in a parchment paper-lined 15x10x1-in. pan. Drizzle with lemon juice, then melted butter.
2. Bake until fish just begins to flake easily with a fork, 11-13 minutes. Meanwhile, mix the remaining ingredients. Remove fish from oven; sprinkle with parsley mixture.
Per 1 fillet: 124 cal., 4g fat (2g sat. fat), 63mg chol., 359mg sod., 1g carb. (0 sugars, 0 fiber), 21g pro.
Diabetic exchanges: 3 lean meat, 1 fat.

SHRIMP & CORN STIR-FRY

I make this seafood stir-fry at summer's end when my garden has plenty of tomatoes, squash, garlic and corn. My family loves it over rice for a quick supper.
—Lindsay Honn, Huntingdon, PA

Start to Finish: 20 min.
Makes: 4 servings

- 2 tablespoons olive oil
- 2 small yellow summer squash, sliced
- 1 small onion, chopped
- 1 pound uncooked shrimp (26-30 per pound), peeled and deveined
- 1½ cups fresh or frozen corn, thawed
- 1 cup chopped tomatoes
- 4 garlic cloves, minced
- ½ teaspoon salt
- ¼ teaspoon pepper
- ¼ teaspoon crushed red pepper flakes, optional
- ¼ cup chopped fresh basil
  Hot cooked brown rice

1. In a large skillet, heat oil over medium-high heat. Add squash and onion; stir-fry until squash is crisp-tender, 2-3 minutes.
2. Add next six ingredients and, if desired, pepper flakes; stir-fry until the shrimp turn pink, 3-4 minutes longer. Top with basil. Serve with brown rice.
Per serving without rice: 239 cal., 9g fat (1g sat. fat), 138mg chol., 443mg sod., 19g carb. (8g sugars, 3g fiber), 22g pro.
Diabetic exchanges: 3 lean meat, 1½ fat, 1 starch, 1 vegetable.

GRILLED SALMON WRAPS

My kids love these wraps. I love them, too, because they contain all five food groups right in one handheld meal. We eat fish on Fridays, so these are a staple in my house.
—Jennifer Krey, Clarence, NY

Start to Finish: 25 min.
Makes: 4 servings

- 1 pound salmon fillet (about 1 inch thick)
- ½ teaspoon salt
- ¼ teaspoon pepper
- ½ cup salsa verde
- 4 whole wheat tortillas (8 inches), warmed
- 1 cup chopped fresh spinach
- 1 medium tomato, seeded and chopped
- ½ cup shredded Monterey Jack cheese
- ½ medium ripe avocado, peeled and thinly sliced

1. Sprinkle salmon with salt and pepper; place on an oiled grill rack over medium heat, skin side down. Grill, covered, 8-10 minutes or until fish just begins to flake easily with a fork.

2. Remove from grill. Break salmon into bite-size pieces, removing skin if desired. Toss gently with salsa. Serve in tortillas. Top with spinach, tomato, cheese and avocado.

Per 1 wrap: 380 cal., 18g fat (5g sat. fat), 69mg chol., 745mg sod., 27g carb. (2g sugars, 5g fiber), 27g pro.
Diabetic exchanges: 3 lean meat, 2 starch, 2 fat.

C **FAST FIX**

GREEK FISH BAKE

*As a military spouse, I had the
opportunity to live overseas and
try many different kinds of cuisine.
Here's a Mediterranean-inspired
recipe that we still love today.*
—Stacey Boyd, Springfield, VA

Start to Finish: 30 min.
Makes: 4 servings

- 4 **cod fillets (6 ounces each)**
- 2 **tablespoons olive oil**
- ¼ **teaspoon salt**
- ⅛ **teaspoon pepper**
- 1 **small green pepper,
  cut into thin strips**
- ½ **small red onion, thinly sliced**
- ¼ **cup pitted Greek
  olives, sliced**
- 1 **can (8 ounces)
  tomato sauce**
- ¼ **cup crumbled feta cheese**

1. Preheat oven to 400°. Place cod
in a greased 13x9-in. baking dish.
Brush with oil; sprinkle with salt and
pepper. Top with green pepper,
onion and olives.

2. Pour tomato sauce over top;
sprinkle with cheese. Bake until fish
just begins to flake easily with a
fork, 15-20 minutes.

Per 1 fillet with toppings: 246 cal.,
12g fat (2g sat. fat), 68mg chol.,
706mg sod., 6g carb. (2g sugars,
2g fiber), 29g pro.

Diabetic exchanges: 4 lean meat,
1½ fat, 1 vegetable.

1. Peel and devein shrimp, removing tails. Cut each shrimp lengthwise in half. Cook pasta according to package directions.
2. In a large nonstick skillet, heat butter and oil over medium-high heat. Add shrimp, green onions and garlic; cook and stir until shrimp turn pink, 2-3 minutes. Remove from pan with a slotted spoon.
3. Add broth, lemon peel, lemon juice, pepper, salt and pepper flakes to same pan. Bring to a boil; cook until liquid is slightly reduced, about 1 minute. Return shrimp to pan; heat through. Remove from heat.
4. Drain pasta; divide among four bowls. Top with shrimp mixture; sprinkle with parsley. If desired, serve with cheese.

Per serving: 378 cal., 10g fat (3g sat. fat), 146mg chol., 405mg sod., 42g carb. (3g sugars, 5g fiber), 29g pro.
Diabetic exchanges: 3 very lean meat, 2½ starch, 1½ fat.

★ ★ ★ ★ ★ **READER REVIEW**

"Anything with shrimp is going to catch my attention, and this one was a huge success. Did not change a thing. Added the optional Parm, and declared this one a winner."

BEEMA TASTEOFHOME.COM

LIGHT & LEMONY SCAMPI

I trimmed the calories in our favorite shrimp scampi recipe. A touch of lemon adds nice flavor. Feel free to sprinkle on Parmesan cheese if you want to indulge.
—Ann Sheehy, Lawrence, MA

Prep: 20 min. • **Cook:** 15 min.
Makes: 4 servings

- 1 pound uncooked shrimp (26-30 per pound)
- 8 ounces uncooked multigrain angel hair pasta
- 1 tablespoon butter
- 1 tablespoon olive oil
- 2 green onions, thinly sliced
- 4 garlic cloves, minced
- ½ cup reduced-sodium chicken broth
- 2 teaspoons grated lemon peel
- 3 tablespoons lemon juice
- ½ teaspoon freshly ground pepper
- ¼ teaspoon salt
- ¼ teaspoon crushed red pepper flakes
- ¼ cup minced fresh parsley
  Grated Parmesan cheese, optional

SKILLET SEA SCALLOPS

Scallops don't need much prep or lots of ingredients to dress them up. Some bread crumbs, garlic and lemon do the trick beautifully.
—Margaret Lowenberg
Kingman, AZ

....

Start to Finish: 25 min.
Makes: 4 servings

- ½ cup dry bread crumbs
- ½ teaspoon salt
- 1 pound sea scallops

- 2 tablespoons butter
- 1 tablespoon olive oil
- ¼ cup white wine or reduced-sodium chicken broth
- 2 tablespoons lemon juice
- 1 garlic clove, minced
- 1 teaspoon minced fresh parsley

1. In a shallow bowl, toss bread crumbs with salt. Dip scallops in crumb mixture to coat both sides, patting to help coating adhere.
2. In a large skillet, heat butter and oil over medium-high heat. Add scallops; cook 1½ to 2 minutes on each side or until firm and opaque. Remove from pan; keep warm.
3. Add wine, lemon juice and garlic to same pan; bring to a boil. Stir in parsley. Drizzle over scallops; serve immediately.

Per serving: 249 cal., 11g fat (4g sat. fat), 52mg chol., 618mg sod., 14g carb. (1g sugars, 1g fiber), 21g pro.
Diabetic exchanges: 3 lean meat, 2 fat, 1 starch.

EASY CRAB CAKES

Ready-to-go crabmeat makes these delicate patties ideal for busy nights. You can also form the crab mixture into four thick patties instead of eight cakes.
—Charlene Spelock, Apollo, PA

Start to Finish: 25 min.
Makes: 4 servings

- 1 cup seasoned bread crumbs, divided
- 2 green onions, finely chopped
- ¼ cup finely chopped sweet red pepper
- 1 large egg, lightly beaten
- ¼ cup reduced-fat mayonnaise
- 1 tablespoon lemon juice
- ½ teaspoon garlic powder
- ⅛ teaspoon cayenne pepper
- 2 cans (6 ounces each) crabmeat, drained, flaked and cartilage removed
- 1 tablespoon butter

1. In a large bowl, combine ⅓ cup bread crumbs, green onions, red pepper, egg, mayonnaise, lemon juice, garlic powder and cayenne; fold in crab.

2. Place remaining bread crumbs in a shallow bowl. Divide mixture into eight portions; shape into 2-in. balls. Gently coat in bread crumbs and shape into ½-in.-thick patties.

3. In a large nonstick skillet, heat butter over medium-high heat. Add crab cakes; cook 3-4 minutes on each side or until golden brown.

Per 2 crab cakes: 239 cal., 11g fat (3g sat. fat), 141mg chol., 657mg sod., 13g carb. (2g sugars, 1g fiber), 21g pro.
Diabetic exchanges: 3 lean meat, 2 fat, 1 starch.

MAHI MAHI & VEGGIE SKILLET

Cooking mahi mahi with a mix of vegetables may seem complex, but I developed a skillet recipe to bring out the wow factor without the hassle and fuss.
—Solomon Wang, Arlington, TX

Start to Finish: 30 min.
Makes: 4 servings

- 3 tablespoons olive oil, divided
- 4 mahi mahi or salmon fillets (6 ounces each)
- 3 medium sweet red peppers, cut into thick strips
- ½ pound sliced baby portobello mushrooms
- 1 large sweet onion, cut into thick rings and separated
- ⅓ cup lemon juice
- ¾ teaspoon salt, divided
- ½ teaspoon pepper
- ¼ cup minced fresh chives
- ⅓ cup pine nuts, optional

1. In a large skillet, heat 2 tablespoons oil over medium-high heat. Add fillets; cook 4-5 minutes on each side or until fish just begins to flake easily with a fork. Remove from pan.

2. Add remaining oil, peppers, mushrooms, onion, lemon juice and ¼ teaspoon salt. Cook, covered, over medium heat until vegetables are tender, stirring occasionally, 6-8 minutes.

3. Place fish over vegetables; sprinkle with pepper and remaining salt. Cook, covered, 2 minutes longer or until heated through. Sprinkle with chives and, if desired, pine nuts before serving.

Per serving: 307 cal., 12g fat (2g sat. fat), 124mg chol., 606mg sod., 15g carb. (9g sugars, 3g fiber), 35g pro.
Diabetic exchanges: 4 lean meat, 3 vegetable, 2 fat.

F **FAST FIX** ▶

TILAPIA WITH FIESTA RICE

PICTURED ON PAGE 112

I often use my husband's fresh-caught bass or catfish for this recipe, but tilapia, salmon and even chicken will do.

—Tarin Hauck, Minneapolis, KS

Start to Finish: 25 min.
Makes: 4 servings

- 4 tilapia fillets (6 ounces each)
- ½ teaspoon chili powder
- ⅛ teaspoon salt
- ⅛ teaspoon ground cumin
- ⅛ teaspoon pepper
- 1 package (8.8 ounces) ready-to-serve brown rice
- 1 can (15 ounces) black beans, rinsed and drained
- 1½ cups frozen corn, thawed
- 1½ cups salsa

1. Place tilapia in a 15x10x1-in. baking pan. Mix chili powder, salt, cumin and pepper; sprinkle over fish. Broil 3-4 in. from heat until fish just begins to flake easily with a fork, 10-12 minutes.
2. Meanwhile, prepare the rice according to package directions. Transfer to a microwave-safe bowl; stir in the beans, corn and salsa. Microwave, covered, on high until heated through, stirring once, 2-3 minutes. Serve with fish.

Per 1 fillet with ¾ cup rice mixture: 424 cal., 3g fat (1g sat. fat), 83mg chol., 874mg sod., 53g carb. (6g sugars, 7g fiber), 41g pro.

FAST FIX ▶

SPEEDY SALMON STIR-FRY

Salmon is a staple where I live, so I tried it in a stir-fry. My recipe has an orange glaze, but I like it with lime, too.

—Joni Hilton, Rocklin, CA

Start to Finish: 30 min.
Makes: 4 servings

- ¼ cup reduced-fat honey mustard salad dressing
- 2 tablespoons orange juice
- 1 tablespoon minced fresh gingerroot
- 1 tablespoon reduced-sodium soy sauce
- 1 tablespoon molasses
- 1 teaspoon grated orange peel
- 4 teaspoons canola oil, divided
- 1 pound salmon fillets, skinned and cut into 1-inch pieces
- 1 package (16 ounces) frozen stir-fry vegetable blend
- 2⅔ cups hot cooked brown rice
- 1 tablespoon sesame seeds, toasted

1. In a small bowl, whisk the first six ingredients. In a large skillet, heat 2 teaspoons oil over medium-high heat. Add salmon; cook and gently stir 3-4 minutes or until fish just begins to flake easily with a fork. Remove from pan.
2. In same pan, heat remaining oil. Add vegetable blend; stir-fry until crisp-tender. Add salad dressing mixture. Return salmon to skillet. Gently combine; heat through. Serve with rice; sprinkle with sesame seeds.

Per 1 cup stir-fry with ⅔ cup rice: 498 cal., 19g fat (3g sat. fat), 57mg chol., 394mg sod., 54g carb. (11g sugars, 5g fiber), 26g pro.

Salsa Bean Burgers
page 139

MEATLESS MAINS

If you're considering cutting back on red meat, fear not. There's still plenty of hearty goodness to enjoy with these protein-packed entrees. They're so good, your family won't even miss the meat!

12 corn tortillas (6 inches)
   Cooking spray
½ medium head iceberg
   lettuce, shredded
3 plum tomatoes, chopped
1 medium ripe avocado,
   peeled and cubed
   Shredded reduced-fat
   cheddar cheese

1. Preheat broiler. For sauce, mix sour cream and salsa.
2. In a large skillet coated with cooking spray, cook and stir red pepper and onion over medium heat until tender, 6-8 minutes. Add garlic; cook and stir 1 minute. Stir in broth, chickpeas, chipotles, cumin and salt; bring to a boil. Reduce heat; simmer, covered, 5 minutes.
3. Coarsely mash mixture with a potato masher; stir in cilantro and lime juice. If desired, cook over low heat to thicken, stirring frequently.
4. In batches, spritz both sides of tortillas with cooking spray and place on a baking sheet; broil 4-5 in. from heat until crisp and lightly browned, about 1 minute per side. To serve, top tortillas with the chickpea mixture, lettuce, tomatoes, avocado and sauce. Sprinkle with cheese.
Per 2 tostadas: 347 cal., 9g fat (1g sat. fat), 5mg chol., 752mg sod., 59g carb. (11g sugars, 12g fiber), 12g pro.

CHICKPEA & CHIPOTLE TOSTADAS

I often take a not-so-healthy dish and revise it into something better for my family. My twins love colorful meals they can eat with their hands, and this one fits the bill.
—Amber Massey, Argyle, TX

Prep: 20 min.
Cook: 25 min.
Makes: 6 servings

¾ cup fat-free sour cream
½ cup salsa verde
1 medium sweet red
   pepper, chopped
1 medium onion, chopped
2 garlic cloves, minced
1 cup vegetable broth
2 cans (15 ounces each)
   chickpeas, rinsed
   and drained
2 chipotle peppers in
   adobo sauce, minced
1 teaspoon ground cumin
½ teaspoon salt
½ cup minced fresh cilantro
2 tablespoons lime juice

SALSA BEAN BURGERS

PICTURED ON PAGE 136

I created these based on a turkey burger recipe, and wanted to make them even healthier. Use a favorite salsa with a heat level of your choice to make it your own.

—Jenny Leighty, West Salem, OH

Prep: 15 min. + chilling
Cook: 10 min.
Makes: 4 servings

- 1 can (15 ounces) black beans, rinsed and drained
- ¾ cup panko (Japanese) bread crumbs
- 1 cup salsa, divided
- 1 large egg, lightly beaten
- 2 tablespoons minced fresh cilantro
- 1 garlic clove, minced
- 2 teaspoons canola oil
- 4 whole wheat hamburger buns, split

1. In a large bowl, mash beans. Mix in bread crumbs, ½ cup salsa, egg, cilantro and garlic. Shape bean mixture into four patties; refrigerate 30 minutes.

2. In a large skillet, heat oil over medium heat. Cook burgers for 3-5 minutes on each side or until a thermometer reads 160°. Serve on buns with remaining salsa.

Per 1 burger: 299 cal., 6g fat (1g sat. fat), 53mg chol., 696mg sod., 49g carb. (7g sugars, 8g fiber), 12g pro.
Diabetic exchanges: 3 starch, 1 lean meat, ½ fat.

M **FAST FIX** ▶

BLACK BEAN & SWEET POTATO RICE BOWLS

I have hungry boys to feed, so dinners need to be quick and filling. This one is a family favorite because it has lots of vegetables, is hearty and offers opportunity to play with different ingredients.

—Kim Van Dunk, Caldwell, NJ

Start to Finish: 30 min.
Makes: 4 servings

- ¾ cup uncooked long grain rice
- ¼ teaspoon garlic salt
- 1½ cups water
- 3 tablespoons olive oil, divided
- 1 large sweet potato, peeled and diced
- 1 medium red onion, finely chopped
- 4 cups chopped fresh kale (tough stems removed)
- 1 can (15 ounces) black beans, rinsed and drained
- 2 tablespoons sweet chili sauce

Lime wedges, optional
Additional sweet chili sauce, optional

1. Place rice, garlic salt and water in a large saucepan; bring to a boil. Reduce heat; simmer, covered, until water is absorbed and rice is tender, 15-20 minutes. Remove from heat; let stand 5 minutes.

2. Meanwhile, heat 2 tablespoons oil in a skillet over medium-high heat; saute potato 8 minutes. Add onion; cook and stir until potato is tender, 4-6 minutes. Add kale; cook and stir until tender, 3-5 minutes. Stir in beans; heat through.

3. Gently stir 2 tablespoons chili sauce and remaining oil into rice; add to potato mixture. If desired, serve with lime wedges and additional chili sauce.

Per 2 cups: 435 cal., 11g fat (2g sat. fat), 0 chol., 405mg sod., 74g carb. (15g sugars, 8g fiber), 10g pro.

S M FAST FIX

PEPPER RICOTTA PRIMAVERA

Garlic, peppers and herbs top creamy ricotta cheese in this meatless skillet meal you can make in just 20 minutes.
—Janet Boulger, Botwood, NL

Start to Finish: 20 min.
Makes: 6 servings

- 1 cup part-skim ricotta cheese
- ½ cup fat-free milk
- 4 teaspoons olive oil
- 1 garlic clove, minced
- ½ teaspoon crushed red pepper flakes
- 1 medium green pepper, julienned
- 1 medium sweet red pepper, julienned
- 1 medium sweet yellow pepper, julienned
- 1 medium zucchini, sliced
- 1 cup frozen peas, thawed
- ¼ teaspoon dried oregano
- ¼ teaspoon dried basil
- 6 ounces fettuccine, cooked and drained

Whisk together ricotta cheese and milk; set aside. In a large skillet, heat oil over medium heat. Add garlic and pepper flakes; saute 1 minute. Add next seven ingredients. Cook and stir over medium heat until vegetables are crisp-tender, about 5 minutes. Add cheese mixture to fettuccine; top with vegetables. Toss to coat. Serve immediately.
Per 1 cup: 229 cal., 7g fat (3g sat. fat), 13mg chol., 88mg sod., 31g carb. (6g sugars, 4g fiber), 11g pro.
Diabetic exchanges: 2 starch, 1 medium-fat meat, ½ fat.

M

ROASTED CURRIED CHICKPEAS & CAULIFLOWER

When there's not much time to cook, try roasting potatoes and cauliflower with chickpeas for a warm-you-up dinner. Add tofu to the sheet pan if you like.
—Pam Correll, Brockport, PA

Prep: 15 min. • **Bake:** 30 min.
Makes: 4 servings

- 2 pounds potatoes (about 4 medium), peeled and cut into ½-inch cubes
- 1 small head cauliflower, broken into florets (about 3 cups)
- 1 can (15 ounces) chickpeas, rinsed and drained
- 3 tablespoons olive oil
- 2 teaspoons curry powder
- ¾ teaspoon salt
- ¼ teaspoon pepper
- 3 tablespoons minced fresh cilantro or parsley

1. Preheat oven to 400°. Place the first seven ingredients in a large bowl; toss to coat. Transfer to a 15x10x1-in. baking pan coated with cooking spray.
2. Roast until vegetables are tender, 30-35 minutes, stirring occasionally. Sprinkle with cilantro.
Per 1½ cups: 339 cal., 13g fat (2g sat. fat), 0 chol., 605mg sod., 51g carb. (6g sugars, 8g fiber), 8g pro.
Diabetic exchanges: 3 starch, 2 fat, 1 lean meat, 1 vegetable.

1. Dissolve yeast in warm water. Combine 2 tablespoons oil, honey, salt, yeast mixture and 1½ cups flour; beat on medium speed until smooth. Stir in enough remaining flour to form a soft dough (dough will be sticky).

2. Turn dough onto a floured surface; knead until smooth and elastic, about 6-8 minutes. Place in a greased bowl, turning once to grease the top. Cover; let rise in a warm place until doubled, about 1 hour.

3. Punch down dough; divide into six portions. On a lightly floured surface, roll each portion into an 8x6-in. rectangle. Place each on a greased piece of foil. Spritz with cooking spray; cover with plastic wrap and let rest 10 minutes.

4. In batches, carefully invert crusts onto greased grill rack; peel off foil. Grill, covered, over medium heat until the bottom is golden brown, 2-3 minutes. Turn; grill until bottom begins to brown, 1-2 minutes.

5. Remove from grill. Brush tops with remaining oil; top with tomatoes. Grill, covered, until bottom is golden brown and tomatoes are heated through, 1-2 minutes. To serve, add basil, drizzle with glaze and, if desired, top with cheese.

Per 1 pizza: 363 cal., 15g fat (2g sat. fat), 0 chol., 115mg sod., 53g carb. (15g sugars, 3g fiber), 6g pro.

M S

GRILLED TOMATO PIZZAS

My husband and I make grilled pizza with a tangy balsamic glaze, and it tastes as if we used a wood-burning oven.
—Michele Tungett, Rochester, IL

Prep: 30 min. + rising
Grill: 5 min./batch
Makes: 6 servings

1   **package (¼ ounce) active dry yeast**
1   **cup warm water (110° to 115°)**
6   **tablespoons olive oil, divided**
1   **tablespoon honey**
¼   **teaspoon salt**
2   **to 3 cups all-purpose flour**
    Cooking spray
6   **cups cherry tomatoes, halved**
1   **cup fresh basil, torn**
½   **cup balsamic glaze**
    Shaved Parmesan cheese, optional

M

PUMPKIN LASAGNA

Even friends who aren't big fans of pumpkin are surprised by this delectable lasagna. Canned pumpkin and no-cook noodles make it a cinch to prepare.
—Tamara Huron, New Market, AL

Prep: 25 min.
Bake: 55 min. + standing
Makes: 6 servings

- ½ **pound sliced fresh mushrooms**
- 1 **small onion, chopped**
- ½ **teaspoon salt, divided**
- 2 **teaspoons olive oil**
- 1 **can (15 ounces) solid-pack pumpkin**
- ½ **cup half-and-half cream**
- 1 **teaspoon dried sage leaves**
  Dash pepper
- 9 **no-cook lasagna noodles**
- 1 **cup reduced-fat ricotta cheese**
- 1 **cup (4 ounces) shredded part-skim mozzarella cheese**
- ¾ **cup shredded Parmesan cheese**

1. In a small skillet, saute the mushrooms, onion and ¼ teaspoon salt in oil until tender; set aside. In a small bowl, combine pumpkin, cream, sage, pepper and the remaining salt.

2. Spread ½ cup pumpkin sauce in an 11x7-in. baking dish coated with cooking spray. Top with three noodles (noodles will overlap slightly). Spread ½ cup pumpkin sauce to edges of noodles. Top with half of mushroom mixture, ½ cup ricotta, ½ cup mozzarella and ¼ cup Parmesan cheese. Repeat layers. Top with remaining noodles and sauce.

3. Cover and bake at 375° for 45 minutes. Uncover; sprinkle with remaining Parmesan cheese. Bake 10-15 minutes longer or until the cheese is melted. Let stand for 10 minutes before cutting.

Freeze option: Cover and freeze unbaked lasagna. To use, partially thaw in refrigerator overnight. Remove from refrigerator 30 minutes before baking. Preheat oven to 375°. Bake as directed, increasing time as necessary to heat through and for a thermometer inserted in center to read 165°.

Per 1 piece: 310 cal., 12g fat (6g sat. fat), 36mg chol., 497mg sod., 32g carb. (7g sugars, 5g fiber), 17g pro.
Diabetic exchanges: 2 starch, 2 fat, 1 lean meat.

M FAST FIX
VEGGIE TACOS

These vegetarian tacos are stuffed with a blend of sauteed cabbage, peppers and black beans that is so filling you won't miss the meat. Top with avocado, cheese or a dollop of sour cream.
—*Taste of Home* Test Kitchen

Start to Finish: 30 min.
Makes: 4 servings

- 2 tablespoons canola oil
- 3 cups shredded cabbage
- 1 medium sweet red pepper, julienned
- 1 medium onion, halved and sliced
- 2 teaspoons sugar
- 1 can (15 ounces) black beans, rinsed and drained
- 1 cup salsa
- 1 can (4 ounces) chopped green chilies
- 1 teaspoon minced garlic
- 1 teaspoon chili powder
- ¼ teaspoon ground cumin
- 8 taco shells, warmed
- ½ cup shredded cheddar cheese
- 1 medium ripe avocado, peeled and sliced

1. In a large skillet, heat oil over medium-high heat; saute cabbage, pepper and onion until crisp-tender, about 5 minutes. Sprinkle with sugar.
2. Stir in beans, salsa, chilies, garlic, chili powder and cumin; bring to a boil. Reduce heat; simmer, covered, until flavors are blended, about 5 minutes.
3. Serve in taco shells. Top with cheese and avocado.
Per 2 tacos: 430 cal., 22g fat (5g sat. fat), 14mg chol., 770mg sod., 47g carb. (8g sugars, 10g fiber), 12g pro.

M
BALSAMIC ROASTED VEGETABLE PRIMAVERA

Roasting makes these end-of-summer veggies irresistible. Toss them with balsamic and pasta for a light but filling dinner.
—Carly Curtin, Ellicott City, MD

Prep: 15 min. • **Bake:** 20 min.
Makes: 4 servings

- 4 medium carrots, sliced
- 2 medium zucchini, coarsely chopped (about 3 cups)
- 1⅔ cups cherry tomatoes
- ¼ cup olive oil
- 3 tablespoons balsamic vinegar
- 1 tablespoon minced fresh thyme or 1 teaspoon dried thyme
- 2 teaspoons minced fresh rosemary or ½ teaspoon dried rosemary, crushed
- 1 teaspoon salt
- ½ teaspoon garlic powder
- 8 ounces uncooked rigatoni or whole wheat rigatoni
- ¼ cup shredded Parmesan cheese

1. Preheat oven to 400°. Combine carrots, zucchini and tomatoes in a greased 15x10x1-in. baking pan. Whisk together next six ingredients; reserve half. Drizzle remaining balsamic mixture over vegetables; toss to coat. Bake until carrots are crisp-tender, 20-25 minutes.
2. Meanwhile, cook rigatoni according to package directions; drain. Toss rigatoni with roasted vegetables, pan juices and reserved balsamic mixture. Sprinkle with Parmesan cheese.
Per 1½ cups: 410 cal., 17g fat (3g sat. fat), 4mg chol., 731mg sod., 56g carb. (12g sugars, 5g fiber), 12g pro.

6 ounces uncooked linguine
2 tablespoons butter
1 tablespoon olive oil
2 medium zucchini, thinly sliced
½ pound fresh mushrooms, sliced
1 large tomato, chopped
2 green onions, chopped
1 garlic clove, minced
½ teaspoon salt
¼ teaspoon pepper
1 cup provolone cheese, shredded
3 tablespoons shredded Parmesan cheese
2 teaspoons minced fresh basil

Cook linguine according to package directions. Meanwhile, in a large skillet, heat butter and oil over medium heat. Add zucchini and mushrooms; saute 3-5 minutes. Add tomato, onions, garlic and seasonings. Reduce heat; simmer, covered, about 3 minutes. Drain linguine; add to vegetable mixture. Sprinkle with cheeses and basil. Toss to coat.

Per 1½ cups: 260 cal., 13g fat (7g sat. fat), 25mg chol., 444mg sod., 26g carb. (3g sugars, 2g fiber), 12g pro.
Diabetic exchanges: 1½ starch, 1½ fat, 1 medium-fat meat, 1 vegetable.

TEST KITCHEN TIP
Handle zucchini carefully; they're thin-skinned and easily damaged. To pick the freshest zucchini, look for a firm heavy squash with a moist stem end and a shiny skin. Smaller squash are generally sweeter and more tender than the larger ones. One medium zucchini (⅓ pound) yields about 2 cups sliced.

M FAST FIX ▶
TOMATO & AVOCADO SANDWICHES

I'm a vegetarian, and this is a tasty, quick and healthy lunch that I could easily eat for every meal. At our house, we call these HATS: hummus, avocado, tomato and shallots. They're ingredients I almost always have on hand.
—Sarah Jaraha, Moorestown, NJ

Start to Finish: 10 min.
Makes: 2 servings

½ medium ripe avocado, peeled and mashed
4 slices whole wheat bread, toasted
1 medium tomato, sliced
2 tablespoons finely chopped shallot
¼ cup hummus

Spread avocado over two slices of toast. Top with tomato and shallot. Spread hummus over remaining toasts; place over tops.

Per 1 sandwich: 278 cal., 11g fat (2g sat. fat), 0 chol., 379mg sod., 35g carb. (6g sugars, 9g fiber), 11g pro.
Diabetic exchanges: 2 starch, 2 fat.

M FAST FIX ▶
VEGETARIAN LINGUINE

Looking for a tasty alternative to meat-and-potatoes meals? Try this colorful pasta dish. My oldest son came up with the stick-to-the-ribs supper, which takes advantage of fresh mushrooms, zucchini and other vegetables as well as basil and provolone cheese.
—Jane Bone, Cape Coral, FL

Start to Finish: 30 min.
Makes: 6 servings

SPINACH & BROCCOLI ENCHILADAS

I top this wonderful meatless meal with lettuce and serve it with extra picante sauce. It's quick, easy, filled with fresh flavor and so satisfying.
—Lesley Tragesser, Charleston, MO

Prep: 25 min. • **Bake:** 25 min.
Makes: 8 servings

- 1 medium onion, chopped
- 2 teaspoons olive oil
- 1 package (10 ounces) frozen chopped spinach, thawed and squeezed dry
- 1 cup finely chopped fresh broccoli
- 1 cup picante sauce, divided
- ½ teaspoon garlic powder
- ½ teaspoon ground cumin
- 1 cup (8 ounces) 1% cottage cheese
- 1 cup shredded reduced-fat cheddar cheese, divided
- 8 flour tortillas (8 inches), warmed

1. Preheat oven to 350°. In a large nonstick skillet over medium heat, cook and stir onion in oil until tender. Add spinach, broccoli, ⅓ cup picante sauce, garlic powder and cumin; heat through.
2. Remove from heat; stir in cottage cheese and ½ cup cheddar cheese. Spoon about ⅓ cup spinach mixture down center of each tortilla. Roll up and place seam side down in a 13x9-in. baking dish coated with cooking spray. Spoon remaining picante sauce over top.
3. Cover and bake 20-25 minutes or until heated through. Uncover; sprinkle with remaining cheese.

Bake 5 minutes longer or until the cheese is melted.
Per 1 enchilada: 246 cal., 8g fat (3g sat. fat), 11mg chol., 614mg sod., 32g carb. (4g sugars, 2g fiber), 13g pro.
Diabetic exchanges: 1½ starch, 1 lean meat, 1 vegetable, ½ fat.

PROVOLONE ZITI BAKE

Instead of waiting for water to boil, I simply toss all the makings for a meatless ziti into one baking dish. After a long day, I like having the oven do the work!
—Vicky Palmer, Albuquerque, NM

Prep: 20 min. • **Bake:** 65 min.
Makes: 8 servings

- 1 tablespoon olive oil
- 1 medium onion, chopped
- 3 garlic cloves, minced
- 2 cans (28 ounces each) Italian crushed tomatoes
- 1½ cups water
- ½ cup dry red wine or reduced-sodium chicken broth
- 1 tablespoon sugar
- 1 teaspoon dried basil
- 1 package (16 ounces) ziti or small tube pasta
- 8 slices provolone cheese

1. Preheat oven to 350°. In a 6-qt. stockpot, heat oil over medium-high heat. Add onion; cook and stir 2-3 minutes or until tender. Add garlic; cook 1 minute longer. Stir in tomatoes, water, wine, sugar and basil. Bring to a boil; remove from heat. Stir in uncooked ziti.
2. Transfer to a 13x9-in. baking dish coated with cooking spray. Bake, covered, 1 hour. Top with cheese. Bake, uncovered, 5-10 minutes longer or until ziti is tender and cheese is melted.
Per 1½ cups: 381 cal., 8g fat (4g sat. fat), 15mg chol., 763mg sod., 60g carb. (13g sugars, 4g fiber), 16g pro.

M FAST FIX ▶

QUINOA & BLACK BEAN-STUFFED PEPPERS

Give these no-fuss peppers a try. They come together with a just few ingredients and put a tasty spin on a low-fat dinner!

—Cindy Reams, Philipsburg, PA

Start to Finish: 30 min.
Makes: 4 servings

- 1½ cups water
- 1 cup quinoa, rinsed
- 4 large green peppers
- 1 jar (16 ounces) chunky salsa, divided
- 1 can (15 ounces) black beans, rinsed and drained
- ½ cup reduced-fat ricotta cheese
- ½ cup shredded Monterey Jack cheese, divided

1. Preheat oven to 400°. In a small saucepan, bring water to a boil. Add the quinoa. Reduce heat; simmer, covered, 10-12 minutes or until the water is absorbed.
2. Meanwhile, cut and discard tops from peppers; remove seeds. Place in a greased 8-in. square baking dish, cut side down. Microwave, uncovered, on high 3-4 minutes or until crisp-tender. Turn peppers cut side up.
3. Reserve ⅓ cup salsa; add the remaining salsa to quinoa. Stir in beans, ricotta cheese and ¼ cup Jack cheese. Spoon mixture into peppers; sprinkle with remaining cheese. Bake, uncovered, until the filling is heated through, 10-15 minutes. Top the peppers with the reserved salsa.

Per 1 stuffed pepper: 393 cal., 8g fat (4g sat. fat), 20mg chol., 774mg sod., 59g carb. (10g sugars, 10g fiber), 18g pro.

M

TOMATO BAGUETTE PIZZA

When my tomatoes ripen all at once, I use them up in simple recipes like this one. Cheesy baguette pizzas, served with a salad, make an ideal lunch—or you can cut them into appetizer sizes.

—Lorraine Caland, Shuniah, ON

Prep: 25 min. • **Bake:** 10 min.
Makes: 6 servings

- 2 teaspoons olive oil
- 8 ounces sliced fresh mushrooms
- 2 medium onions, halved and sliced
- 2 garlic cloves, minced
- ½ teaspoon Italian seasoning
- ¼ teaspoon salt
  Dash pepper
- 1 French bread baguette (10½ ounces), halved lengthwise
- 1½ cups shredded part-skim mozzarella cheese, divided
- ¾ cup thinly sliced fresh basil leaves, divided
- 3 medium tomatoes, sliced

1. Preheat oven to 400°. In a large skillet, heat oil over medium-high heat; saute mushrooms and onions until tender. Add the garlic and seasonings; cook and stir 1 minute.
2. Place baguette halves on a baking sheet, cut side up; sprinkle with half of the cheese and ½ cup basil. Top with mushroom mixture, tomatoes and remaining cheese.
3. Bake until cheese is melted, 10-15 minutes. Sprinkle with the remaining basil. Cut each half into three portions.

Per 1 piece: 260 cal., 7g fat (4g sat. fat), 18mg chol., 614mg sod., 36g carb. (5g sugars, 3g fiber), 13g pro.
Diabetic exchanges: 2 starch, 1 medium-fat meat, 1 vegetable.

TEST KITCHEN TIP
To quickly chop basil, stack several leaves and roll them into a tight tube. Slice the leaves widthwise into narrow pieces to create long thin strips. If you'd like smaller pieces, chop the strips again.

M FAST FIX
NO-FRY BLACK BEAN CHIMICHANGAS

My chimichangas get lovin' from the oven, so they're a bit healthier than the traditional kind. This recipe is a smart way to use up leftover rice.
—Kimberly Hammond Kingwood, TX

Start to Finish: 25 min.
Makes: 6 servings

- 2 cans (15 ounces each) black beans, rinsed and drained
- 1 package (8.8 ounces) ready-to-serve brown rice
- ⅔ cup frozen corn
- ⅔ cup minced fresh cilantro
- ⅔ cup chopped green onions
- ½ teaspoon salt
- 6 whole wheat tortillas (8 inches), warmed if necessary
- 4 teaspoons olive oil Guacamole and salsa, optional

1. Preheat broiler. In a large microwave-safe bowl, mix beans, rice and corn; microwave, covered, for 4-5 minutes or until heated through, stirring halfway. Stir in cilantro, green onions and salt.
2. To assemble, spoon ¾ cup bean mixture across the center of each tortilla. Fold bottom and sides of tortilla over filling and roll up. Place on a greased baking sheet, seam side down.
3. Brush tops with 2 teaspoons oil. Broil 3-4 in. from heat until golden brown, 45-60 seconds. Turn over; brush tops with remaining oil. Broil 45-60 seconds longer or until golden brown. If desired, serve with guacamole and salsa.

Per 1 chimichanga: 337 cal., 5g fat (0 sat. fat), 0 chol., 602mg sod., 58g carb. (2g sugars, 10g fiber), 13g pro.

F M FAST FIX
TOMATO-GARLIC LENTIL BOWLS

An Ethiopian recipe was the inspiration behind this feel-good dinner that's packed with comfort.
—Rachael Cushing, Portland, OR

Start to Finish: 30 min.
Makes: 6 servings

- 1 tablespoon olive oil
- 2 medium onions, chopped
- 4 garlic cloves, minced
- 2 cups dried lentils, rinsed
- 1 teaspoon salt
- ½ teaspoon ground ginger
- ½ teaspoon paprika
- ¼ teaspoon pepper
- 3 cups water
- ¼ cup lemon juice
- 3 tablespoons tomato paste
- ¾ cup fat-free plain Greek yogurt

Chopped tomatoes and minced fresh cilantro, optional

1. In a large saucepan, heat oil over medium-high heat; saute onions 2 minutes. Add the garlic; cook 1 minute. Stir in lentils, seasonings and water; bring to a boil. Reduce heat; simmer, covered, until lentils are tender, 25-30 minutes.
2. Stir in lemon juice and tomato paste; heat through. Serve with yogurt and, if desired, tomatoes and cilantro.

HEALTH TIP Cup for cup, lentils have twice as much protein and iron as quinoa.

Per ¾ cup: 294 cal., 3g fat (0 sat. fat), 0 chol., 419mg sod., 49g carb. (5g sugars, 8g fiber), 21g pro.
Diabetic exchanges: 3 starch, 2 lean meat, ½ fat.

2. Meanwhile, in a large skillet, heat oil over medium-high heat; saute zucchini until crisp-tender, 2-4 minutes. Add garlic; cook and stir 30 seconds. Stir in tomatoes, beans, olives and pepper; bring to a boil. Reduce heat; simmer, uncovered, until the tomatoes are softened, 3-5 minutes, stirring occasionally.

3. Stir in pasta and pasta water to moisten as desired. Stir in cheese.

HEALTH TIP Boost protein in meatless pasta dishes by using whole wheat noodles, adding white beans or stirring in a little cheese—or all three!

Per 1½ cups: 348 cal., 9g fat (2g sat. fat), 8mg chol., 394mg sod., 52g carb. (4g sugars, 11g fiber), 15g pro.

M **FAST FIX**
ROMAINE WITH WARM RICE & PINTOS

My college roommate taught me how to cook vegetarian dishes like brown rice with pintos. It's highly versatile: You can also turn it into a wrap or a casserole.
—Natalie Van Apeldoorn
Vancouver, BC

....

Start to Finish: 30 min.
Makes: 4 servings

- 1   tablespoon olive oil
- 1   cup frozen corn
- 1   small onion, chopped
- 2   garlic cloves, minced
- 1½   teaspoons chili powder
- 1½   teaspoons ground cumin
- 1   can (15 ounces) pinto beans, rinsed and drained
- 1   package (8.8 ounces) ready-to-serve brown rice

- 1   can (4 ounces) chopped green chilies
- ½   cup salsa
- ¼   cup chopped fresh cilantro
- 1   bunch romaine, quartered lengthwise through the core
- ¼   cup finely shredded cheddar cheese

1. In a large skillet, heat oil over medium-high heat. Add corn and onion; cook and stir 4-5 minutes or until onion is tender. Stir in garlic, chili powder and cumin; cook and stir 1 minute longer.

2. Add beans, rice, green chilies, salsa and cilantro; heat through, stirring occasionally.

3. Serve over romaine wedges. Sprinkle with cheese.

Per serving: 331 cal., 8g fat (2g sat. fat), 7mg chol., 465mg sod., 50g carb. (5g sugars, 9g fiber), 12g pro.
Diabetic exchanges: 2½ starch, 2 vegetable, 1 lean meat, ½ fat.

M **FAST FIX**
WHITE BEANS & BOW TIES

When we have fresh veggies, we toss them with fun pasta shapes such as penne or bow ties. What a tasty way to enjoy a meatless meal!
—Angela Buchanan, Longmont, CO

....

Start to Finish: 25 min.
Makes: 4 servings

- 2½   cups uncooked whole wheat bow tie pasta (about 6 ounces)
- 1   tablespoon olive oil
- 1   medium zucchini, sliced
- 2   garlic cloves, minced
- 2   large tomatoes, chopped (about 2½ cups)
- 1   can (15 ounces) cannellini beans, rinsed and drained
- 1   can (2¼ ounces) sliced ripe olives, drained
- ¾   teaspoon freshly ground pepper
- ½   cup crumbled feta cheese

1. Cook pasta according to package directions. Drain, reserving ½ cup pasta water.

M **FAST FIX** ▶
ROASTED SWEET POTATO & CHICKPEA PITAS

Looking for something different for your next meal? You'll love the flavorful Mediterranean spin in my pitas. Sweet potatoes tucked inside make them extra hearty.
—Beth Jacobson, Milwaukee, WI

Start to Finish: 30 min.
Makes: 6 servings

- 2 medium sweet potatoes (about 1¼ pounds), peeled and cubed
- 2 cans (15 ounces each) chickpeas or garbanzo beans, rinsed and drained
- 1 medium red onion, chopped
- 3 tablespoons canola oil, divided
- 2 teaspoons garam masala
- ½ teaspoon salt, divided
- 2 garlic cloves, minced
- 1 cup plain Greek yogurt
- 1 tablespoon lemon juice
- 1 teaspoon ground cumin
- 2 cups arugula or baby spinach
- 12 whole wheat pita pocket halves, warmed
- ¼ cup minced fresh cilantro

1. Preheat oven to 400°. Place potatoes in a large microwave-safe bowl; microwave, covered, on high 5 minutes. Stir in chickpeas and onion; toss with 2 tablespoons oil, garam masala and ¼ teaspoon salt.
2. Spread into a 15x10x1-in. pan. Roast until potatoes are tender, about 15 minutes. Cool slightly.
3. Place garlic and remaining oil in a small microwave-safe bowl; microwave on high until garlic is lightly browned, 1-1½ minutes. Stir in yogurt, lemon juice, cumin and remaining salt.
4. Toss the potato mixture with arugula. Spoon into pitas; top with sauce and cilantro.

Per 2 filled pita halves: 462 cal., 15g fat (3g sat. fat), 10mg chol., 662mg sod., 72g carb. (13g sugars, 12g fiber), 14g pro.

M **C**
ZUCCHINI CRUST PIZZA

My mother-in-law shared this recipe with me. Its nutritious zucchini crust makes it just right for brunch, lunch or a light supper.
—Ruth Denomme, Englehart, ON

Prep: 20 min. • **Bake:** 25 min.
Makes: 6 slices

- 2 cups shredded zucchini (1 to 1½ medium), squeezed dry
- ½ cup egg substitute or 2 large eggs, lightly beaten
- ¼ cup all-purpose flour
- ¼ teaspoon salt
- 2 cups shredded part-skim mozzarella cheese, divided
- ½ cup grated Parmesan cheese, divided
- 2 small tomatoes, halved, seeded and sliced
- ½ cup chopped onion
- ½ cup julienned green pepper
- 1 teaspoon dried oregano
- ½ teaspoon dried basil

1. Preheat oven to 450°. In a bowl, combine the first four ingredients; stir in ½ cup mozzarella cheese and ¼ cup Parmesan cheese. Transfer to a 12-in. pizza pan generously coated with cooking spray; spread to an 11-in. circle.
2. Bake until golden brown, 13-16 minutes. Reduce oven to 400°. Add remaining mozzarella; top with the tomatoes, onion, pepper, herbs and remaining Parmesan cheese. Bake until edges are golden brown and cheese is melted, 10-15 minutes.

Per 1 slice: 188 cal., 10g fat (5g sat. fat), 30mg chol., 514mg sod., 12g carb. (4g sugars, 1g fiber), 14g pro.
Diabetic exchanges: 2 lean meat, 2 vegetable, ½ fat.

Red Potato Salad
Dijon *page 159*

SALADS & SOUPS

Whether paired for a meal, served on the side or simply enjoyed alone, salads and soups are perfect choices for today's health-minded cooks. Dig in!

FAST FIX ▶
VEGGIE CHOWDER

Packed with potatoes, carrots and corn, this soup is a great healthy dinner choice. It's not too heavy, so it also makes a nice light partner for a sandwich.
—Vicki Kerr, Portland, ME

Start to Finish: 30 min.
Makes: 7 servings (1¾ quarts)

- 2 cups cubed peeled potatoes
- 2 cups reduced-sodium chicken broth
- 1 cup chopped carrots
- ½ cup chopped onion
- 1 can (14¾ ounces) cream-style corn
- 1 can (12 ounces) fat-free evaporated milk
- ¾ cup shredded reduced-fat cheddar cheese
- ½ cup sliced fresh mushrooms
- ¼ teaspoon pepper
- 2 tablespoons bacon bits

1. In a large saucepan, combine potatoes, broth, carrots and onion; bring to a boil. Reduce the heat; simmer, uncovered, 10-15 minutes or until vegetables are tender.
2. Add the corn, milk, cheese, mushrooms and pepper; cook and stir 4-6 minutes longer or until heated through. Sprinkle with bacon bits.
Per 1 cup: 191 cal., 5g fat (2g sat. fat), 15mg chol., 505mg sod., 29g carb. (10g sugars, 2g fiber), 11g pro.
Diabetic exchanges: 2 starch, ½ fat.

F S C M FAST FIX ▶
SPRING PEA & RADISH SALAD

Winters can be very long in New Hampshire, so I always look forward to the first veggies of spring. I love making lighter dishes such as this fresh salad.
—Jolene Martinelli, Fremont, NH

Start to Finish: 20 min.
Makes: 6 servings

- ½ pound fresh wax or green beans
- ½ pound fresh sugar snap peas
- 2 cups water
- 6 large radishes, halved and thinly sliced
- 2 tablespoons honey
- 1 teaspoon dried tarragon
- ¼ teaspoon kosher salt
- ¼ teaspoon coarsely ground pepper

1. Snip ends off beans and sugar snap peas; remove strings from sugar snaps. In a large saucepan, bring water to a boil over high heat. Add beans, reduce heat; simmer, covered, 4-5 minutes. Add sugar snap peas; simmer, covered, until both beans and peas are crisp-tender, another 2-3 minutes. Drain.
2. Toss beans and peas with the radishes. Stir together honey, tarragon, salt and pepper. Drizzle over vegetables.
Per ⅔ cup: 50 cal., 0 fat (0 sat. fat), 0 chol., 86mg sod., 11g carb. (8g sugars, 2g fiber), 2g pro.
Diabetic exchanges: 1 vegetable, ½ starch.

PICTURED ON PAGE 156

RED POTATO SALAD DIJON

My mother made the best warm potato salad, and now it's a tradition at all of our tables. Sometimes I use Yukon Gold potatoes to make it even prettier.
—Patricia Swart, Galloway, NJ

Prep: 25 min. • **Cook:** 15 min.
Makes: 12 servings (¾ cup each)

3½ **pounds red potatoes (about 12 medium), cubed**
¼ **cup Dijon-mayonnaise blend**
3 **tablespoons seasoned rice vinegar**
3 **tablespoons olive oil**
4 **teaspoons minced fresh tarragon**
1½ **teaspoons salt**
¾ **teaspoon pepper**
6 **green onions, thinly sliced**

1. Place potatoes in a Dutch oven; add water to cover. Bring to a boil. Reduce heat; cook, uncovered, 10-15 minutes or until tender. Drain; transfer to a large bowl.
2. In a small bowl, mix mayonnaise blend, vinegar, oil, tarragon, salt and pepper. Drizzle over potatoes; toss to coat. Gently stir in the green onions. Serve warm. Refrigerate the leftovers.
Per ¾ cup: 139 cal., 4g fat (1g sat. fat), 0 chol., 557mg sod., 24g carb. (3g sugars, 2g fiber), 3g pro.
Diabetic exchanges: 1½ starch, 1 fat.

SPLIT PEA SOUP WITH HAM

To liven up pea soup, I load mine with potatoes and veggies. It's peppery rather than smoky, and I pass it around with corn bread for a heartwarming meal.
—Barbara Link, Alta Loma, CA

Prep: 15 min. • **Cook:** 1¼ hours
Makes: 12 servings (3 quarts)

1 **package (16 ounces) dried green split peas**
8 **cups water**
¾ **pound potatoes (about 2 medium), cubed**
2 **large onions, chopped**
2 **medium carrots, chopped**
2 **cups cubed fully cooked ham (about 10 ounces)**
1 **celery rib, chopped**
5 **teaspoons reduced-sodium chicken bouillon granules**
1 **teaspoon dried marjoram**
1 **teaspoon poultry seasoning**
1 **teaspoon rubbed sage**
½ **to 1 teaspoon pepper**
½ **teaspoon dried basil**

Place all ingredients in a Dutch oven; bring to a boil. Reduce heat; simmer, covered, 1¼-1½ hours or until the peas and vegetables are tender, stirring occasionally.
Per 1 cup: 202 cal., 2g fat (0 sat. fat), 14mg chol., 396mg sod., 33g carb. (5g sugars, 11g fiber), 15g pro.
Diabetic exchanges: 2 starch, 1 lean meat.

S C M

MARINATED CAULIFLOWER SALAD

I sometimes serve this salad as an appetizer alongside a meat and cheese tray.
—Stephanie Hase, Lyons, CO

....

Prep: 20 min. + marinating
Makes: 12 servings

¼	cup red wine vinegar
¼	cup olive oil
2	tablespoons water
5	cups fresh cauliflowerets
1	bay leaf
1	garlic clove, minced
¼	teaspoon salt
¼	teaspoon coarsely ground pepper
1	medium carrot, shredded
1	small red onion, chopped
¼	cup minced fresh parsley
¼	teaspoon dried basil

1. In a small saucepan, bring vinegar, oil and water just to a boil.
2. Meanwhile, place next five ingredients in a large heatproof bowl. Add hot oil mixture; toss to coat. Refrigerate, covered, at least 6 hours or overnight, stirring the mixture occasionally.
3. Add carrot, onion, parsley and basil; toss to coat. Refrigerate, covered, 2 hours longer. Discard bay leaf. Serve with a slotted spoon.
Per ⅔ cup: 58 cal., 5g fat (1g sat. fat), 0 chol., 67mg sod., 4g carb. (1g sugars, 1g fiber), 1g pro.
Diabetic exchanges: 1 vegetable, 1 fat.

M **FAST FIX**

QUICK MUSHROOM BARLEY SOUP

I surprised my mother with a visit some years ago, and she was preparing this soup when I walked in. It was so wonderful that I asked for the recipe, and I've been fixing it ever since.
—Edie Irwin, Cornwall, NY

....

Start to Finish: 30 min.
Makes: 6 servings

1	tablespoon olive oil
1	cup sliced fresh mushrooms
½	cup chopped carrot
⅓	cup chopped onion
2	cups water
¾	cup quick-cooking barley
2	tablespoons all-purpose flour
3	cups whole milk
1½	teaspoons salt
½	teaspoon pepper

1. In a large saucepan, heat oil over medium heat. Add mushrooms, carrot and onion; cook and stir for 5-6 minutes or until tender. Add water and barley. Bring to a boil. Reduce heat; simmer the mixture, uncovered, 12-15 minutes or until barley is tender.
2. In a small bowl, mix flour, milk, salt and pepper until smooth; stir into soup. Return to a boil, stirring constantly; cook and stir for 1-2 minutes or until thickened.
Per 1 cup: 196 cal., 7g fat (3g sat. fat), 12mg chol., 654mg sod., 27g carb. (7g sugars, 5g fiber), 8g pro.
Diabetic exchanges: 1½ starch, ½ whole milk, ½ fat.

C M

CITRUS FENNEL SALAD

My family really enjoys crunchy fennel, which pairs well with citrus vinaigrette. I think this salad makes a nice addition to any meal.
—Denise Elder, Hanover, ON

Prep: 20 min.+ chilling
Makes: 5 servings

- 1 large fennel bulb, thinly sliced
- 1 small apple, thinly sliced
- ¼ cup sliced sweet onion

DRESSING
- ⅓ cup olive oil
- ½ teaspoon grated lemon peel
- 2 tablespoons lemon juice
- ½ teaspoon grated orange peel
- 2 tablespoons orange juice
- ½ teaspoon Dijon mustard
- ½ teaspoon salt
- ⅛ teaspoon pepper

Combine fennel, apple and onion. In another bowl, whisk together dressing ingredients. Pour over salad; toss to coat. Refrigerate the salad until serving.

To make ahead: Prepare dressing up to 3 days before serving.
Per ¾ cup: 160 cal., 15g fat (2g sat. fat), 0 chol., 273mg sod., 8g carb. (5g sugars, 2g fiber), 1g pro.
Diabetic exchanges: 3 fat, ½ starch.

GREEK TOMATO SOUP WITH ORZO

My recipe for manestra, which means orzo in Greek, is so easy . A few steps is all it takes to transform simple ingredients into a creamy, tomatoey one-pot-wonder. It's a fast, hearty meal the whole family will enjoy!
—Kiki Vagianos, Melrose, MA

Prep: 10 min. • **Cook:** 25 min.
Makes: 4 servings

- 2 tablespoons olive oil
- 1 medium onion, chopped
- 1¼ cups uncooked whole wheat orzo pasta
- 2 cans (14½ ounces each) whole tomatoes, undrained, coarsely chopped
- 3 cups reduced-sodium chicken broth
- 2 teaspoons dried oregano
- ¼ teaspoon salt
- ¼ teaspoon pepper
  Crumbled feta cheese and minced fresh basil, optional

1. In large saucepan, heat oil over medium heat; saute onion until tender, 3-5 minutes. Add orzo; cook and stir until lightly toasted.
2. Stir in tomatoes, broth and seasonings; bring to a boil. Reduce heat; simmer, covered, until orzo is tender, 15-20 minutes, stirring occasionally. If desired, top with feta and basil.

Freeze option: Freeze cooled soup in freezer containers. To use, partially thaw in refrigerator overnight. Heat through in a saucepan, stirring soup occasionally and adding a little broth or water if necessary.

Per 1 cup: 299 cal., 8g fat (1g sat. fat), 0 chol., 882mg sod., 47g carb. (7g sugars, 12g fiber), 11g pro.

SO EASY GAZPACHO

My daughter got this recipe from a friend a few years ago. Now I serve it often as a first course. It's always the talk of the party!
—Lorna Sirtoli, Cortland, NY

Prep: 10 min. + chilling
Makes: 5 servings

- 2 cups tomato juice
- 4 medium tomatoes, peeled and finely chopped
- ½ cup chopped seeded peeled cucumber
- ⅓ cup finely chopped onion
- ¼ cup olive oil
- ¼ cup cider vinegar
- 1 teaspoon sugar
- 1 garlic clove, minced
- ¼ teaspoon salt
- ¼ teaspoon pepper

In a large bowl, combine all the ingredients. Cover and refrigerate at least 4 hours or until chilled.
Per 1 cup: 146 cal., 11g fat (2g sat. fat), 0 chol., 387mg sod., 11g carb. (8g sugars, 2g fiber), 2g pro.
Diabetic exchanges: 2 vegetable, 2 fat.

★ ★ ★ ★ ★ **READER REVIEW**

"Really good! I've never tried gazpacho before and this made me a fan! Not only is it really healthy...but absolutely delicious!"
ZAS1207 TASTEOFHOME.COM

SIMPLE WALDORF SALAD

This is my go-to salad when I need a quick little something for a meal. Sometimes, when I want the salad to have a sweeter taste, I use half mayonnaise and half plain yogurt or whipped cream.
—Wendy Masters
East Garafraxa, ON

Start to Finish: 10 min.
Makes: 6 servings

- 2 large Gala or Honeycrisp apples, unpeeled and chopped (about 3 cups)
- 2 cups chopped celery
- ¼ cup raisins
- ¼ cup chopped walnuts, toasted
- ⅓ cup reduced-fat mayonnaise
- ⅓ cup plain yogurt

Combine apples, celery, raisins and walnuts. Add mayonnaise and yogurt; toss to coat. Refrigerate, covered, until serving.
Note: To toast nuts, bake in a shallow pan in a 350° oven for 5-10 minutes or cook in a skillet over low heat until lightly browned, stirring occasionally.
Per ¾ cup: 140 cal., 8g fat (1g sat. fat), 6mg chol., 119mg sod., 17g carb. (12g sugars, 3g fiber), 2g pro.
Diabetic exchanges: 1½ fat, 1 fruit.

C M FAST FIX ▶
NECTARINE & BEET SALAD

Beets and nectarines sprinkled with feta cheese make a simply scrumptious blend for a colorful mixed green salad. The unique combination of ingredients may seems unlikely, but I think it will become a favorite.
—Nicole Werner, Ann Arbor, MI

Start to Finish: 10 min.
Makes: 8 servings

- 2 packages (5 ounces each) spring mix salad greens
- 2 medium nectarines, sliced
- ½ cup balsamic vinaigrette
- 1 can (14½ ounces) sliced beets, drained
- ½ cup crumbled feta cheese

On a serving dish, toss greens and nectarines with vinaigrette. Top with beets and cheese; serve the salad immediately.

Per 1 cup: 84 cal., 4g fat (1g sat. fat), 4mg chol., 371mg sod., 10g carb. (6g sugars, 3g fiber), 3g pro.
Diabetic exchanges: 2 vegetable, ½ fat.

TEST KITCHEN TIP
Eight servings of the beet salad a bit too much for your home? It's easy to cut the ingredients in half for a smaller serving yield. Be sure to pick up an 8.25-oz. can of sliced beets.

C FAST FIX ▶
MEXICAN CABBAGE ROLL SOUP

I love sharing our humble and hearty soup made with beef, cabbage and green chilies. A blast of cilantro gives it a sunshiny finish.
—Michelle Beal, Powell, TN

Start to Finish: 30 min.
Makes: 6 servings (2 quarts)

- 1 pound lean ground beef (90% lean)
- ½ teaspoon salt
- ¾ teaspoon garlic powder
- ¼ teaspoon pepper
- 1 tablespoon olive oil
- 1 medium onion, chopped
- 6 cups chopped cabbage (about 1 small head)
- 3 cans (4 ounces each) chopped green chilies
- 2 cups water
- 1 can (14½ ounces) reduced-sodium beef broth
- 2 tablespoons minced fresh cilantro

Pico de gallo and reduced-fat sour cream, optional

1. In a large saucepan, cook and crumble beef with seasonings over medium-high heat until no longer pink, 5-7 minutes. Remove from the pan.

2. In the same pan, heat oil over medium-high heat; saute onion and cabbage until crisp-tender, 4-6 minutes. Stir in beef, chilies, water and broth; bring to a boil. Reduce heat; simmer, covered, to allow flavors to blend, about 10 minutes. Stir in cilantro. If desired, top with pico de gallo and sour cream.

Freeze option: Freeze cooled soup in freezer containers without optional toppings. To use, partially thaw in refrigerator overnight. Heat through in a saucepan, stirring occasionally.

Per 1⅓ cups: 186 cal., 9g fat (3g sat. fat), 49mg chol., 604mg sod., 10g carb. (4g sugars, 4g fiber), 17g pro.
Diabetic exchanges: 2 lean meat, 2 vegetable, ½ fat.

LENTIL & CHICKEN SAUSAGE STEW

This hearty and healthy stew will warm your family right down to their toes! Serve with corn bread or rolls to soak up every last delicious morsel.

—Jan Valdez, Chicago, IL

....

Prep: 15 min. • **Cook:** 8 hours
Makes: 6 servings

- 1 carton (32 ounces) reduced-sodium chicken broth
- 1 can (28 ounces) diced tomatoes, undrained
- 3 fully cooked spicy chicken sausage links (3 ounces each), cut into ½-inch slices
- 1 cup dried lentils, rinsed
- 1 medium onion, chopped
- 1 medium carrot, chopped
- 1 celery rib, chopped
- 2 garlic cloves, minced
- ½ teaspoon dried thyme

In a 4- or 5-qt. slow cooker, combine all ingredients. Cover and cook on low for 8-10 hours or until lentils are tender.

Per 1½ cups: 231 cal., 4g fat (1g sat. fat), 33mg chol., 803mg sod., 31g carb. (8g sugars, 13g fiber), 19g pro.
Diabetic exchanges: 2 lean meat, 2 vegetable, 1 starch.

★ ★ ★ ★ ★ **READER REVIEW**

"This was delicious. My kids even liked it. I doubled the carrots and added a couple of potatoes."

JRLECH TASTEOFHOME.COM

C S M **FAST FIX**

KALE SLAW SPRING SALAD

My parents and in-laws are retired and like to spend their winters in Florida. This tangy spring salad welcomes the snowbirds back for spring celebrations!

—Jennifer Gilbert, Brighton, MI

....

Start to Finish: 25 min.
Makes: 10 servings

- 5 cups chopped fresh kale
- 3 cups torn romaine
- 1 package (14 ounces) coleslaw mix
- 1 medium fennel bulb, thinly sliced
- 1 cup chopped fresh broccoli
- ½ cup shredded red cabbage
- 1 cup crumbled feta cheese
- ¼ cup sesame seeds, toasted
- ⅓ cup extra virgin olive oil
- 3 tablespoons sesame oil
- 2 tablespoons honey
- 2 tablespoons cider vinegar
- 2 tablespoons lemon juice
- ⅓ cup pureed strawberries
   Sliced fresh strawberries

1. Combine kale and romaine. Add coleslaw mix, fennel, broccoli and red cabbage; sprinkle with feta cheese and sesame seeds. Toss to combine ingredients.
2. Stir together olive oil and sesame oil. Whisk in honey, vinegar and lemon juice. Add the pureed strawberries. Whisk until well combined. Dress salad just before serving; top with the sliced fresh strawberries.

Per 1⅓ cups: 192 cal., 15g fat (3g sat. fat), 6mg chol., 140mg sod., 12g carb. (7g sugars, 3g fiber), 4g pro.
Diabetic exchanges: 3 fat, 1 starch.

LAYERED GARDEN BEAN SALAD

For easy entertaining, you can cover and refrigerate this salad a few hours before guests arrive so you don't have to bother with last-minute assembly. Turn it into a light lunch by adding sliced rotisserie chicken, salmon or tuna.
—Melissa Wharton, Cincinnati, OH

Start to Finish: 20 min.
Makes: 16 servings

- 2 **cups shredded romaine**
- 2 **cans (15 ounces each) black beans, rinsed and drained**
- 2 **tablespoons chopped red onion**
- 2 **cups frozen corn, thawed**
- 2 **English cucumbers, chopped**
- 4 **medium tomatoes, chopped**
- ½ **cup reduced-fat ranch salad dressing**
- 1 **teaspoon cumin seeds**

In a 4-qt. glass bowl, layer the first six ingredients. In a small bowl, mix salad dressing and cumin seeds; drizzle over salad.

Per 1 cup: 93 cal., 2g fat (0 sat. fat), 2mg chol., 180mg sod., 15g carb. (3g sugars, 4g fiber), 4g pro.
Diabetic exchanges: 1 starch.

F

PEA SOUP WITH QUINOA

This soup is low in fat, high in fiber, and has a fantastically fresh flavor. Best of all, it's simple to make!
—Jane Hacker, Milwaukee, WI

Prep: 10 min.
Cook: 25 min.
Makes: 6 servings

- 1 **cup water**
- ½ **cup quinoa, rinsed**
- 2 **teaspoons canola oil**
- 1 **medium onion, chopped**
- 2½ **cups frozen peas (about 10 ounces)**
- 2 **cans (14½ ounces each) reduced-sodium chicken broth or vegetable broth**
- ½ **teaspoon salt**
- ¼ **teaspoon pepper**
   Optional toppings: plain yogurt, croutons, shaved Parmesan cheese and cracked pepper

1. In a small saucepan, bring water to a boil. Add quinoa. Reduce heat; simmer, covered, until the water is absorbed, 12-15 minutes.
2. Meanwhile, in a large saucepan, heat oil over medium-high heat; saute onion until tender. Stir in peas and broth; bring to a boil. Reduce heat; simmer, uncovered, until peas are tender, about 5 minutes.
3. Puree soup using an immersion blender. Or cool slightly and puree soup in a blender; return to pan. Stir in quinoa, salt and pepper; heat through. Serve soup with toppings as desired.

Per 1 cup: 126 cal., 3g fat (0 sat. fat), 0 chol., 504mg sod., 19g carb. (4g sugars, 4g fiber), 7g pro.
Diabetic exchanges: 1 starch, ½ fat.

F

ZESTY CHICKEN SOUP

This spicy soup is chock-full of chicken and vegetables. Best of all, it freezes nicely, making a second meal with little effort.
—Gwen Nelson, Castro Valley, CA

Prep: 25 min. • **Cook:** 40 min.
Makes: 10 servings (3¾ quarts)

1¼ pounds boneless skinless chicken breasts
4 cups water
1 tablespoon canola oil
1 medium onion, chopped
2 celery ribs, chopped
4 garlic cloves, minced
1 can (14½ ounces) Mexican diced tomatoes
1 can (14½ ounces) diced tomatoes
1 can (8 ounces) tomato sauce
1 cup medium salsa
3 medium zucchini, halved and sliced
2 medium carrots, sliced
1 cup frozen white corn
1 can (4 ounces) chopped green chilies
3 teaspoons ground cumin
2 teaspoons chili powder
1 teaspoon dried basil
Shredded cheddar cheese and tortilla chips, optional

1. Place chicken in a Dutch oven; add water. Bring to a boil; reduce heat. Simmer, covered, 10-15 minutes or until chicken juices run clear. Remove chicken; cut into ½-in. cubes and set aside.
2. In a large skillet, heat oil over medium-high heat. Add onion, celery and garlic; cook and stir until tender.

3. Add to cooking juices in Dutch oven. Stir in tomatoes, tomato sauce, salsa, zucchini, carrots, corn, chilies, cumin, chili powder and basil. Bring to a boil. Reduce heat; simmer, covered, 20-25 minutes or until vegetables are tender. Add chicken; heat through.
4. If desired, serve with cheese and tortilla chips.
Per 1½ cups: 152 cal., 3g fat (1g sat. fat), 31mg chol., 518mg sod., 16g carb. (8g sugars, 5g fiber), 14g pro.
Diabetic exchanges: 2 vegetable, 1 lean meat, ½ starch.

C **M** **FAST FIX**
LEMONY ZUCCHINI RIBBONS

Fresh zucchini gets a shave and a drizzle of lemony goodness in this fabulous salad.
Plus the ribbons are so pretty and fun to eat. Sprinkle on the goat cheese or feta and dive right in.
—Ellie Martin Cliffe, Milwaukee, WI

Start to Finish: 15 min.
Makes: 4 servings

1 tablespoon olive oil
½ teaspoon grated lemon peel
1 tablespoon lemon juice
½ teaspoon salt
¼ teaspoon pepper
3 medium zucchini
⅓ cup crumbled goat or feta cheese

1. For dressing, in a small bowl, mix the first five ingredients. Using a vegetable peeler, shave zucchini lengthwise into very thin slices; arrange on a serving plate.
2. To serve, drizzle with dressing, toss lightly , and top with cheese.
HEALTH TIP Making this colorful salad with zucchini instead of cooked pasta saves 130 calories.
Per ¾ cup: 83 cal., 6g fat (2g sat. fat), 12mg chol., 352mg sod., 5g carb. (3g sugars, 2g fiber), 3g pro.
Diabetic exchanges: 1 vegetable, 1 fat.

TEST KITCHEN TIP
Turn a bumper crop of zucchini into a main meal! Simply add cooked cubed chicken breast to Lemony Zucchini Ribbons for a fast fix dinner.

M

BEET, GRAPEFRUIT & ONION SALAD

My husband loves pickled beets, so I paired them with a little citrus for a spring salad. It has such a great color combination!
—Michelle Clair, Seattle, WA

....

Prep: 15 min.
Bake: 50 min. + cooling
Makes: 8 servings

  6 medium fresh beets
      (about 2 pounds)
  ¼ cup extra virgin olive oil
  3 tablespoons lemon juice
  2 tablespoons cider vinegar
  2 tablespoons honey
  ¼ teaspoon salt
  ¼ teaspoon pepper
  2 large ruby red grapefruit,
      peeled and sectioned
  2 small red onions, halved
      and thinly sliced

1. Preheat oven to 425°. Scrub beets, trimming tops to 1 in. Wrap in foil; bake beets on a baking sheet until tender, about 50-60 minutes. Remove foil; cool completely. Peel, halve and thinly slice beets. Place in a serving bowl.
2. Whisk together the next six ingredients. Pour over beets; add grapefruit and onion. Toss mixture gently to coat.
Per ¾ cup: 161 cal., 7g fat (1g sat. fat), 0 chol., 162mg sod., 24g carb. (20g sugars, 4g fiber), 3g pro.
Diabetic exchanges: 1½ fat, 1 starch, 1 vegetable.

F **S** **M** **FAST FIX**

MINTY PINEAPPLE FRUIT SALAD

Fresh mint adds bright flavor to this easy, quick and low-fat pineapple salad. You can give it a berry twist by using blueberries and raspberries in place of the grapes, but don't forget the secret dressing ingredient—lemonade!
—Janie Colle, Hutchinson, KS

Start to Finish: 15 min.
Makes: 8 servings

- 4 **cups cubed fresh pineapple**
- 2 **cups sliced fresh strawberries**
- 1 **cup green grapes**
- 3 **tablespoons thawed lemonade concentrate**
- 2 **tablespoons honey**
- 1 **tablespoon minced fresh mint**

Place fruit in a large bowl. In another bowl, mix the remaining ingredients; stir gently into fruit. Refrigerate, covered, until serving.

Per ¾ cup: 99 cal., 0 fat (0 sat. fat), 0 chol., 4mg sod., 26g carb. (21g sugars, 2g fiber), 1g pro.
Diabetic exchanges: 1½ fruit, ½ starch.

Roasted Green Beans
with Lemon & Walnuts
page 183

SIDES & BREADS

Colorful veggies and low-carb breads make it easy to create healthy menus. Round out your meals with any of the 21 easy options you'll find here.

1 teaspoon salt
2 packages (¼ ounce each) active dry yeast
½ cup warm water (110° to 115°)
2 to 2½ cups all-purpose flour
1½ cups whole wheat flour
½ cup canned pumpkin
½ teaspoon ground cinnamon
¼ teaspoon ground ginger
¼ teaspoon ground nutmeg

1. In a small saucepan, heat the milk, brown sugar, 4 tablespoons butter and salt to 110°-115°; set mixture aside.

2. In a large bowl, dissolve yeast in warm water. Stir in milk mixture. Add 1½ cups all-purpose flour, whole wheat flour, pumpkin, cinnamon, ginger and nutmeg. Beat until smooth. Add enough of the remaining all-purpose flour to form a soft dough.

3. Turn onto a floured surface; knead until smooth and elastic, for 6-8 minutes. Place in a greased bowl, turning once to grease top. Cover and let rise in a warm place until doubled, about 1 hour.

4. Punch dough down. Divide into 20 pieces; shape into balls. Place in a greased 13x9-in. baking pan. Cover and let rise for 30 minutes or until doubled.

5. Preheat oven to 375°. Melt the remaining butter; brush over dough. Bake 20-25 minutes or until golden brown. Remove from pan to a wire rack. Serve warm.

Per 1 roll: 124 cal., 3g fat (2g sat. fat), 9mg chol., 154mg sod., 21g carb. (5g sugars, 2g fiber), 3g pro.
Diabetic exchanges: 1½ starch, ½ fat.

S C M FAST FIX ▶
LEMON GARLIC MUSHROOMS

I baste whole mushrooms with a lemony sauce to prepare this simple side dish. Using skewers or a basket makes it easy to turn them as they grill to perfection.
—Diane Hixon, Niceville, FL

Start to Finish: 15 min.
Makes: 4 servings

¼ cup lemon juice
3 tablespoons minced fresh parsley
2 tablespoons olive oil
3 garlic cloves, minced
Pepper to taste
1 pound large fresh mushrooms

1. For dressing, whisk together first five ingredients. Toss mushrooms with 2 tablespoons dressing.

2. Grill mushrooms, covered, over medium-high heat until tender, for 5-7 minutes per side. Toss with remaining dressing before serving.

Per serving: 94 cal., 7g fat (1g sat. fat), 0mg chol., 2mg sod., 6g carb. (0g sugars, 0g fiber), 3g pro.
Diabetic exchanges: 1 vegetable, 1½ fat.

F M
PUMPKIN PAN ROLLS

Serve these spicy-sweet pumpkin rolls for dinner—or any time of day—and get ready to hear a chorus of "yums" in your kitchen!
—Linnea Rein, Topeka, KS

Prep: 20 min. + rising
Bake: 20 min.
Makes: 20 rolls

¾ cup whole milk
⅓ cup packed brown sugar
5 tablespoons butter, divided

C M

ROASTED BEET WEDGES

This recipe makes ordinary beets taste delicious with just a few ingredients: so sweet, tender and good for you.
—Wendy Stenman
Germantown, WI

....

Prep: 15 min.
Bake: 1¼ hours
Makes: 4 servings

1 **pound medium fresh beets, peeled**
4 **teaspoons olive oil**
½ **teaspoon kosher salt**
3 **to 5 fresh rosemary sprigs**

1. Preheat oven to 400°. Cut each beet into six wedges; place in a large resealable plastic bag. Add olive oil and salt; seal and shake to coat.
2. Place a piece of heavy-duty foil 12 in. long in a 15x10x1-in. baking pan. Arrange beets on foil; top with rosemary. Seal foil tightly.

3. Bake until tender, about 1 hour. Open foil carefully to allow steam to escape. Discard rosemary sprigs.

Per 3 wedges: 92 cal., 5g fat (1g sat. fat), 0 chol., 328mg sod., 12g carb. (9g sugars, 3g fiber), 2g pro.
Diabetic exchanges: 1 vegetable, 1 fat.

GRANOLA BLUEBERRY MUFFINS

I wanted to put a new spin on muffins, so I mixed in granola that contained lots of nuts, pumpkin seeds and shredded coconut. Then I brought the muffins in to work the next morning. What a success!
—Megan Weiss, Menomonie, WI

Prep: 20 min.
Bake: 15 min.
Makes: 1 dozen

- 1½ cups whole wheat flour
- ½ cup all-purpose flour
- ¼ cup packed brown sugar
- 2 teaspoons baking powder
- ½ teaspoon salt
- ½ teaspoon baking soda
- 1 cup granola without raisins, divided
- 1 large egg
- 1 cup buttermilk
- ¼ cup canola oil
- 2 tablespoons orange juice
- 1 tablespoon lemon juice
- 1 cup fresh or frozen unsweetened blueberries

1. Preheat oven to 400°. In a small bowl, whisk flours, brown sugar, baking powder, salt and baking soda. Stir in ½ cup granola. In another bowl, whisk the egg, buttermilk, oil and juices until blended. Add to flour mixture; stir just until moistened. Fold in the blueberries.
2. Fill 12 greased muffin cups three-fourths full; sprinkle the remaining granola over batter. Bake 12-15 minutes or until a toothpick inserted in center comes out clean. Cool 5 minutes before removing from pan to a wire rack.
Freeze option: Freeze cooled muffins in resealable plastic freezer bags. To use, thaw at room temperature or, if desired, microwave each muffin on high for 20-30 seconds or until heated through.
Note: If using frozen blueberries, use without thawing to avoid discoloring the batter.
Per 1 muffin: 188 cal., 7g fat (1g sat. fat), 18mg chol., 251mg sod., 28g carb. (8g sugars, 4g fiber), 6g pro.
Diabetic Exchanges: 2 starch, 1 fat.

C M FAST FIX

ROASTED GREEN BEANS WITH LEMON & WALNUTS

PICTURED ON PAGE 178
I first tasted roasted green beans in a Chinese restaurant and fell in love with the texture and flavor. This is my Americanized version, and it's always a big hit at family get-togethers and holidays.
—Lily Julow, Lawrenceville, GA

Start to Finish: 25 min.
Makes: 8 servings

- 2 pounds fresh green beans, trimmed
- 2 shallots, thinly sliced
- 6 garlic cloves, crushed
- 2 tablespoons olive oil
- ¾ teaspoon salt
- ¼ teaspoon pepper
- 2 teaspoons grated lemon peel
- ½ cup chopped walnuts, toasted

1. Preheat oven to 425°. In a large bowl, combine the green beans, shallots and garlic; drizzle with oil and sprinkle with salt and pepper. Transfer to two 15x10x1-in. baking pans coated with cooking spray.
2. Roast 15-20 minutes or until tender and lightly browned, stirring occasionally. Remove from oven; stir in 1 teaspoon of the lemon peel. Sprinkle with walnuts and remaining lemon peel.
Note: To toast nuts, bake in a shallow pan in a 350° oven for 5-10 minutes or cook in a skillet over low heat until lightly browned, stirring occasionally.
Per serving: 119 cal., 8g fat (1g sat. fat), 0 chol., 229mg sod., 11g carb. (3g sugars, 4g fiber), 3g pro.
Diabetic exchanges: 2 vegetable, 1½ fat.

C **M** **FAST FIX**
SPICY GRILLED EGGPLANT

This four-ingredient recipe goes well with pasta or grilled meats. Thanks to the Cajun seasoning, it gets more attention than an ordinary side dish.
—Greg Fontenot
The Woodlands, TX

....

Start to Finish: 20 min.
Makes: 8 servings

- 2 **small eggplants, cut into ½-inch slices**
- ¼ **cup olive oil**
- 2 **tablespoons lime juice**
- 3 **teaspoons Cajun seasoning**

1. Brush eggplant slices with oil. Drizzle with lime juice; sprinkle with Cajun seasoning. Let slices stand for 5 minutes.
2. Grill eggplant, covered, over medium heat or broil 4 in. from heat until tender, 4-5 minutes per side.
Per serving: 88 cal., 7g fat (1g sat. fat), 0 chol., 152mg sod., 7g carb. (3g sugars, 4g fiber), 1g pro.
Diabetic Exchanges: 1½ fat, 1 vegetable.

F **S** **M**
HONEY-OAT PAN ROLLS

These tender rolls are a welcome addition to any meal. Whole wheat flour and oats boost the nutrients a bit, too.
—Arlene Butler, Ogden, UT

....

Prep: 45 min. + rising
Bake: 20 min.
Makes: 2 dozen

- 2½ to 2¾ cups all-purpose flour
- ¾ cup whole wheat flour
- ½ cup old-fashioned oats
- 2 packages (¼ ounce each) active dry yeast
- 1 teaspoon salt
- 1 cup water
- ¼ cup honey
- 5 tablespoons butter, divided
- 1 large egg

1. In a large bowl, mix 1 cup all-purpose flour, whole wheat flour, oats, yeast and salt. In a small saucepan, heat the water, honey and 4 tablespoons butter to 120°-130°. Add to dry ingredients; beat on medium speed 2 minutes. Add egg; beat on high 2 minutes. Stir in enough of the remaining all-purpose flour to form a soft dough (the dough will be sticky).
2. Turn dough onto a floured surface; knead until smooth and elastic, about 6-8 minutes. Place in a greased bowl, turning once to grease the top. Cover with plastic wrap and let rise in a warm place until doubled, about 1 hour.
3. Punch down dough. Turn onto a lightly floured surface; divide and shape into 24 balls. Place in a greased 13x9-in. baking pan. Cover with a kitchen towel; let rise in a warm place until doubled, for about 30 minutes.
4. Preheat oven to 375°. Bake 20-22 minutes or until golden brown. Melt remaining butter; brush over rolls. Remove from pan to a wire rack.
Per 1 roll: 103 cal., 3g fat (2g sat. fat), 15mg chol., 126mg sod., 17g carb. (3g sugars, 1g fiber), 3g pro.
Diabetic exchanges: 1 starch, ½ fat.

5. Bake at 400° for 10-15 minutes or until golden brown. Brush again with butter while hot.

Per 1 butterhorn: 137 cal., 4g fat (2g sat. fat), 10mg chol., 237mg sod., 23g carb. (5g sugars, 2g fiber), 3g pro.

M **FAST FIX**

CONFETTI QUINOA

If you've never tried quinoa, start with my easy side, brimming with colorful veggies. I serve it with orange-glazed chicken.
—Kim Ciepluch, Kenosha, WI

Start to Finish: 30 min.
Makes: 4 servings

- 2 **cups water**
- 1 **cup quinoa, rinsed**
- ½ **cup chopped fresh broccoli**
- ½ **cup coarsely chopped zucchini**
- ¼ **cup shredded carrots**
- ½ **teaspoon salt**
- 1 **tablespoon lemon juice**
- 1 **tablespoon olive oil**

In a large saucepan, bring water to a boil. Add next five ingredients. Reduce heat; simmer, covered, until liquid is absorbed, 12-15 minutes. Stir in lemon juice and oil; heat through. Remove from heat; fluff with a fork.

Per ⅔ cup: 196 cal., 6g fat (1g sat. fat), 0 chol., 307mg sod., 29g carb. (1g sugars, 4g fiber), 7g pro.
Diabetic exchanges: 2 starch, ½ fat.

M

WHOLE WHEAT BUTTERHORNS

I take these buttery delights to potluck suppers, and when I serve them to guests, I can count on many requesting the recipe. They're a favorite at home with the family, too. Best of all, the rolls aren't hard to make, so we have them often.
—Mary Jane Mullins, Livonia, MO

Prep: 30 min. + rising
Bake: 10 min.
Makes: 24 rolls

- 2¾ **cups all-purpose flour**
- 2 **packages (¼ ounce each) active dry yeast**
- 1¾ **cups water**
- ⅓ **cup packed brown sugar**
- ½ **cup butter, divided**
- 2 **tablespoons honey**
- 2 **teaspoons salt**
- 2 **cups whole wheat flour**

1. In a large bowl, combine 1½ cups all-purpose flour and yeast.

2. Heat the water, brown sugar, 3 tablespoons butter, honey and salt to 120°-130°; add to flour mixture. Beat on low for 30 seconds with electric mixer; increase speed to high and continue beating for 3 minutes. Stir in whole wheat flour and enough remaining all-purpose flour to form a soft dough.

3. Turn out onto a lightly floured surface and knead until smooth and elastic, about 6-8 minutes. Place in a greased bowl, turning once to grease the top. Cover with plastic wrap and let rise in a warm place until doubled, about 1½ hours. Punch dough down and divide into thirds. Shape each into a ball, cover and let rest 10 minutes.

4. On a lightly floured surface, roll the balls into three 12-in. circles. Cut each circle into 6-8 wedges. Roll wedges into crescent shapes, starting at the wide end. Place on greased baking sheets. Cover and let rolls rise in a warm place until doubled, about 1 hour. Melt the remaining butter and brush some on each crescent.

M FAST FIX
CHOCOLATE BANANA BRAN MUFFINS

So easy to make, these treats are healthy, but they still satisfy my chocolate-loving family. Stir in raisin bran instead of bran flakes for a little extra fun.
—Tracy Chappell, Hamiota, MB

Start to Finish: 25 min.
Makes: 1 dozen

- 1 **cup all-purpose flour**
- ½ **cup sugar**
- 2 **tablespoons baking cocoa**
- 1 **teaspoon baking powder**
- 1 **teaspoon baking soda**
- ½ **teaspoon salt**
- 1 **cup bran flakes**
- 2 **large eggs**
- 1 **cup mashed ripe bananas (about 2 medium)**
- ⅓ **cup canola oil**
- ¼ **cup buttermilk**

1. Preheat oven to 400°. In a large bowl, whisk the first six ingredients. Stir in bran flakes. In another bowl, whisk the eggs, bananas, oil and buttermilk until blended. Add to flour mixture; stir just until moistened.
2. Fill foil-lined muffin cups three-fourths full. Bake 12-14 minutes or until a toothpick inserted in center comes out clean. Cool 5 minutes before removing from pan to a wire rack. Serve muffins warm.
Per 1 muffin: 169 cal., 7g fat (1g sat. fat), 35mg chol., 278mg sod., 24g carb. (12g sugars, 2g fiber), 3g pro.
Diabetic exchanges: 1½ starch, 1½ fat.

M FAST FIX
LEMON & GARLIC NEW POTATOES

When I was in the Peace Corps in Costa Rica, my host family made a version of this dish. I simplified it some, and it has become a very popular side at my house.
—Katie Bartle, Parkville, MO

Start to Finish: 25 min.
Makes: 4 servings

- 1 **pound small red potatoes**
- 2 **tablespoons olive oil**
- 2 **garlic cloves, minced**
- ¼ **cup shredded Parmesan cheese**
- 2 **tablespoons lemon juice**
- ¼ **teaspoon salt**
- ¼ **teaspoon pepper**

Cut the scrubbed potatoes into wedges; place in a large saucepan. Add water to cover; bring to a boil. Cook, covered, until tender, 10-15 minutes; drain. In the same pan, heat oil over medium-high heat. Add potatoes; cook until browned, 4-6 minutes. Add the garlic; cook 1 minute longer. Remove from heat. Stir in remaining ingredients.
Per ¾ cup: 166 cal., 8g fat (2g sat. fat), 4mg chol., 240mg sod., 19g carb. (1g sugars, 2g fiber), 4g pro.
Diabetic exchanges: 1 starch, 1½ fat.

SOUR CREAM-LEEK BISCUITS

These biscuits are a wonderful pairing for soups. I've made them with all-purpose white flour as well as whole wheat, and both work equally well.
—Bonnie Appleton, Canterbury, CT

Start to Finish: 30 min.
Makes: about 1 dozen

⅓ cup cold unsalted butter, divided
1½ cups finely chopped leeks (white portion only)
2 cups white whole wheat flour
2½ teaspoons baking powder
½ teaspoon salt
¼ teaspoon baking soda
¾ cup reduced-fat sour cream
¼ cup water

1. Preheat oven to 400°. In a small skillet over medium heat, melt 1 tablespoon butter. Add leeks; cook until tender, 6-7 minutes. Cool.
2. Whisk together flour, baking powder, salt and baking soda. Cut in remaining butter until mixture resembles coarse crumbs. Stir in leeks, sour cream and water just until moistened. Turn onto a lightly floured surface; knead 8-10 times.
3. Pat or roll out to ½-in. thickness; cut with a floured 2½-in. biscuit cutter. Place biscuits 2 in. apart on an ungreased baking sheet; bake until golden brown, 12-16 minutes. Serve warm.
Per 1 biscuit: 166 cal., 7g fat (4g sat. fat), 20mg chol., 241mg sod., 20g carb. (2g sugars, 3g fiber), 4g pro.
Diabetic exchanges: 1½ fat, 1 starch.

C M FAST FIX

EGGPLANT SNACK STICKS

Coated with Italian seasoning, Parmesan cheese and garlic salt, my veggie sticks are broiled so there's no guilt when you crunch into them.

—Mary Murphy, Atwater, CA

Start to Finish: 20 min.
Makes: 6 servings

- 2 **large eggs**
- ½ **cup grated Parmesan cheese**
- ½ **cup toasted wheat germ**
- 1 **teaspoon Italian seasoning**
- ¾ **teaspoon garlic salt**
- 1 **medium eggplant (about 1¼ pounds)**
  Cooking spray
- 1 **cup meatless pasta sauce, warmed**

1. Preheat broiler. In a shallow bowl, whisk eggs. In another shallow bowl, mix cheese, wheat germ and the seasonings.

2. Trim ends of eggplant; cut the eggplant lengthwise into ½-in.-thick slices. Cut slices lengthwise into ½-in. strips. Dip eggplant in eggs, then coat with cheese mixture. Place on a baking sheet coated with cooking spray.

3. Spritz eggplant with additional cooking spray. Broil 4 in. from heat for 3 minutes. Turn eggplant; spritz with additional cooking spray. Broil until golden brown, 1-2 minutes. Serve immediately with meatless pasta sauce.

Per serving: 135 cal., 5g fat (2g sat. fat), 68mg chol., 577mg sod., 15g carb. (6g sugars, 4g fiber), 9g pro.
Diabetic exchanges: 1 medium-fat meat, 1 vegetable, ½ starch.

BAKED SWEET POTATO FRIES

I can never get enough of these baked fries! Even though grocery stores sell them in the frozen foods section, I still love to make my own using the fresh spuds from my garden.
—Amber Massey, Argyle, TX

Prep: 10 min. • **Bake:** 35 min.
Makes: 4 servings

- 2 large sweet potatoes, cut into thin strips
- 2 tablespoons canola oil
- 1 teaspoon garlic powder
- 1 teaspoon paprika
- 1 teaspoon kosher salt
- ¼ teaspoon cayenne pepper

Preheat oven to 425°. Combine all ingredients; toss to coat. Spread fries in a single layer on two baking sheets. Bake until crisp, 35-40 minutes. Serve immediately.
Per serving: 243 cal., 7g fat (1g sat. fat), 0 chol., 498mg sod., 43g carb. (17g sugars, 5g fiber), 3g pro.

ELVIS BANANA BREAD

As a toddler, my son really loved bananas, so we always had them in the house. We didn't always eat them all before they were too ripe, so we experimented beyond basic banana bread. That's how we came up with Elvis bread!
—Elizabeth Somppi, Greenfield, WI

Prep: 30 min.
Bake: 45 min. + cooling
Makes: 3 mini loaves
(6 slices each)

- 2 cups all-purpose flour
- 1 cup sugar
- 1 teaspoon baking powder
- 1 teaspoon baking soda
- 1 teaspoon salt
- 1 teaspoon pumpkin pie spice
- 4 medium ripe bananas, mashed
- 2 large eggs
- ½ cup creamy peanut butter
- ¼ cup unsweetened applesauce
- ¼ cup canola oil
- 2 teaspoons vanilla extract
- ⅔ cup semisweet chocolate chips

1. Preheat oven to 350°. In a large bowl, whisk the first six ingredients. In another bowl, whisk bananas, eggs, peanut butter, applesauce, oil and vanilla until blended. Add to flour mixture; stir just until moistened. Fold in chocolate chips.
2. Transfer to three 5¾x3x2-in. loaf pans coated with cooking spray. Bake 45-50 minutes or until a toothpick inserted in the center comes out clean. Cool bread in pans 10 minutes before removing to a wire rack to cool.
Freeze option: Freeze cooled loaves in resealable plastic freezer bags. To use, thaw at room temperature or, if desired, microwave each loaf on high for 60-75 seconds or until heated through.
Per 1 slice: 227 cal., 9g fat (2g sat. fat), 24mg chol., 266mg sod., 34g carb. (19g sugars, 2g fiber), 4g pro.

M **FAST FIX**

COLCANNON IRISH POTATOES

My mother came from Ireland when she was a teen and brought this homey recipe with her. I find that it's a great way to get my family to eat cooked cabbage... hidden in Grandma's potatoes!
—Marie Pagel, Lena, WI

Start to Finish: 30 min.
Makes: 10 servings

- 2½ **pounds potatoes (about 6 medium), peeled and cut into 1-inch pieces**
- 2 **cups chopped cabbage**
- 1 **large onion, chopped**
- 1 **teaspoon salt**
- ¼ **teaspoon pepper**
- ¼ **cup butter, softened**
- 1 **cup 2% milk**

1. Place potatoes in a 6-qt. stockpot; add water to cover. Bring to a boil. Reduce heat to medium; cook, covered, until potatoes are almost tender, 8-10 minutes.
2. Add cabbage and onion; cook, covered, until cabbage is tender, 5-7 minutes. Drain; return to pot. Add salt and pepper; mash to desired consistency, gradually adding butter and milk.
Per ¾ cup: 129 cal., 5g fat (3g sat. fat), 14mg chol., 290mg sod., 19g carb. (4g sugars, 2g fiber), 3g pro.
Diabetic exchanges: 1 starch, 1 fat.

C **M** **FAST FIX**

PARMESAN ROASTED BROCCOLI

Sure, it's simple and healthy but, oh, is this roasted broccoli delicious! Cutting the stalks into tall trees turns this ordinary veggie into a standout side dish.
—Holly Sander, Wellesley, MA

Start to Finish: 30 min.
Makes: 4 servings

- 2 **small broccoli crowns (about 8 ounces each)**
- 3 **tablespoons olive oil**
- ½ **teaspoon salt**
- ½ **teaspoon pepper**
- ¼ **teaspoon crushed red pepper flakes**
- 4 **garlic cloves, thinly sliced**
- 2 **tablespoons grated Parmesan cheese**
- 1 **teaspoon grated lemon peel**

1. Preheat oven to 425°. Cut broccoli crowns into quarters from top to bottom. Drizzle with oil; sprinkle with salt, pepper and red pepper flakes. Place in a parchment paper-lined 15x10x1-in. pan.
2. Roast until crisp-tender, 10-12 minutes. Sprinkle with garlic; roast 5 minutes. Sprinkle with cheese; roast until cheese is melted and the stalks are tender, 2-4 minutes more. Sprinkle with the lemon peel.
Per 2 broccoli pieces: 144 cal., 11g fat (2g sat. fat), 2mg chol., 378mg sod., 9g carb. (2g sugars, 3g fiber), 4g pro.
Diabetic exchanges: 2 fat, 1 vegetable.

SPRING ASPARAGUS

This impressive side dish is delicious served warm or cold. I get lots of compliments on the homemade dressing.
—Millie Vickery, Lena, IL

....

Start to Finish: 25 min.
Makes: 8 servings

1½ pounds fresh asparagus, trimmed and cut into 2-inch pieces
2 small tomatoes, cut into wedges
3 tablespoons cider vinegar
¾ teaspoon Worcestershire sauce
⅓ cup sugar
1 tablespoon grated onion
½ teaspoon salt
½ teaspoon paprika
⅓ cup canola oil
⅓ cup sliced almonds, toasted
⅓ cup crumbled blue cheese, optional

1. In a large saucepan, bring 1 cup water to a boil. Add asparagus; cook, covered, until crisp-tender, 3-5 minutes. Drain; place in a large bowl. Add tomatoes; cover and keep warm.
2. Place vinegar, Worcestershire sauce, sugar, onion, salt and paprika in a blender; cover and process until smooth. While processing, gradually add oil in a steady stream. Toss with asparagus mixture. Top with the toasted almonds and, if desired, cheese.
Per ¾ cup: 154 cal., 11g fat (1g sat. fat), 0 chol., 159mg sod., 12g carb. (10g sugars, 1g fiber), 2g pro.
Diabetic exchanges: 2 fat, 1 vegetable, ½ starch.

SUNFLOWER SEED & HONEY WHEAT BREAD

I've tried other bread recipes, but this one is a staple in our home. I had a loaf stored in the freezer, and I thawed it out to enter a baking contest. It won a prize!
—Mickey Turner, Grants Pass, OR

....

Prep: 40 min. + rising
Bake: 35 min. + cooling
Makes: 3 loaves (12 slices each)

2 packages (¼ ounce each) active dry yeast
3¼ cups warm water (110° to 115°)
¼ cup bread flour
⅓ cup canola oil
⅓ cup honey
3 teaspoons salt
6½ to 7½ cups whole wheat flour
½ cup sunflower kernels
3 tablespoons butter, melted

1. In a large bowl, dissolve yeast in warm water. Add the bread flour, oil, honey, salt and 4 cups whole wheat flour. Beat until smooth. Stir in sunflower kernels and enough remaining flour to form a firm dough.
2. Turn onto a floured surface; knead until smooth and elastic, about 6-8 minutes. Place in a greased bowl, turning once to grease the top. Cover and let rise in a warm place until doubled, about 1 hour.
3. Punch dough down; divide into three portions. Shape into loaves; place in three greased 8x4-in. loaf pans. Cover and let rise until doubled, about 30 minutes.
4. Bake at 350° for 35-40 minutes or until golden brown. Brush with melted butter. Remove from pans to wire racks to cool.
Freeze option: Securely wrap and freeze cooled loaves in foil; place in resealable plastic freezer bags. To use, thaw at room temperature.
Per 1 slice: 125 cal., 4g fat (1g sat. fat), 3mg chol., 212mg sod., 19g carb. (3g sugars, 3g fiber), 4g pro.
Diabetic exchanges: 1 starch, 1 fat.

CRUSTY HOMEMADE BREAD

F M

Crackling homemade bread makes an average day extraordinary. Enjoy this beautiful loaf as is, or stir in a few favorites such as cheese, garlic, herbs and dried fruits.
—Megumi Garcia, Milwaukee, WI

....

Prep: 20 min. + rising
Bake: 50 min. + cooling
Makes: 1 loaf (16 slices)

- 1½ **teaspoons active dry yeast**
- 1¾ **cups water (70° to 75°)**
- 3½ **cups plus 1 tablespoon all-purpose flour, divided**
- 2 **teaspoons salt**
- 1 **tablespoon cornmeal or additional flour**

1. In a small bowl, dissolve yeast in water. In a large bowl, mix 3½ cups flour and salt. Using a rubber spatula, stir in yeast mixture to form a soft, sticky dough. Do not knead. Cover with plastic wrap; let rise at room temperature 1 hour.
2. Punch down dough. Turn onto a lightly floured surface; pat into a 9-in. square. Fold the square into thirds, forming a 9x3-in. rectangle. Fold rectangle into thirds, forming a 3-in. square. Turn dough over; place in a greased bowl. Cover with plastic wrap; let rise at room temperature until almost doubled, about 1 hour.
3. Punch down dough and repeat folding process. Return dough to the bowl; refrigerate, covered, overnight.
4. Dust bottom of a disposable foil roasting pan with cornmeal. Turn dough onto a floured surface. Knead gently 6-8 times; shape into

a 6-in. round loaf. Place in prepared pan; dust top with remaining 1 tablespoon flour. Cover pan with plastic wrap; let rise at room temperature until dough expands to a 7½-in. loaf, about 1¼ hours.
5. Preheat oven to 500°. Using a sharp knife, make a slash (¼ in. deep) across top of loaf. Cover pan tightly with foil. Bake on lowest oven rack 25 minutes.
6. Reduce oven setting to 450°. Remove foil; bake bread until deep golden brown, 25-30 minutes. Remove loaf to a wire rack to cool.
Per 1 slice: 105 cal., 0 fat (0 sat. fat), 0 chol., 296mg sod., 22g carb. (0 sugars, 1g fiber), 3g pro.

MOM'S APPLE CORN BREAD STUFFING

My speedy stuffing is the end-all and be-all side dish for our family. We never have leftovers.
—Marie Forte, Raritan, NJ

....

Prep: 15 min. • **Bake:** 35 min.
Makes: 16 servings

- 6 **large Granny Smith apples, peeled and chopped**
- 1 **package (14 ounces) crushed corn bread stuffing**
- ½ **cup butter, melted**
- 1 **can (14½ ounces) chicken broth**

1. Preheat oven to 350°. Combine apples, stuffing and melted butter. Add broth; mix well.
2. Transfer to a greased 13x9-in. baking dish. Bake until golden brown, 35-40 minutes.
Per ¾ cup: 183 cal., 7g fat (4g sat. fat), 16mg chol., 434mg sod., 28g carb. (8g sugars, 2g fiber), 3g pro.
Diabetic exchanges: 2 starch, 1½ fat.

Cinnamon Nut Bars
page 211

COOKIES, BARS & BROWNIES

Life is too short to pass on dessert. Now you can give into temptation without much guilt when you bake up a batch of these sweet delights—they're light on calories but big on taste!

F S C
CHEWY COCONUT MACAROONS

These chewy macaroons are my husband's favorite cookie, so he requests them often. I like to make them on cold winter days when we're stuck indoors. I keep them in an airtight bowl on the kitchen counter, but they never last long!
—Peggy Key, Grant, AL

....

Prep: 10 min. • **Bake:** 20 min.
Makes: 32 cookies

- 2½ cups sweetened shredded coconut
- ¾ cup all-purpose flour
- ⅛ teaspoon salt
- 1 can (14 ounces) fat-free sweetened condensed milk
- 1½ teaspoons almond extract

1. In a bowl, toss the coconut, flour and salt. Stir in milk and extract until blended (mixture will be thick and sticky).

2. Drop by level tablespoons 3 in. apart on lightly greased baking sheets. Bake at 300° for 18-22 minutes or just until golden brown. Cool for 2 minutes before removing from pans to wire racks.

Per 1 cookie: 83 cal., 3g fat (2g sat. fat), 2mg chol., 41mg sod., 13g carb. (11g sugars, 0 fiber), 1g pro.

Diabetic exchanges: 1 starch, ½ fat.

S C
SWIRLED PUMPKIN CHEESECAKE BARS

Enjoy this holiday dessert without worrying about calories. It is so luscious that no one will guess it's light!
—Jean Ecos, Hartland, WI

Prep: 30 min.
Bake: 20 min. + chilling
Makes: 16 servings

- 1 cup graham cracker crumbs
- 2 tablespoons sugar
- 2 tablespoons reduced-fat butter, melted

FILLING
- 11 ounces reduced-fat cream cheese
- ⅓ cup reduced-fat sour cream
- ⅓ cup sugar
- 2 teaspoons all-purpose flour
- ½ teaspoon vanilla extract
- 1 large egg, lightly beaten
- ½ cup canned pumpkin
- 1 tablespoon brown sugar

1. In a small bowl, combine cracker crumbs and sugar; stir in butter. Press onto the bottom of a 9-in. square baking dish coated with cooking spray. Bake at 325° for 7-10 minutes or until set. Cool on a wire rack.

2. For filling, in a large bowl, beat the cream cheese, sour cream, sugar, flour and vanilla until mixture is smooth. Add the egg; beat on low just until combined. Remove ¾ cup batter to a small bowl; stir in the pumpkin and brown sugar until well blended.

3. Pour plain batter over crust. Drop pumpkin batter by single tablespoons over plain batter. Cut through batter with a knife to swirl. Bake at 325° for 20-25 minutes or until center is almost set. Cool on a wire rack for 1 hour. Cover and refrigerate for at least 2 hours. Refrigerate leftovers.

Note: This recipe was tested with Land O'Lakes light stick butter.

Per 1 bar: 117 cal., 6g fat (4g sat. fat), 31mg chol., 135mg sod., 13g carb. (9g sugars, 0 fiber), 3g pro.

Diabetic exchanges: 1 starch, 1 fat.

S

ALMOND BLONDIES

Here's a sweet change from the typical chocolate brownie. When I bake up a batch, they never last long at my house.
—Cindy Pruitt, Grove, OK

Prep: 15 min.
Bake: 25 min. + cooling
Makes: 16 servings

- 2 large eggs
- ½ cup sugar
- ½ cup packed brown sugar
- ⅓ cup butter, melted
- 1 teaspoon vanilla extract
- ¼ teaspoon almond extract
- 1⅓ cups all-purpose flour
- ½ teaspoon baking powder
- ¼ teaspoon salt
- ¼ cup chopped almonds

1. In a large bowl, beat the eggs, sugar and brown sugar for 3 minutes. Add butter and extracts; mix well. Combine the flour, baking powder and salt. Gradually add to the creamed mixture, beating just until blended. Fold in almonds.
2. Pour into an 8-in. square baking pan coated with cooking spray. Bake at 350° for 25-30 minutes or until a toothpick inserted in the center comes out clean. Cool on a wire rack. Cut into squares.
Per 1 bar: 143 cal., 6g fat (3g sat. fat), 36mg chol., 88mg sod., 21g carb. (13g sugars, 1g fiber), 2g pro.
Diabetic exchanges: 1½ starch, 1 fat.

TEST KITCHEN TIP
Cover a pan of uncut brownies and bars with foil, or put the pan in a large resealable plastic bag. (If they're made with perishable ingredients, like cream cheese, they should be covered and refrigerated.) Store the bars in an airtight container after cutting.

APPLESAUCE BROWNIES

Cinnamon-flavored brownies are a cinch to make from scratch. This recipe can also be doubled and baked in a jelly-roll pan.
—Bernice Pebley, Cozad, NE

Prep: 15 min.
Bake: 25 min. + cooling
Makes: 16 brownies

- ¼ **cup butter, softened**
- ¾ **cup sugar**
- 1 **large egg**

- 1 **cup all-purpose flour**
- 1 **tablespoon baking cocoa**
- ½ **teaspoon baking soda**
- ½ **teaspoon ground cinnamon**
- 1 **cup applesauce**

TOPPING

- ½ **cup chocolate chips**
- ½ **cup chopped walnuts or pecans**
- 1 **tablespoon sugar**

1. In a bowl, cream butter and sugar. Beat in egg. Combine the flour, cocoa, baking soda and cinnamon; gradually add to the creamed mixture and mix well.

Stir in applesauce. Pour into an 8-in. square baking pan coated with cooking spray.

2. Combine topping ingredients; sprinkle over batter. Bake at 350° for 25 minutes or until toothpick inserted near the center comes out clean. Cool on a wire rack. Cut the brownies into squares.

Per 1 brownie: 154 cal., 7g fat (3g sat. fat), 21mg chol., 65mg sod., 22g carb. (15g sugars, 1g fiber), 2g pro.
Diabetic exchanges: 1½ starch, 1½ fat.

You'd never guess these rich, velvety chocolate treats contain a can of black beans. They make a great gluten-free dessert.
—Kathy Hewitt, Cranston, RI

Prep: 15 min.
Bake: 20 min. + cooling
Makes: 1 dozen

- 1   can (15 ounces) black beans, rinsed and drained
- ½   cup semisweet chocolate chips, divided
- 3   tablespoons canola oil
- 3   large eggs
- ⅔   cup packed brown sugar
- ½   cup baking cocoa
- 1   teaspoon vanilla extract
- ½   teaspoon baking powder
- ⅛   teaspoon salt

1. Place the beans, ¼ cup chocolate chips and oil in a food processor; cover and process until blended. Add eggs, brown sugar, cocoa, vanilla, baking powder and salt; cover and process until smooth.
2. Transfer batter to a parchment paper-lined 8-in. square baking pan. Sprinkle with remaining chocolate chips. Bake at 350° for 20-25 minutes or until a toothpick inserted in center comes out clean. Cool on a wire rack. Cut into bars.
Per 1 brownie: 167 cal., 7g fat (2g sat. fat), 53mg chol., 131mg sod., 24g carb. (16g sugars, 2g fiber), 4g pro.
Diabetic exchanges: 1½ starch, 1 fat.

F S

RASPBERRY OAT BARS

You'll love the fruity raspberry and sweet almond flavors in these tempting bars. They're wonderful with hot coffee or cold milk.
—Mary Nourse, South Deerfield, MA

Prep: 20 min.
Bake: 25 min. + cooling
Makes: 2 dozen

- 2   tablespoons sugar
- 2   tablespoons cornstarch
- 1   package (10 ounces) frozen sweetened raspberries, thawed
- ¼   teaspoon almond extract
- 1   cup quick-cooking oats
- ¾   cup all-purpose flour
- ⅔   cup packed brown sugar
- ¼   cup whole wheat flour
- ¼   teaspoon salt
- 1   teaspoon vanilla extract
- ⅓   cup cold butter, cubed

1. In a small saucepan, combine sugar and cornstarch. Gradually stir in raspberries until blended. Bring to a boil; cook and stir for 1-2 minutes or until thickened. Remove from the heat; stir in extract. Cool.
2. In a large bowl, combine the oats, flour, brown sugar, wheat flour, salt and vanilla. Cut in the butter until mixture resembles coarse crumbs. Press 2½ cups crumb mixture into a 9-in. square baking pan coated with cooking spray. Spread with cooled berry mixture. Sprinkle top with the remaining crumbs.
3. Bake at 350° for 25-30 minutes or until golden brown. Cool on a wire rack. Cut into bars.
Per 1 bar: 95 cal., 3g fat (2g sat. fat), 7mg chol., 45mg sod., 17g carb. (10g sugars, 1g fiber), 1g pro.
Diabetic exchanges: 1 starch, ½ fat.

F S C
MOLASSES CRACKLE COOKIES

You can treat yourself to one or two of my crackle cookies without guilt. They contain less sugar than most and don't call for butter but taste super spicy and delicious!
—Jean Ecos, Hartland, WI

Prep: 20 min. + chilling
Bake: 10 min./batch
Makes: 2½ dozen

- ⅔ cup sugar
- ¼ cup canola oil
- 1 large egg
- ⅓ cup molasses
- 2 cups white whole wheat flour
- 1½ teaspoons baking soda
- 1 teaspoon ground cinnamon
- ½ teaspoon salt
- ¼ teaspoon ground ginger
- ¼ teaspoon ground cloves
- 1 tablespoon confectioners' sugar

1. In a small bowl, beat sugar and oil until blended. Beat in the egg and molasses. Combine the flour, baking soda, cinnamon, salt, ginger and cloves; gradually add to sugar mixture and mix well. Cover and refrigerate at least 2 hours.
2. Preheat oven to 350°. Shape dough into 1-in. balls; roll in confectioners' sugar. Place 2 in. apart on baking sheets coated with cooking spray; flatten slightly. Bake 7-9 minutes or until set. Remove to wire racks to cool.
Per 1 cookie: 77 cal., 2g fat (0 sat. fat), 7mg chol., 106mg sod., 14g carb. (7g sugars, 1g fiber), 1g pro.
Diabetic exchanges: 1 starch.

LEMONY CREAM CHEESE BARS

This recipe is special to me because it's been passed down in my family for several generations. I use reduced-fat cream cheese to lighten it up while still keeping the same flavor.
—Patti Lavell, Islamorada, FL

Prep: 15 min.
Bake: 25 min. + cooling
Makes: 2 dozen

- 1 package lemon cake mix (regular size)
- ½ cup egg substitute, divided
- ⅓ cup canola oil
- 1 package (8 ounces) reduced-fat cream cheese
- ⅓ cup sugar
- 1 teaspoon lemon juice

1. Preheat oven to 350°. In a large bowl, combine cake mix, ¼ cup egg substitute and oil; mix until blended. Reserve ½ cup mixture for topping. Press remaining mixture onto the bottom of a 13x9-in. baking pan coated with cooking spray. Bake 11-13 minutes or until edges are light brown.
2. In a small bowl, beat the cream cheese, sugar and lemon juice until smooth. Add the remaining egg substitute; beat on low speed just until blended. Spread over crust. Crumble reserved topping over cream cheese filling.
3. Bake 11-13 minutes longer or until filling is set. Cool on a wire rack 1 hour. Cut into bars. Refrigerate any leftovers.
Per 1 bar: 149 cal., 7g fat (2g sat. fat), 7mg chol., 190mg sod., 20g carb. (12g sugars, 0 fiber), 3g pro.
Diabetic exchanges: 1½ fat, 1 starch.

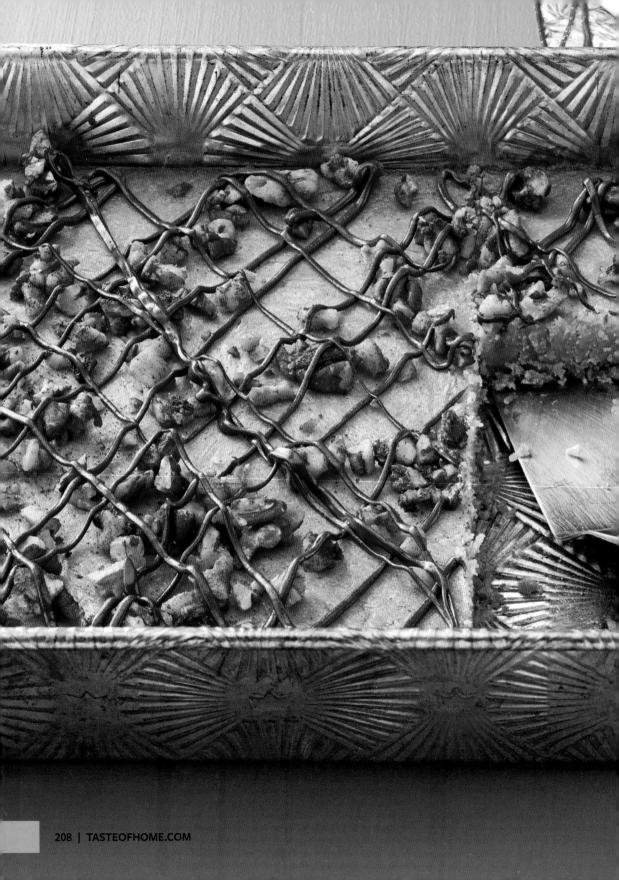

NUT-LICIOUS PEANUT BUTTER BARS

My friends were astonished to find that these bars, my favorite go-to treat, are not button-busting. Each one is just 189 calories!
—Hannah Wolters, Culleoka, TN

....

Prep: 45 min.
Bake: 15 min. + chilling
Makes: 2 dozen

CRUST
1½ cups reduced-fat graham cracker crumbs (about 10 whole crackers)
⅓ cup honey
2 tablespoons butter, melted

NUT TOPPING
¼ cup chopped pecans
¼ cup chopped walnuts
2 tablespoons honey
1½ teaspoons ground cinnamon

FILLING
12 ounces fat-free cream cheese
⅔ cup peanut butter
3 tablespoons butter, softened
½ cup confectioners' sugar
½ cup honey
1 large egg
1 teaspoon vanilla extract
¼ teaspoon maple flavoring
¼ cup all-purpose flour
¼ teaspoon baking powder

DRIZZLE
⅓ cup semisweet chocolate chips, melted

1. In a small bowl, combine crust ingredients. Press onto the bottom of a 13x9-in. baking pan coated with cooking spray. Bake at 350° for 8 minutes or until golden brown. Cool on a wire rack.

2. Meanwhile, combine the nuts, honey and cinnamon. Transfer to a baking sheet lined with parchment paper and coated with cooking spray. Bake at 350° for 5-7 minutes or until toasted and fragrant, stirring occasionally. Cool nuts completely. Crumble mixture and set aside.

3. In a small bowl, beat the cream cheese, peanut butter, butter, confectioners' sugar and honey until smooth. Beat in the egg, vanilla and maple flavoring. Combine flour and baking powder; gradually beat into cream cheese mixture. Spread over cooled crust. Bake for 14-16 minutes or until set.

4. Sprinkle nut mixture over warm filling; press in slightly. Drizzle with melted chocolate. Cool completely on a wire rack. Chill for 2 hours or until firm. Cut into bars. Refrigerate leftover bars.

Per 1 bar: 189 cal., 9g fat (3g sat. fat), 16mg chol., 175mg sod., 24g carb. (17g sugars, 1g fiber), 5g pro.

TEST KITCHEN TIP
If you use lots of nuts in your cooking and baking, you don't want to run out at a crucial time. To keep an ample supply on hand, buy large bags of walnuts, pecans and other nuts from wholesale stores, pour them into freezer bags, label them and store them in the freezer. When making a recipe, just pour out the amount of nuts called for and put the rest back in the freezer.

F S C

LOW-FAT CHOCOLATE COOKIES

These soft, cakelike cookies have a mild cocoa flavor and a cute chocolate chip topping. Better still, they're quick to make and contain only 2 grams of fat!
—Mary Houchin, Lebanon, IL

Prep: 15 min. + chilling
Bake: 10 min./batch
Makes: about 3½ dozen

½ cup unsweetened applesauce
⅓ cup canola oil
3 large egg whites
¾ cup sugar
¾ cup packed brown sugar
2 teaspoons vanilla extract
2⅔ cups all-purpose flour
½ cup baking cocoa
1 teaspoon baking soda
½ teaspoon salt
¼ cup miniature semisweet chocolate chips

1. In a large bowl, combine the applesauce, oil and egg whites. Beat in sugars and vanilla. Combine the flour, cocoa, baking soda and salt; gradually add to the applesauce mixture and mix well. Cover and refrigerate for 2 hours or until slightly firm.
2. Drop the dough by rounded teaspoonfuls 2 in. apart onto baking sheets coated with cooking spray. Sprinkle with the chocolate chips. Bake cookies at 350° for 8-10 minutes or until set. Remove to wire racks.
Per 1 cookie: 78 cal., 2g fat (0 sat. fat), 0 chol., 63mg sod., 14g carb. (0 sugars, 1g fiber), 1g pro.
Diabetic exchanges: 1 starch.

S

WHITE CHIP CRANBERRY GRANOLA BARS

These high-energy bars are great for late-night snacks, road trips, lunch boxes and care packages. The tart cranberries balance the sweet white chocolate nicely.
—Janis Loomis, Madison, VA

Prep: 25 min.
Bake: 20 min. + cooling
Makes: 2 dozen

¼ cup maple syrup
¼ cup honey
¼ cup packed brown sugar
2 tablespoons peanut butter
1 large egg white
1 tablespoon evaporated milk
1 teaspoon vanilla extract
1 cup whole wheat flour
½ teaspoon baking soda
½ teaspoon ground cinnamon
2 cups old-fashioned oats
1½ cups crisp rice cereal
½ cup vanilla or white chips
½ cup dried cranberries
¼ cup chopped walnuts

1. In a bowl, combine the maple syrup, honey, brown sugar, peanut butter, egg white, evaporated milk and vanilla; beat until smooth. Combine the flour, baking soda and cinnamon; stir into maple syrup mixture. Fold in the oats, cereal, vanilla chips, cranberries and chopped walnuts.
2. Press into a greased 13x9-in. baking pan. Bake at 350° for 18-20 minutes or until golden brown. Cool on a wire rack. Cut into bars. Store in an airtight container.
Per 1 bar: 140 cal., 4g fat (2g sat. fat), 2mg chol., 59mg sod., 24g carb. (9g sugars, 2g fiber), 3g pro.
Diabetic exchanges: 1½ starch, ½ fat.

S
CINNAMON NUT BARS
PICTURED ON PAGE 196

A classic bar meets good-for-you ingredients in this updated recipe. If you have the patience, store the cooled bars in a tin for 24 hours to allow the flavors to meld. They taste even better the next day.
—Heidi Lindsey, Prairie du Sac, WI

Prep: 20 min.
Bake: 15 min. + cooling
Makes: 2 dozen

- ½ cup whole wheat flour
- ½ cup all-purpose flour
- ½ cup sugar
- 1½ teaspoons ground cinnamon
- 1¼ teaspoons baking powder
- ¼ teaspoon baking soda
- 1 large egg, beaten
- ⅓ cup canola oil
- ¼ cup unsweetened applesauce
- ¼ cup honey
- 1 cup chopped walnuts

ICING
- 1 cup confectioners' sugar
- 2 tablespoons butter, melted
- 1 teaspoon vanilla extract
- 1 tablespoon water
- 2 tablespoons honey

1. Preheat oven to 350°. In a large bowl, combine the flours, sugar, cinnamon, baking powder and baking soda. In another bowl, combine egg, oil, applesauce and honey. Stir into dry ingredients just until moistened. Fold in walnuts.
2. Spread batter into a 13x9-in. baking pan coated with cooking spray. Bake 15-20 minutes or until a toothpick inserted in the center comes out clean.

3. Combine icing ingredients; spread over warm bars. Let bars cool completely before cutting.
Per 1 bar: 142 cal., 7g fat (1g sat. fat), 11mg chol., 44mg sod., 18g carb. (13g sugars, 1g fiber), 2g pro.
Diabetic exchanges: 1 starch, 1 fat.

F S
MINT-MALLOW SANDWICH COOKIES

My whoopie pies have a refreshing peppermint twist. Their gooey marshmallow filling makes them a big hit with kids, especially around the holidays.
—Dion Frischer, Ann Arbor, MI

Prep: 30 min.
Bake: 10 min./batch
Makes: 2 dozen

- ⅓ cup butter, softened
- 1¼ cups sugar
- 1 large egg white
- 1 teaspoon vanilla extract
- 1 cup all-purpose flour
- ⅓ cup baking cocoa
- ¼ teaspoon baking soda

FILLING
- ⅓ cup marshmallow creme
- ⅛ teaspoon peppermint extract
- 1 drop red food coloring, optional

1. In a large bowl, beat the butter and sugar until crumbly, about 2 minutes. Beat in egg white and vanilla. Combine the flour, cocoa and baking soda; gradually add to sugar mixture, and mix well.
2. Shape into ¾-in. balls; place 2 in. apart on baking sheets coated with cooking spray. Bake at 350° for 7-9 minutes or until set. Remove to wire racks to cool completely.
3. In a small bowl, combine the marshmallow creme, extract and, if desired, food coloring. Spread on the bottoms of half of the cookies; top with remaining cookies. Store in an airtight container.
Per 1 sandwich cookie: 91 cal., 3g fat (2g sat. fat), 7mg chol., 35mg sod., 16g carb. (11g sugars, 0 fiber), 1g pro.

Frozen Berry
& Yogurt Swirls
page 229 o ———————————➔

SPECIAL TREATS & DESSERTS

Yes, you can have your cake and eat it, too! It's possible to stick to a healthy eating plan even when you crave something sweet. These better-for-you desserts let you enjoy the best of both worlds.

PLUM UPSIDE-DOWN CAKE

The delicate flavor of plums is a pleasing change of pace in this cake that bakes in a skillet.
—Bobbie Talbott, Veneta, OR

Prep: 15 min. • **Bake:** 40 min.
Makes: 10 servings

⅓ cup butter
½ cup packed brown sugar
1¾ to 2 pounds medium plums, pitted and halved
2 large eggs
⅔ cup sugar
1 cup all-purpose flour
1 teaspoon baking powder
¼ teaspoon salt
⅓ cup hot water
½ teaspoon lemon extract
Whipped cream, optional

1. Melt butter in a 10-in. cast-iron or ovenproof skillet. Sprinkle brown sugar over butter. Arrange plum halves, cut side down, in a single layer over sugar; set aside.

2. In a large bowl, beat eggs until thick and lemon-colored; gradually beat in sugar. Combine the flour, baking powder and salt; add to egg mixture and mix well. Blend water and lemon extract; beat into batter. Pour over plums.

3. Bake at 350° for 40-45 minutes or until a toothpick inserted near the center comes out clean. Immediately invert onto a serving plate. Serve warm, with whipped cream if desired.

Per 1 piece: 245 cal., 7g fat (4g sat. fat), 53mg chol., 173mg sod., 43g carb. (32g sugars, 1g fiber), 3g pro.

CHUNKY MONKEY CUPCAKES

Peanut butter is a favorite of ours, and it brings a fun element to these banana cupcakes. Sprinkle additional peanuts on top for extra crunch if you like.
—Holly Jones, Kennesaw, GA

Prep: 30 min.
Bake: 20 min. + cooling
Makes: 2 dozen

- 2 **cups mashed ripe bananas (about 5 medium)**
- 1½ **cups sugar**
- 3 **large eggs**
- ½ **cup unsweetened applesauce**
- ¼ **cup canola oil**
- 3 **cups all-purpose flour**
- 1 **teaspoon baking soda**
- ½ **teaspoon baking powder**
- ½ **teaspoon salt**
- 1 **cup semisweet chocolate chunks**

FROSTING
- 4 **ounces reduced-fat cream cheese**
- ¼ **cup creamy peanut butter**
- 3 **tablespoons butter, softened**
- 1 **to 1¼ cups confectioners' sugar**
  Chopped salted peanuts, optional

1. Preheat the oven to 350°. Line 24 muffin cups with paper liners.
2. Beat first five ingredients until well blended. In another bowl, whisk together flour, baking soda, baking powder and salt; gradually beat into banana mixture. Fold in chocolate chunks.
3. Fill prepared cups three-fourths full. Bake until a toothpick inserted in center comes out clean, 20-25 minutes. Cool in pans 10 minutes before removing to wire racks to cool completely.
4. For frosting, beat cream cheese, peanut butter and butter until smooth. Gradually beat in enough confectioners' sugar to reach desired consistency. Spread over cupcakes. If desired, sprinkle with peanuts. Refrigerate leftovers.

Per 1 cupcake: 250 cal., 9g fat (4g sat. fat), 30mg chol., 165mg sod., 40g carb. (25g sugars, 2g fiber), 4g pro.

FRUIT & CAKE KABOBS

A neighbor served these kabobs at a family picnic and brought some over for us to sample. I was pleasantly surprised at the tasty toasted cake and juicy grilled fruit.
—Mary Ann Dell, Phoenixville, PA

Start to Finish: 25 min.
Makes: 8 servings

- ½ cup apricot preserves
- 1 tablespoon water
- 1 tablespoon butter
- ⅛ teaspoon ground cinnamon
- ⅛ teaspoon ground nutmeg
- 3 medium nectarines, quartered
- 3 medium peaches, quartered
- 3 medium plums, quartered
- 1 loaf (10¾ ounces) frozen pound cake, thawed and cut into 1½-inch cubes

1. In a small saucepan, combine the first five ingredients; cook and stir over medium heat until blended. Remove from heat.

2. On eight metal or soaked wooden skewers, alternately thread fruit and the pound cake. Place on a greased rack over medium heat. Grill, uncovered, until fruit is lightly browned and tender, brushing occasionally with apricot mixture.

Per serving: 1 kabob: 259 cal., 8g fat (4g sat. fat), 58mg chol., 161mg sod., 46g carb. (33g sugars, 3g fiber), 4g pro.

FAMILY-FAVORITE PEANUT BUTTER CAKE

My grandmother and aunts used to serve this alongside homemade ice cream. I now share it at special family gatherings.
—Keith Gable, Goddard, KS

Prep: 20 min.
Bake: 15 min. + cooling
Makes: 24 servings

- ½ cup creamy peanut butter
- 6 tablespoons butter, cubed
- 1 cup water
- 2 cups all-purpose flour
- 1½ cups sugar
- ½ cup buttermilk
- ¼ cup unsweetened applesauce
- 2 large eggs, lightly beaten
- 1¼ teaspoons baking powder
- 1 teaspoon vanilla extract
- ½ teaspoon salt
- ¼ teaspoon baking soda

FROSTING

- ¼ cup butter, cubed
- ¼ cup creamy peanut butter
- 2 tablespoons fat-free milk
- 1¾ cups confectioners' sugar
- 1 teaspoon vanilla extract

1. In a large saucepan, bring the peanut butter, butter and water just to a boil. Immediately remove mixture from the heat; stir in the flour, sugar, buttermilk, applesauce, eggs, baking powder, vanilla, salt and baking soda until smooth.

2. Pour into a 15x10x1-in. baking pan coated with cooking spray. Bake at 375° for 15-20 minutes or until golden brown and a toothpick inserted near the center comes out clean. Cool on a wire rack for 20 minutes.

3. In a small saucepan, melt butter and peanut butter over medium heat; add milk. Bring to a boil. Remove from the heat. Gradually whisk in confectioners' sugar and vanilla until smooth. Spread over warm cake. Cool completely on a wire rack. Refrigerate leftovers.

Per 1 piece: 220 cal., 9g fat (4g sat. fat), 30mg chol., 166mg sod., 31g carb. (22g sugars, 1g fiber), 4g pro.
Diabetic exchanges: 2 starch, 1½ fat.

MANGO RICE PUDDING

Mangoes are my son's favorite fruit, so I was ecstatic to incorporate them into a healthy dessert. You can also use ripe bananas instead of mango, almond extract instead of vanilla or regular milk in place of soy.
—Melissa McCabe, Victor, NY

Prep: 5 min. • **Cook:** 50 min.
Makes: 4 servings

- 2 cups water
- ¼ teaspoon salt
- 1 cup uncooked long grain brown rice
- 1 medium ripe mango
- 1 cup vanilla soy milk
- 2 tablespoons sugar
- ½ teaspoon ground cinnamon
- 1 teaspoon vanilla extract
  Chopped peeled mango, optional

1. In a large heavy saucepan, bring water and salt to a boil; stir in rice. Reduce heat; simmer, covered, 35-40 minutes or until water is absorbed and rice is tender.
2. Meanwhile, peel, seed and slice mango. Mash mango with a potato masher or fork.
3. Stir milk, sugar, cinnamon and mashed mango into rice. Cook, uncovered, on low 10-15 minutes longer or until liquid is almost absorbed, stirring occasionally.
4. Remove from heat; stir in vanilla. Serve warm or cold, with chopped mango if desired.
Per 1 cup: 275 cal., 3g fat (0 sat. fat), 0 chol., 176mg sod., 58g carb. (20g sugars, 3g fiber), 6g pro.

SPICED BUTTERNUT SQUASH PIE

My mom made this dessert with her homegrown squash. It was my dad's favorite after-dinner treat. I continue to make it to this day.
—Johnna Poulson, Celebration, FL

Prep: 20 min.
Bake: 40 min. + cooling
Makes: 8 servings

- 1 refrigerated pie pastry
- 3 large eggs
- 1½ cups mashed cooked butternut squash
- 1 cup fat-free milk
- ⅔ cup fat-free evaporated milk
- ¾ cup sugar
- ½ teaspoon salt
- 1 teaspoon ground cinnamon
- ½ teaspoon ground ginger
- ¼ teaspoon ground nutmeg
- ¼ teaspoon ground cloves
  Sweetened whipped cream, optional

1. Preheat oven to 450°. Unroll pastry sheet into a 9-in. pie plate; flute edge. Place eggs, squash, milks, sugar, salt and spices in a food processor; process until smooth. Pour into crust. Bake on a lower oven rack 10 minutes.
2. Reduce oven setting to 350°. Bake 30-40 minutes longer or until a knife inserted near the center comes out clean. Cool on a wire rack; serve or refrigerate within 2 hours. If desired, serve with whipped cream.
Per 1 piece: 266 cal., 9g fat (4g sat. fat), 76mg chol., 313mg sod., 41g carb. (24g sugars, 2g fiber), 7g pro.

HONEYDEW GRANITA

When melons are ripe and flavorful, this is a refreshing summer treat that's so easy to make. I like to garnish each serving with a sprig of mint or a small slice of honeydew.

—Bonnie Hawkins, Elkhorn, WI

Prep: 10 min.
Cook: 5 min. + freezing
Makes: 5½ cups

- 1 **cup sugar**
- 1 **cup water**
- 6 **cups cubed peeled honeydew**
- 2 **tablespoons sweet white wine**

1. In a small saucepan, bring sugar and water to a boil over medium-high heat. Cook and stir until sugar is dissolved. Cool.
2. Pulse honeydew, sugar syrup and wine in batches in a food processor until smooth, 1-2 minutes. Transfer to an 8-in. square dish. Freeze 1 hour. Stir with a fork. Freeze, stirring every 30 minutes, until frozen, 2-3 hours longer. Stir again with a fork just before serving.
Per ½ cup: 107 cal., 0 fat (0 sat. fat), 0 chol., 17mg sod., 27g carb. (26g sugars, 1g fiber), 1g pro.
Diabetic exchanges: 1½ starch, ½ fruit.

HEALTHY APPLE CRISP

This easy dish—a tradition in my family—is a mouthwatering ending to any meal. It's as quick as a boxed cake mix but it's a healthier dessert choice. It's ideal in autumn, when it seems that everyone has a bag or two of fresh apples to give away!
—Terri Wetzel, Roseburg, OR

Start to Finish: 20 min.
Makes: 6 servings

- 4 **medium tart apples, peeled and thinly sliced**
- ¼ **cup sugar**
- 1 **tablespoon all-purpose flour**
- 2 **teaspoons lemon juice**
- ¼ **teaspoon ground cinnamon**

TOPPING
- ⅔ **cup old-fashioned oats**
- ½ **cup packed brown sugar**
- ¼ **cup all-purpose flour**
- ½ **teaspoon ground cinnamon**
- 3 **tablespoons cold butter**
  Vanilla ice cream, optional

1. Toss apples with sugar, flour, lemon juice and cinnamon. Transfer to a greased microwave-safe 9-in. deep-dish pie plate.
2. Mix first four topping ingredients. Cut in butter until crumbly; sprinkle over filling.
3. Cover topping with waxed paper. Microwave on high until apples are tender, 5-7 minutes. If desired, serve with ice cream.
Per serving: 1 cup: 252 cal., 7g fat (4g sat. fat), 15mg chol., 66mg sod., 49g carb. (35g sugars, 3g fiber), 2g pro.

OLD-FASHIONED HONEY BAKED APPLES

My baked apple recipe is very old-fashioned yet tried-and-true. It's definitely a comfort food.
—Rachel Hamilton, Greenville, PA

Prep: 10 min. • **Bake:** 35 min.
Makes: 2 servings

 2 medium tart apples
 ¼ cup dried cranberries
 ⅔ cup water
 ¼ cup packed brown sugar
 1 tablespoon honey
  Vanilla ice cream or sweetened whipped cream, optional

1. Preheat oven to 350°. Core apples, leaving bottoms intact; peel top third of each. Place in a greased 8x4-in. glass loaf pan; fill with cranberries.
2. In a small saucepan, combine water, brown sugar and honey; cook and stir over medium heat until sugar is dissolved. Pour over the apples.
3. Bake, uncovered, until apples are tender, 35-40 minutes, basting occasionally with juices. If desired, serve with ice cream.

Per 1 baked apple: 253 cal., 0 fat (0 sat. fat), 0 chol., 13mg sod., 67g carb. (59g sugars, 4g fiber), 0 pro.

MOCHA FROSTED SNACK CAKE

Here's a lighter version of a chocolate mocha cake I've been baking for my family for over 30 years. I replaced part of the sugar with a lower-calorie sugar blend and some of the canola oil with applesauce. It turned out just as delicious.
—Donna Roberts, Manhattan, KS

Prep: 20 min.
Bake: 35 min. + cooling
Makes: 9 servings

 1 teaspoon instant coffee granules
 1 cup boiling water
 1¼ cups all-purpose flour
 ½ cup packed brown sugar
 ¼ cup cornstarch
 ¼ cup sugar blend
 3 tablespoons baking cocoa
 1 teaspoon baking soda
 ½ teaspoon salt
 ¼ cup unsweetened applesauce
 2 tablespoons canola oil
 1 tablespoon white vinegar
 ½ teaspoon vanilla extract
FROSTING
 ½ teaspoon instant coffee granules
 1 tablespoon fat-free milk
 1½ cups confectioners' sugar
 2 tablespoons baking cocoa
 3 tablespoons reduced-fat butter, softened
 ½ teaspoon vanilla extract

1. Preheat oven to 350°. In a small bowl, dissolve coffee granules in boiling water; cool slightly. Coat an 8-in. square baking dish with cooking spray.
2. In a large bowl, whisk flour, brown sugar, cornstarch, sugar blend, cocoa, baking soda and salt. Whisk applesauce, oil, vinegar and vanilla into coffee mixture. Add to the flour mixture; stir just until moistened.
3. Transfer to prepared dish. Bake 35-40 minutes or until a toothpick inserted in center comes out clean. Cool completely on a wire rack.
4. For frosting, in a small bowl, dissolve coffee granules in milk. In a large bowl, mix confectioners' sugar and cocoa until blended; beat in butter, vanilla and enough coffee mixture to reach a spreading consistency. Spread over cake.
Note: This recipe was tested with Splenda Sugar Blend for Baking and Land O'Lakes light stick butter.
Per 1 piece: 280 cal., 6g fat (2g sat. fat), 7mg chol., 301mg sod., 56g carb. (32g sugars, 1g fiber), 3g pro.

LIGHT CHEESECAKE

*Our family adores cheesecake,
but I wanted to serve something
healthier. I came up with this
lighter version that we all love.*
—Diane Roth, Adams, WI

....

Prep: 25 min.
Bake: 1 hour + chilling
Makes: 12 servings

- 1¼ cups crushed reduced-
  fat vanilla wafers
  (about 40 wafers)
- 2 tablespoons butter, melted
- 1 teaspoon plus
  1¼ cups sugar, divided
- 2 packages (8 ounces each)
  reduced-fat cream cheese
- 1 package (8 ounces)
  fat-free cream cheese
- 1 cup (8 ounces)
  reduced-fat sour cream
- 2 tablespoons cornstarch
- 1 teaspoon vanilla extract
- 2 large eggs, lightly beaten
- 2 large egg whites,
  lightly beaten
- 1 cup sliced fresh
  strawberries

1. Preheat oven to 350°. In a small
bowl, combine wafer crumbs,
butter and 1 teaspoon sugar. Press
onto the bottom and ½ in. up sides

of a greased 9-in. springform pan.
Bake 8 minutes. Cool on a wire
rack. Reduce oven setting to 325°.
2. In a large bowl, beat cream
cheeses and remaining 1¼ cups
sugar until smooth. Beat in sour
cream, cornstarch and vanilla. Add
eggs and egg whites; beat on low
speed just until blended. Pour into
crust. Place pan on a baking sheet.
3. Bake 60-65 minutes or until
center is almost set. Cool on a wire
rack 10 minutes. Loosen sides from
pan with a knife. Cool 1 hour longer.
Refrigerate overnight, covering
when completely cooled.
4. Remove rim from pan. Top
cheesecake with strawberries.
Per 1 slice: 311 cal., 13g fat (7g sat.
fat), 74mg chol., 310mg sod., 39g carb.
(0 sugars, 0 fiber), 10g pro.

SPICED PEACH
COBBLER

*This warm cobbler with cinnamon
and cardamom is a slimmed-down
dessert, so flirt with the possibility
of ice cream on top.*
—Mary Relyea, Canastota, NY

....

Prep: 20 min. • **Bake:** 30 min.
Makes: 8 servings

- ½ cup sugar
- 3 tablespoons cornstarch
- ½ teaspoon ground cinnamon
- ¼ teaspoon ground cardamom
- 12 medium peaches, peeled
  and sliced (about 8 cups)
- 1 tablespoon lemon juice

TOPPING
- 1 cup all-purpose flour
- ¼ cup sugar
- 2 teaspoons grated
  orange peel
- ¾ teaspoon baking powder
- ¼ teaspoon salt

- ¼ teaspoon baking soda
- 3 tablespoons cold butter
- ¾ cup buttermilk

1. Preheat oven to 375°. In a large
bowl, mix sugar, cornstarch,
cinnamon and cardamom. Add
peaches and lemon juice; toss to
combine. Transfer mixture to an
11x7-in. baking dish coated with
cooking spray.
2. In a small bowl, whisk the first six
topping ingredients; cut in butter
until mixture resembles coarse
crumbs. Add buttermilk; stir just
until moistened. Drop mixture by
tablespoonfuls over peach mixture.
3. Bake, uncovered, 30-35 minutes
or until topping is golden brown.
Serve warm.

HEALTH TIP To dollop or not to
dollop? Here are the calories per ¼ cup
of optional topping: whipped topping,
50; light ice cream, 50; ice cream, 70;
sweetened whipped cream, 114.
Per serving: 246 cal., 5g fat (3g sat.
fat), 12mg chol., 206mg sod., 49g carb.
(32g sugars, 3g fiber), 4g pro.

FRESH BLUEBERRY PIE

We live in blueberry country, and this pie is a delicious way to showcase the luscious berries. A kind neighbor made this dessert for us when we had a death in the family several years ago. We loved it so much that we have made it several times since.
—R. Ricks, Kalamazoo, MI

Prep: 20 min. + chilling
Makes: 8 servings

¾ cup sugar
3 tablespoons cornstarch
⅛ teaspoon salt
¼ cup water
4 cups fresh blueberries, divided
1 graham cracker crust (9 inches)
Whipped cream

1. In a large saucepan, combine the sugar, cornstarch and salt. Gradually add water, stirring until smooth. Stir in 2 cups blueberries. Bring to a boil; cook and stir until thickened, 1-2 minutes. Remove from the heat; cool mixture to room temperature.
2. Gently stir remaining blueberries into cooled blueberry mixture. Spoon into crust. Refrigerate, covered, until chilled, 1-2 hours. Serve with whipped cream.
Per 1 piece (without whipped cream): 230 cal., 6g fat (1g sat. fat), 0 chol., 159mg sod., 46g carb. (35g sugars, 2g fiber), 1g pro.

MOIST LEMON CHIFFON CAKE

This fluffy tube cake is a real treat, especially when drizzled with the sweet-tart lemon glaze.
—Rebecca Baird, Salt Lake City, UT

Prep: 15 min.
Bake: 45 min. + cooling
Makes: 16 servings

½ cup fat-free evaporated milk
½ cup reduced-fat sour cream
¼ cup lemon juice
2 tablespoons canola oil
2 teaspoons vanilla extract
1 teaspoon grated lemon peel
1 teaspoon lemon extract
2 cups cake flour
1½ cups sugar
1 tablespoon baking powder
½ teaspoon salt
1 cup egg whites (about 7)
½ teaspoon cream of tartar

LEMON GLAZE
1¾ cups confectioners' sugar
3 tablespoons lemon juice

1. In a large bowl, combine the first seven ingredients. Sift together the flour, sugar, baking powder and salt; gradually beat into lemon mixture until smooth. In a small bowl, beat egg whites until foamy. Add cream of tartar; beat until stiff peaks form. Gently fold into the lemon mixture.
2. Pour into an ungreased 10-in. tube pan. Bake at 325° for 45-55 minutes or until cake springs back when lightly touched. Immediately invert pan; cool completely. Remove cake to a serving platter. Combine glaze ingredients; drizzle over cake.
Per 1 slice: 230 cal., 3g fat (1g sat. fat), 3mg chol., 189mg sod., 47g carb. (33g sugars, 0 fiber), 4g pro.

S

STRAWBERRY-HAZELNUT MERINGUE SHORTCAKES

In early summer, the strawberry farms in our area open to the public for picking. These shortcakes really show off the big juicy berries of our harvest.

—Barb Estabrook, Appleton, WI

Prep: 25 min.
Bake: 45 min. + cooling
Makes: 8 servings

 2 **large egg whites**
 ½ **cup sugar**
 ¼ **cup finely chopped hazelnuts**
 6 **cups fresh strawberries, hulled and sliced**
 4 **cups low-fat frozen yogurt**

1. Place egg whites in a small bowl; let stand at room temperature for 30 minutes.

2. Preheat oven to 250°. Beat egg whites on medium speed until foamy. Gradually add the sugar, 1 tablespoon at a time, beating on high after each addition until sugar is dissolved. Continue beating until stiff glossy peaks form.

3. Using a measuring cup and spatula or an ice cream scoop, drop meringue into eight even mounds on a parchment paper-lined baking sheet. With the back of a spoon, shape into 3-in. cups. Sprinkle with hazelnuts. Bake 45-50 minutes or until set and dry. Turn off oven (do not open oven door); leave the meringues in oven 1 hour. Remove from oven; cool completely on baking sheets. Remove meringues from paper.

4. Place 3 cups strawberries in a large bowl; mash slightly. Stir in remaining strawberries. Just before serving, top meringues with frozen yogurt and strawberries.

Per serving: 212 cal., 4g fat (1g sat. fat), 5mg chol., 74mg sod., 40g carb. (36g sugars, 3g fiber), 7g pro.

How to Make Meringue Cups

1. Line a baking sheet with parchment paper. Drop meringue into mounds on the paper. Using the back of a spoon, make a well in the center of each mound to form a 3-inch cup.

2. Bake as the recipe directs. After drying in the oven, remove meringues to cool completely. Once cooled, store in an airtight container at room temperature up to 2 days.

frosting between layers and over top of cake. Refrigerate leftovers.

Per 1 slice: 241 cal., 9g fat (3g sat. fat), 49mg chol., 375mg sod., 36g carb. (19g sugars, 1g fiber), 5g pro.

S

CHUNKY BANANA CREAM FREEZE

With its sweet banana-almond flavor and chunky texture, this appealing frozen dessert is a crowd-pleaser. People who ask me for the recipe can't believe how easy it is to make.
—Kristen Bloom, APO, AP

Prep: 15 min. + freezing
Makes: 3 cups

- 5 **medium bananas, peeled and frozen**
- ⅓ **cup almond milk**
- 2 **tablespoons unsweetened finely shredded coconut**
- 2 **tablespoons creamy peanut butter**
- 1 **teaspoon vanilla extract**
- ¼ **cup chopped walnuts**
- 3 **tablespoons raisins**

1. Place the bananas, milk, coconut, peanut butter and vanilla in a food processor; cover and process until blended.

2. Transfer to a freezer container; stir in walnuts and raisins. Freeze for 2-4 hours before serving.

Note: Look for unsweetened coconut in the baking or health food section.

Per ½ cup: 181 cal., 7g fat (2g sat. fat), 0 chol., 35mg sod., 29g carb. (16g sugars, 4g fiber), 3g pro.

Diabetic exchanges: 1 fruit, 1 fat, ½ starch.

SPICED CARROT CAKE

My mom made this cake for my birthday one year because carrot cake is her favorite. It became my favorite, too! Now when I make it, I add lots of spice. The pumpkin pie spice is a perfect shortcut, but you could also use a custom blend of cinnamon, ginger, nutmeg and cloves.
—Jaris Dykas, Knoxville, TN

Prep: 30 min.
Bake: 20 min. + cooling
Makes: 16 servings

- 3 **large eggs**
- 1 **cup packed brown sugar**
- ¾ **cup fat-free plain yogurt**
- ¼ **cup canola oil**
- 2 **teaspoons vanilla extract**
- 2½ **cups all-purpose flour**
- 3 **teaspoons pumpkin pie spice**
- 2 **teaspoons baking soda**
- 1 **teaspoon salt**
- 3 **cups shredded carrots (about 6 medium)**

FROSTING
- ½ **cup heavy whipping cream**
- 4 **ounces reduced-fat cream cheese**
- ½ **cup confectioners' sugar**

1. Preheat oven to 350°. Line the bottoms of two greased 9-in. round baking pans with parchment paper; grease paper.

2. Beat first five ingredients until well blended. In another bowl, whisk together flour, pie spice, baking soda and salt; stir into egg mixture. Fold in carrots.

3. Transfer to prepared pans. Bake until a toothpick inserted in center comes out clean, 20-25 minutes. Cool in pans 10 minutes before removing to wire racks; remove paper. Cool completely.

4. For frosting, beat cream until soft peaks form. In another bowl, beat the cream cheese and confectioners' sugar until smooth; gradually fold in whipped cream.

5. If cakes are domed, trim tops with a serrated knife. Spread

FROZEN BERRY & YOGURT SWIRLS

PICTURED ON PAGE 212

These pops are a welcome treat on a warm summer day! They're a favorite at our annual summer block party.
—Colleen Ludovice, Wauwatosa, WI

Prep: 15 min. + freezing
Makes: 10 pops

- 10 plastic or paper cups (3 ounces each)
- 2¾ cups fat-free honey Greek yogurt
- 1 cup mixed fresh berries
- ¼ cup water
- 2 tablespoons sugar
- 10 wooden pop sticks

1. Fill each cup with about ¼ cup yogurt. Place berries, water and sugar in a food processor; pulse until berries are finely chopped. Spoon 1½ tablespoons berry mixture into each cup. Stir gently with a pop stick to swirl.
2. Top cups with foil; insert pop sticks through foil. Freeze until firm.
Per 1 pop: 60 cal., 0 fat (0 sat. fat), 0 chol., 28mg sod., 9g carb. (8g sugars, 1g fiber), 6g pro.
Diabetic exchanges: 1 starch.

LIME BASIL PIE

If you love citrus pies, you're sure to enjoy this one, which gets a unique taste from basil. It also contains fewer calories and less fat than the traditional key lime pie.
—Samara Donald, Redmond, WA

Prep: 15 min.
Bake: 15 min. + chilling
Makes: 8 servings

- 1 package (8 ounces) reduced-fat cream cheese
- 1 can (14 ounces) fat-free sweetened condensed milk
- 1 tablespoon grated lime peel
- ½ cup lime juice
- 2 large egg yolks
- ¼ cup minced fresh basil
- 1 reduced-fat graham cracker crust (8 inches) Sweetened whipped cream or creme fraiche, optional

1. Preheat oven to 325°. In a large bowl, beat cream cheese until smooth; gradually beat in milk. Add lime peel, juice and egg yolks; beat just until blended. Stir in basil. Pour into crust.
2. Bake 15-18 minutes or until center is set. Cool 1 hour on a wire rack. Refrigerate at least 2 hours before serving. If desired, serve with whipped cream.
Per 1 piece: 328 cal., 10g fat (5g sat. fat), 72mg chol., 268mg sod., 49g carb. (39g sugars, 0 fiber), 9g pro.

GRAPEFRUIT, LIME & MINT YOGURT PARFAIT

Tart grapefruit and lime are balanced with a bit of honey in this cool and easy parfait. Try them for desserts, after-school snacks or even for a light breakfast.

—Lois Enger, Colorado Springs, CO

Start to Finish: 15 min.
Makes: 6 servings

4 **large red grapefruit**
4 **cups (32 ounces) reduced-fat plain yogurt**
2 **teaspoons grated lime peel**
2 **tablespoons lime juice**
3 **tablespoons honey**
  Torn fresh mint leaves

1. Cut a thin slice from the top and bottom of each grapefruit; stand fruit upright on a cutting board. With a knife, cut off peel and outer membrane from grapefruit. Cut along the membrane of each segment to remove fruit.

2. In a large bowl, mix yogurt, lime peel and juice. Layer half of the grapefruit and half of the yogurt mixture into six parfait glasses. Repeat layers. Drizzle with honey; top with mint.

Per 1 parfait: 207 cal., 3g fat (2g sat. fat), 10mg chol., 115mg sod., 39g carb. (36g sugars, 3g fiber), 10g pro.

S

PRETTY PEACH TART

I love peaches. So when the blushed golden fruit finally arrives at fruit stands, this is the first dessert I think of. To me, it's pure perfection. You can make the tart with other varieties of fruit, too.

—Lorraine Caland, Shuniah, ON

Prep: 30 min.
Bake: 40 min. + cooling
Makes: 8 servings

- ¼ cup butter, softened
- 3 tablespoons sugar
- ¼ teaspoon ground nutmeg
- 1 cup all-purpose flour

FILLING

- 2 pounds peaches (about 7 medium), peeled and sliced
- ⅓ cup sugar
- 2 tablespoons all-purpose flour
- ¼ teaspoon ground cinnamon
- ⅛ teaspoon almond extract
- ¼ cup sliced almonds
  Whipped cream, optional

1. Preheat oven to 375°. Cream butter, sugar and nutmeg until light and fluffy. Beat in flour until blended (mixture will be dry). Press firmly onto bottom and up sides of an ungreased 9-in. fluted tart pan with removable bottom.

2. Place on a baking sheet. Bake on a middle oven rack until lightly browned, 10-12 minutes. Cool on a wire rack.

3. In a large bowl, toss peaches with sugar, flour, cinnamon and extract; add to crust. Sprinkle with almonds.

4. Bake tart on a lower oven rack until crust is golden brown and peaches are tender, 40-45 minutes. Cool on a wire rack. If desired, serve with whipped cream.

Per 1 piece: 222 cal., 8g fat (4g sat. fat), 15mg chol., 46mg sod., 36g carb. (21g sugars, 3g fiber), 4g pro.

TEST KITCHEN TIP
Purchase peaches that have an intense fragrance and that give slightly to palm pressure. Avoid those that are hard or have soft spots. Store ripe peaches in a plastic bag in the refrigerator for up to 5 days.

SKILLET BLUEBERRY SLUMP

My mother-in-law made a slump of wild blueberries with dumplings and served it warm with a pitcher of farm cream. We've been eating it for nearly 60 years!

—Eleanore Ebeling, Brewster, MN

....

Prep: 25 min. • **Bake:** 20 min.
Makes: 6 servings

4	cups fresh or frozen blueberries
½	cup sugar
½	cup water
1	teaspoon grated lemon peel
1	tablespoon lemon juice
1	cup all-purpose flour
2	tablespoons sugar
2	teaspoons baking powder
½	teaspoon salt
1	tablespoon butter
½	cup 2% milk
	Vanilla ice cream

1. Preheat oven to 400°. In a 10-in. ovenproof skillet, combine the first five ingredients; bring to a boil. Reduce heat; simmer, uncovered, 9-11 minutes or until slightly thickened, stirring occasionally.

2. Meanwhile, in a small bowl, whisk flour, sugar, baking powder and salt. Cut in butter until mixture resembles coarse crumbs. Add milk; stir just until moistened.

3. Drop batter in six portions on top of berry mixture. Transfer to oven. Bake, uncovered, 17-20 minutes or until dumplings are golden brown. Serve warm with ice cream.

Per 1 serving without ice cream:
239 cal., 3g fat (2g sat. fat), 7mg chol., 355mg sod., 52g carb. (32g sugars, 3g fiber), 4g pro.

F S
LIGHT & CREAMY CHOCOLATE PUDDING

This pudding is exactly what its name promises: light and creamy. Since it uses soy milk, it's a smart choice if you're lactose intolerant or you're serving a guest who doesn't consume milk.
—Deborah Williams, Peoria, AZ

Prep: 10 min.
Cook: 15 min. + chilling
Makes: 4 servings

- 3 tablespoons cornstarch
- 2 tablespoons sugar
- 2 tablespoons baking cocoa
- ⅛ teaspoon salt
- 2 cups chocolate soy milk
- 1 teaspoon vanilla extract

1. In a small heavy saucepan, mix cornstarch, sugar, cocoa and salt. Whisk in milk. Cook and stir over medium heat until thickened and bubbly. Reduce heat to low; cook and stir 2 minutes longer.
2. Remove mixture from heat. Stir in vanilla. Cool 15 minutes, stirring occasionally.
3. Transfer to dessert dishes. Refrigerate, covered, 30 minutes or until cold.
Per ½ cup: 127 cal., 2g fat (0 sat. fat), 0 chol., 112mg sod., 25g carb. (16g sugars, 1g fiber), 3g pro.
Diabetic exchanges: 1½ starch.

F
SONORAN SUNSET WATERMELON ICE

If you didn't think watermelon and cilantro could go together, this refreshing dessert will give you a pleasant surprise! Sprinkle some pomegranate seeds and a sprig of cilantro on top for extra flair.
—Jeanne Holt
Mendota Heights, MN

Prep: 15 min. + cooling
Process: 10 min. + freezing
Makes: 6 servings

½ cup sugar
¼ cup water
4 cups seedless cubed watermelon
3 tablespoons lime juice
2 tablespoons pomegranate juice
1 tablespoon minced fresh cilantro
   Dash salt

1. In a small saucepan, bring sugar and water to a boil; cook and stir until the sugar is dissolved. Cool completely.
2. Puree watermelon in a blender. Transfer to a large bowl; stir in sugar syrup and the remaining ingredients. Refrigerate until cold.
3. Pour watermelon mixture into cylinder of ice cream maker; freeze according to the manufacturer's directions. Transfer to freezer containers, allowing headspace for expansion. Freeze for 4 hours or until firm.
Per ½ cup: 100 cal., 0 fat (0 sat. fat), 0 chol., 246mg sod., 26g carb. (24g sugars, 0 fiber), 1g pro.
Diabetic exchanges: 1½ starch, ½ fruit.

BIRTHDAY CAKE FREEZER POPS

On my quest to find birthday cake ice cream—my favorite flavor—I came up with these easy freezer pops. Now, instead of going to the store whenever a craving hits, I just head to my freezer.
—Dawn Lopez, Westerly, RI

Prep: 25 min. + freezing
Makes: 1½ dozen

⅔ **cup sprinkles, divided**
18 **disposable plastic or paper cups (3 ounces each)**
2 **cups cold 2% milk**
1 **package (3.4 ounces) instant vanilla pudding mix**
1 **carton (8 ounces) frozen whipped topping, thawed**
2 **cups crushed vanilla wafers (about 60 wafers)**
18 **wooden pop sticks**

1. Spoon 1 teaspoon sprinkles into each cup.
2. In a large bowl, whisk the milk and pudding mix 2 minutes. Let stand until pudding is soft-set, about 2 minutes. Stir in whipped topping, crushed wafers and the remaining sprinkles.
3. Cut a 1-in. hole in the tip of a pastry bag or in a corner of a food-safe plastic bag; fill bag with pudding mixture. Pipe into the prepared cups. Top cups with foil and insert pop sticks through foil.
4. Freeze until firm, about 4 hours. Let stand at room temperature 5 minutes before gently removing pops from cups.
Per 1 pop: 161 cal., 7g fat (3g sat. fat), 4mg chol., 96mg sod., 23g carb. (15g sugars, 0 fiber), 1g pro.
Diabetic exchanges: 1½ starch, 1½ fat.

Slow-Cooked Potatoes
with Spring Onions
page 244

BONUS: SKINNY SLOW COOKER

A dish cooked in the slow cooker stirs up excitement for a comforting, down-home dinner. Enjoy all that hot, steamy goodness without expanding your waistline with these trimmed-down slow cooker specialties.

C

TERIYAKI PORK ROAST

I'm always looking for no-fuss recipes, so I was thrilled to find this one. The tender teriyaki pork has become a family favorite.
—Roxanne Hulsey, Gainesville, GA

Prep: 10 min. • **Cook:** 7 hours
Makes: 8 servings

- ¾ cup unsweetened apple juice
- 2 tablespoons sugar
- 2 tablespoons reduced-sodium soy sauce
- 1 tablespoon white vinegar
- 1 teaspoon ground ginger
- ¼ teaspoon garlic powder
- ⅛ teaspoon pepper
- 1 boneless pork loin roast (about 3 pounds), halved
- 7½ teaspoons cornstarch
- 3 tablespoons cold water

1. In a greased 3-qt. slow cooker, combine the first seven ingredients. Add roast and turn to coat. Cover and cook on low for 7-8 hours or until meat is tender.

2. Remove pork to a serving platter; keep warm. Skim fat from cooking juices; transfer to a small saucepan. Bring liquid to a boil. Combine cornstarch and water until smooth. Gradually stir into the pan. Bring to a boil; cook and stir for 2 minutes or until thickened. Serve with meat.

Per 4 ounces cooked pork: 247 cal., 8g fat (3g sat. fat), 85mg chol., 194mg sod., 9g carb. (5g sugars, 0 fiber), 33g pro.

Diabetic exchanges: 4 lean meat, ½ starch.

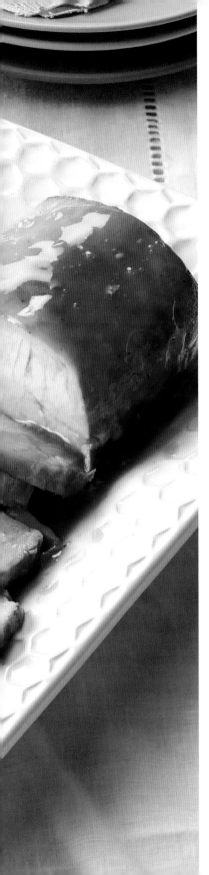

APPLE CHICKEN STEW

My husband and I enjoy visiting the apple orchards in nearby Nebraska City. We always buy cider to use in this sensational slow-cooked stew.
—Carol Mathias, Lincoln, NE

Prep: 35 min. • **Cook:** 3 hours
Makes: 8 servings

1½ teaspoons salt
¾ teaspoon dried thyme
½ teaspoon pepper
¼ to ½ teaspoon
   caraway seeds
1½ pounds potatoes
   (about 4 medium), cut
   into ¾-inch pieces
4 medium carrots, cut
   into ¼-inch slices
1 medium red onion,
   halved and sliced
1 celery rib, thinly sliced
2 pounds boneless skinless
   chicken breasts, cut
   into 1-inch pieces
2 tablespoons olive oil

1 bay leaf
1 large tart apple, peeled
   and cut into 1-inch cubes
1 tablespoon cider vinegar
1¼ cups apple cider or juice
   Minced fresh parsley

1. Mix the first four ingredients. In a 5-qt. slow cooker, layer vegetables; sprinkle vegetables with half of the salt mixture.
2. Toss chicken with oil and remaining salt mixture. In a large skillet over medium-high heat, brown chicken in batches. Add to slow cooker. Top with bay leaf and apple. Add vinegar and cider.
3. Cook, covered, on high until chicken is no longer pink and vegetables are tender, 3 -3½ hours. Discard bay leaf. Stir before serving. Sprinkle with parsley.

Per 1 cup: 284 cal., 6g fat (1g sat. fat), 63mg chol., 533mg sod., 31g carb. (9g sugars, 4g fiber), 26g pro.
Diabetic exchanges: 3 lean meat, 2 starch, 1 fat.

TANDOORI CHICKEN PANINI

The tandoori-style spices in this slow-cooked chicken give it a bold flavor that's impossible to resist. It tastes incredible tucked between pieces of naan, then grilled for an Indian-inspired panini.
—Yasmin Arif, Manassas, VA

Prep: 25 min. • **Cook:** 3 hours
Makes: 6 servings

1½ **pounds boneless skinless chicken breasts**
¼ **cup reduced-sodium chicken broth**
2 **garlic cloves, minced**
2 **teaspoons minced fresh gingerroot**
1 **teaspoon paprika**
¼ **teaspoon salt**
¼ **to ½ teaspoon cayenne pepper**
¼ **teaspoon ground turmeric**
6 **green onions, chopped**
6 **tablespoons chutney**
6 **naan flatbreads**

1. Place first eight ingredients in a 3-qt. slow cooker. Cook, covered, on low until the chicken is tender, 3-4 hours.
2. Shred chicken with two forks. Stir in green onions.
3. Spread chutney over one side of each naan. Top chutney side of three naan with chicken mixture; top with remaining naan.
4. Cook sandwiches, covered, until golden brown, 6-8 minutes. To serve, cut each sandwich in half.
Per ½ panini: 351 cal., 6g fat (2 sat. fat), 68mg chol., 830mg sod., 44g carb. (12g sugars, 2 fiber), 27g pro.
Diabetic exchanges: 3 lean meat, 3 starch.

BURGUNDY BEEF

When my adult children come over for dinner, this is their top request. All three of them and their significant others love this dish. Yum!

—Urilla Cheverie, Andover, MA

Prep: 10 min. • **Cook:** 8¼ hours
Makes: 10 servings

4 pounds beef top sirloin steak, cut into 1-inch cubes
3 large onions, sliced
1 cup water
1 cup burgundy wine or beef broth
1 cup ketchup
¼ cup quick-cooking tapioca
¼ cup packed brown sugar
¼ cup Worcestershire sauce
4 teaspoons paprika
1½ teaspoons salt
1 teaspoon minced garlic
1 teaspoon ground mustard
2 tablespoons cornstarch
3 tablespoons cold water
Hot cooked noodles

1. In a 5-qt. slow cooker, combine the first 12 ingredients. Cook, covered, on low until meat is tender, 8-9 hours.

2. Combine cornstarch and water until smooth; stir into pan juices. Cook, covered, on high until gravy is thickened, about 15 minutes. Serve with noodles.

Per 1 cup: 347 cal., 8g fat (3g sat. fat), 74mg chol., 811mg sod., 24g carb. (15g sugars, 1g fiber), 40g pro.

SLOW COOKER STUFFED SHELLS

There's no need to precook the shells in this simple pasta dish. It's almost like magic when you open the lid and find the deliciousness waiting in the slow cooker. Add garlic bread, and you're golden!
—Sherry Day, Pinckney, MI

Prep: 30 min. • **Cook:** 4 hours
Makes: 10 servings

- 1 carton (15 ounces) part-skim ricotta cheese
- 1 package (10 ounces) frozen chopped spinach, thawed and squeezed dry
- 2½ cups shredded Italian cheese blend
- ½ cup diced red onion
- ½ teaspoon garlic powder
- 2 teaspoons dried basil
- ½ teaspoon dried oregano
- ½ teaspoon dried thyme
- 2 jars (24 ounces each) roasted garlic Parmesan pasta sauce
- 1 package (12 ounces) jumbo pasta shells
- 2 cups water
  Additional shredded Italian cheese blend and sliced fresh basil

1. Mix the first eight ingredients (mixture will be stiff). In a greased 6-qt. slow cooker, mix one jar pasta sauce with water. Fill shells with ricotta mixture; layer in slow cooker. Top with remaining jar of pasta sauce.
Cook, covered, on low until pasta is tender, 4-5 hours. If desired, serve with additional cheese and fresh basil.

HEALTH TIP Relative to other cheeses, ricotta is especially high in calcium. Just ¼ cup provides almost 20 percent of the daily value.

Per 4 stuffed shells: 303 cal., 10g fat (6g sat. fat), 34mg chol., 377mg sod., 34g carb. (4g sugars, 3g fiber), 17g pro.
Diabetic exchanges: 2 starch, 2 medium-fat meat.

SWEET & TANGY PULLED PORK

The slow cooker makes these sandwiches a convenient option for busy weeknights. The apricot preserves lend a sweet flavor to the pork.
—Megan Klimkewicz, Kaiser, MO

Prep: 15 min. • **Cook:** 8 hours
Makes: 12 servings

- 1 jar (18 ounces) apricot preserves
- 1 large onion, chopped
- 2 tablespoons reduced-sodium soy sauce
- 2 tablespoons Dijon mustard
- 1 boneless pork shoulder butt roast (3 to 4 pounds)
  Hamburger buns, split, optional

1. Mix first four ingredients. Place roast in a 4- or 5-qt. slow cooker; top with preserves mixture. Cook, covered, on low until the meat is tender, 8-10 hours.
2. Remove pork from slow cooker. Skim fat from cooking juices. Shred pork with two forks; return to slow cooker and heat through. If desired, serve on buns.

Per ½ cup: 296 cal., 11g fat (4g sat. fat), 67mg chol., 248mg sod., 29g carb. (16g sugars, 0 fiber), 20g pro.
Diabetic exchanges: 3 lean meat, 2 starch.

SLOW-COOKED MEXICAN BEEF SOUP

My family loves this stew, and I'm happy to make it for them since it's so simple. Serve with corn bread instead of corn chips to make it even more filling.
—Angela Lively, Conroe, TX

Prep: 15 min. • **Cook:** 6 hours
Makes: 8 servings (2 quarts)

- 1 pound beef stew meat (1¼-inch pieces)
- ¾ pound potatoes (about 2 medium), cut into ¾-inch cubes
- 2 cups frozen corn (about 10 ounces), thawed
- 2 medium carrots, cut into ½-inch slices
- 1 medium onion, chopped
- 2 garlic cloves, minced
- 1½ teaspoons dried oregano
- 1 teaspoon ground cumin
- ½ teaspoon salt
- ¼ teaspoon crushed red pepper flakes
- 2 cups beef stock
- 1 can (10 ounces) diced tomatoes and green chilies, undrained
  Sour cream and tortilla chips, optional

In a 5- or 6-qt. slow cooker, combine first 12 ingredients. Cook, covered, on low until the meat is tender, 6-8 hours. If desired, serve with sour cream and chips.
Per serving: 218 cal., 6g fat (2g sat. fat), 47mg chol., 602mg sod., 24g carb. (5g sugars, 3 fiber), 19g pro.
Diabetic exchanges: 2 lean meat, 1½ starch.

S SLOW COOKER BERRY COBBLER

Even during warm weather, you can still enjoy the amazing flavor of homemade cobbler without heating up your kitchen.
—Karen Jarocki, Yuma, AZ

Prep: 15 min. • **Cook:** 1¾ hours
Makes: 8 servings

- 1¼ cups all-purpose flour, divided
- 2 tablespoons plus 1 cup sugar, divided
- 1 teaspoon baking powder
- ¼ teaspoon ground cinnamon
- 1 large egg
- ¼ cup fat-free milk
- 2 tablespoons canola oil
- ⅛ teaspoon salt
- 2 cups fresh or frozen raspberries, thawed
- 2 cups fresh or frozen blueberries, thawed
  Low-fat vanilla frozen yogurt, optional

1. Whisk together 1 cup flour, 2 tablespoons sugar, baking powder and cinnamon. In another bowl, whisk together egg, milk and oil; add to dry ingredients, stirring just until moistened (batter will be thick). Spread onto bottom of a 5-qt. slow cooker coated with cooking spray.
2. Mix salt and the remaining flour and sugar; toss with berries. Spoon over batter. Cook, covered, on high until berry mixture is bubbly, 1¾-2 hours. If desired, serve with frozen yogurt.
Per serving: 260 cal., 5g fat (1g sat. fat), 23mg chol., 110mg sod., 53g carb. (34g sugars, 3g fiber), 4g pro.

FRENCH DIP SANDWICHES

These sandwiches make a standout addition to any buffet line. Make sure to have plenty of small cups of broth for everyone to grab. It's dipping perfection!
—Holly Neuharth, Mesa, AZ

Prep: 15 min. • **Cook:** 8 hours
Makes: 12 servings

- 1 beef rump or bottom round roast (3 pounds)
- 1½ teaspoons onion powder
- 1½ teaspoons garlic powder
- ½ teaspoon Creole seasoning
- 1 carton (26 ounces) beef stock
- 12 whole wheat hoagie buns, split
- 6 ounces Havarti cheese, cut into 12 slices

1. Cut roast in half. Mix onion powder, garlic powder and Creole seasoning; rub onto beef. Place in a 5-qt. slow cooker; add stock. Cook, covered, on low 8-10 hours or until meat is tender.

2. Remove beef; cool slightly. Skim fat from cooking juices. When cool enough to handle, shred the beef with two forks and return to the slow cooker.

3. Place buns on ungreased baking sheets, cut side up. Using tongs, place beef on bun bottoms. Place cheese on bun tops. Broil 3-4 in. from heat 1-2 minutes or until cheese is melted. Close sandwiches; serve with cooking juices.

Note: The following spices may be substituted for 1 teaspoon Creole seasoning: ¼ teaspoon each salt, garlic powder and paprika; and a pinch each of dried thyme, ground cumin and cayenne pepper.

Per 1 sandwich with ⅓ cup juices: 456 cal., 14g fat (5g sat. fat), 81mg chol., 722mg sod., 50g carb. (9g sugars, 7g fiber), 35g pro.

S M
SLOW-COOKED POTATOES WITH SPRING ONIONS

PICTURED ON PAGE 236
I love the simplicity of this recipe, as well as the ease of preparation using my slow cooker. Everyone loves the roasted potatoes, even my pickiest child. If you like, top with shredded cheese.
—Theresa Gomez, Stuart, FL

Prep: 5 min. • **Cook:** 6 hours
Makes: 12 servings

- 4 pounds small red potatoes
- 8 green onions, chopped (about 1 cup)
- 1 cup chopped sweet onion
- ¼ cup olive oil
- ½ teaspoon salt
- ½ teaspoon pepper

In a 5- or 6-qt. slow cooker, combine all ingredients. Cook, covered, on low 6-8 hours or until potatoes are tender.

Per serving: 157 cal., 5g fat (1g sat. fat), 0 chol., 110mg sod., 26g carb. (2g sugars, 3g fiber), 3g pro. **Diabetic exchanges:** 1½ starch, 1 fat.

My crew looks forward to this side dish every holiday. I add sliced almonds for crunch and garlic for a little kick.
—Cheryl Wittman, Bergen, NY

EASY GREEN BEANS WITH MUSHROOMS

Prep: 10 min. • **Cook:** 5 hours
Makes: 10 servings

- 2 **pounds fresh green beans, trimmed**
- 1 **pound sliced fresh mushrooms**
- 1 **large onion, finely chopped**
- 2 **tablespoons butter, melted**
- 2 **tablespoons olive oil**
- 3 **garlic cloves, minced**
- ½ **teaspoon salt**
- ¼ **teaspoon pepper**
- ½ **cup sliced almonds, toasted**

In a 6-qt. slow cooker, combine all ingredients except almonds. Cook, covered, on low until beans are tender, 5-6 hours. Remove with a slotted spoon. Top with almonds.

Note: To toast nuts, bake in a shallow pan in a 350° oven for 5-10 minutes or cook in a skillet over low heat until lightly browned, stirring occasionally.

Per serving: 116 cal., 8g fat (2g sat. fat), 6mg chol., 145mg sod., 11g carb. (4g sugars, 4g fiber), 4g pro.
Diabetic exchanges: 1½ fat, 1 vegetable.

AUTUMN PUMPKIN CHILI

I prepare this chili often and everyone loves it, even my most finicky grandchildren. My family and friends have all given it a big thumbs-up. It's a definite keeper in my book!
—Kimberly Nagy, Port Hadlock, WA

Prep: 20 min. • **Cook:** 7 hours
Makes: 4 servings

- 1 **medium onion, chopped**
- 1 **small green pepper, chopped**
- 1 **small sweet yellow pepper, chopped**
- 1 **tablespoon canola oil**
- 1 **garlic clove, minced**
- 1 **pound ground turkey**
- 1 **can (15 ounces) solid-pack pumpkin**
- 1 **can (14½ ounces) diced tomatoes, undrained**
- 4½ **teaspoons chili powder**
- ¼ **teaspoon pepper**
- ¼ **teaspoon salt**
  Optional toppings: shredded cheddar cheese, sour cream and sliced green onions

1. Saute the onion and green and yellow peppers in oil in a large skillet until tender. Add the garlic; cook 1 minute longer. Crumble turkey into skillet. Cook over medium heat until meat is no longer pink.
2. Transfer to a 3-qt. slow cooker. Stir in the pumpkin, tomatoes, chili powder, pepper and salt. Cover and cook on low for 7-9 hours. Serve with toppings of your choice.

Per 1¼ cups: 281 cal., 13g fat (3g sat. fat), 75mg chol., 468mg sod., 20g carb. (9g sugars, 7g fiber), 25g pro.
Diabetic exchanges: 3 lean meat, 1 starch, 1 vegetable, 1 fat.

C
SLOW COOKER PORK CHOPS

Everyone will enjoy these fork-tender pork chops with a creamy, light gravy. Serve with a green vegetable, mashed potatoes and coleslaw or a salad.
—Sue Bingham, Madisonville, TN

Prep: 15 min. • **Cook:** 2 hours
Makes: 4 servings

- ½ cup all-purpose flour, divided
- ½ teaspoon ground mustard
- ½ teaspoon garlic pepper blend
- ¼ teaspoon seasoned salt
- 4 boneless pork loin chops (4 ounces each)
- 2 tablespoons canola oil
- 1 can (14½ ounces) chicken broth

1. In a large resealable plastic bag, combine ¼ cup flour, mustard, garlic pepper and seasoned salt. Add pork chops, one at a time, and shake to coat. In a large skillet, brown chops in oil on both sides.
2. Transfer to a 5-qt. slow cooker. Pour broth over chops. Cook, covered, on low for 2-3 hours or until meat is tender.
3. Remove pork to a serving plate and keep warm. Whisk remaining flour into cooking juices until smooth; cook, covered, on high until sauce is thickened.
Per 1 pork chop: 279 cal., 14g fat (3g sat. fat), 57mg chol., 606mg sod., 12g carb. (1g sugars, 0 fiber), 24g pro.
Diabetic exchanges: 3 lean meat, 1½ fat, 1 starch.

SWEET AND SOUR BRISKET

Here's one dish that never gets old. The brisket is tender and juicy with a great sweet-sour twist.
—Jolie Albertazzie, Moreno Valley, CA

Prep: 15 min. • **Cook:** 8 hours
Makes: 10 servings

- 1 can (28 ounces) crushed tomatoes
- 1 medium onion, halved and thinly sliced
- ½ cup raisins
- ¼ cup packed brown sugar
- 2 tablespoons lemon juice
- 3 garlic cloves, minced
- 1 fresh beef brisket (3 pounds)
- ½ teaspoon salt
- ¼ teaspoon pepper

1. In a small bowl, combine the tomatoes, onion, raisins, brown sugar, lemon juice and garlic. Pour half into a 4- or 5-qt. slow cooker coated with cooking spray. Sprinkle meat with salt and pepper. Transfer to slow cooker. Top with remaining tomato mixture. Cover and cook on low for 8-10 hours or until meat is tender.
2. Remove brisket to a serving platter and keep warm. Skim fat from cooking juices. Thinly slice meat across the grain. Serve with tomato mixture.
Note: This is a fresh beef brisket, not corned beef.
Per 4 ounces cooked beef with ⅓ cup sauce: 248 cal., 6g fat (2g sat. fat), 58mg chol., 272mg sod., 19g carb. (11g sugars, 2g fiber), 30g pro.
Diabetic exchanges: 4 lean meat, 1 starch.

EASY TURKEY SLOPPY JOES

Letting all the flavors combine in the slow cooker is the key to these mildly sweet sloppy joes. This recipe is sure to be one you'll turn to again, and because it calls for turkey, you can feel good about serving it to your family.
—Lisa Ann Panzino DiNunzio, Vineland, NJ

Prep: 20 min. • **Cook:** 4 hours
Makes: 10 servings

- 2 pounds lean ground turkey
- 1 medium onion, finely chopped
- 1 small green pepper, chopped
- 2 cans (8 ounces each) no-salt-added tomato sauce
- 1 cup water
- 2 envelopes sloppy joe mix
- 1 tablespoon brown sugar
- 10 hamburger buns, split

1. In a large nonstick skillet coated with cooking spray, cook the turkey, onion and pepper over medium heat until the meat is no longer pink; drain. Transfer to a 3-qt. slow cooker.
2. Stir in the tomato sauce, water, sloppy joe mix and brown sugar. Cover and cook on low until flavors are blended, 4-5 hours. Spoon ½ cup onto each bun.

Per serving: 304 cal., 9g fat (3g sat. fat), 72mg chol., 870mg sod., 33g carb. (8g sugars, 2g fiber), 20g pro.

F C
SLOW COOKER CHICKEN TACO SALAD

We use this seasoned chicken across several meals, including tacos, enchiladas, sandwiches, omelets and this colorful salad.
—Karie Houghton, Lynnwood, WA

Prep: 10 min. • **Cook:** 3 hours
Makes: 6 servings

- 3 teaspoons chili powder
- 1 teaspoon each ground cumin, seasoned salt and pepper
- ½ teaspoon each white pepper, ground chipotle pepper and paprika
- ¼ teaspoon dried oregano
- ¼ teaspoon crushed red pepper flakes
- 1½ pounds boneless skinless chicken breasts
- 1 cup chicken broth
- 9 cups torn romaine
  Optional toppings: sliced avocado, shredded cheddar cheese, chopped tomato, sliced green onions and ranch salad dressing

1. Mix seasonings; rub over chicken. Place in a 3-qt. slow cooker. Add broth. Cook, covered, on low until chicken is tender, 3-4 hours.
2. Remove chicken; cool slightly. Shred with two forks. Serve over romaine; top as desired.
 HEALTH TIP Switch to a baby kale salad blend for more fiber, vitamin C, calcium and iron.
Per 1¾ cups: 143 cal., 3g fat (1g sat. fat), 63mg chol., 516mg sod., 4g carb. (1g sugars, 2g fiber), 24g pro.
Diabetic exchanges: 3 lean meat, 1 vegetable.

M
ITALIAN SPAGHETTI SQUASH

If you're searching for a tasty meatless dish to make in the slow cooker, give my spaghetti squash a try. Fill the squash with whatever type of sauce or other ingredients score big at your house.
—Melissa Brooks, Sparta, WI

Prep: 15 min. • **Cook:** 6¼ hours
Makes: 4 servings

- 1 **medium spaghetti squash (3 pounds)**
- 1 **can (14½ ounces) diced tomatoes, undrained**
- 1 **cup sliced fresh mushrooms**
- ½ **teaspoon salt**
- ½ **teaspoon dried oregano**
- ¼ **teaspoon pepper**
- ¾ **cup shredded part-skim mozzarella cheese**

1. Halve squash lengthwise; discard seeds. Fill with tomatoes and mushrooms; sprinkle with the seasonings. Place in an oval 7-qt. slow cooker, tilting one squash half slightly to fit.
2. Cook, covered, on low until squash is tender, 6-8 hours. Sprinkle with cheese. Cook, covered, on low until cheese is melted, 10-15 minutes. To serve, cut each half into two portions.
Per ¾ cup: 195 cal., 6g fat (3g sat. fat), 14mg chol., 661mg sod., 31g carb. (4g sugars, 7g fiber), 9g pro.
Diabetic exchanges: 2 starch, 1 medium-fat meat.

STEAK SAN MARINO

As a busy wife and mom, I count on this delicious, budget-friendly dish to help my day run more smoothly. The steak is so tender and flavorful, my kids gobble it up and my husband asks for seconds.
—Lael Griess, Hull, IA

Prep: 15 min. • **Cook:** 7 hours
Makes: 6 servings

- ¼ **cup all-purpose flour**
- ½ **teaspoon salt**
- ½ **teaspoon pepper**
- 1 **beef top round steak (1½ pounds), cut into six pieces**
- 2 **large carrots, sliced**
- 1 **celery rib, sliced**
- 1 **can (8 ounces) tomato sauce**
- 2 **garlic cloves, minced**
- 1 **bay leaf**
- 1 **teaspoon Italian seasoning**
- ½ **teaspoon Worcestershire sauce**
- 3 **cups hot cooked brown rice**

1. In a large resealable plastic bag, combine the flour, salt and pepper. Add beef, a few pieces at a time, and shake to coat. Transfer to a 4-qt. slow cooker.
2. In a small bowl, combine the carrots, celery, tomato sauce, garlic, bay leaf, Italian seasoning and Worcestershire sauce. Pour over beef. Cover and cook on low for 7-9 hours or until beef is tender. Discard bay leaf. Serve with rice.
Freeze option: Place cooked steak and vegetables in freezer containers; top with sauce. Cool and freeze. To use, partially thaw in refrigerator overnight. Heat through in a covered saucepan, gently stirring and adding a little water if necessary.
Per 3 ounces cooked beef with ½ cup rice and ⅓ cup sauce: 286 cal., 5g fat (1g sat. fat), 64mg chol., 368mg sod., 30g carb. (2g sugars, 3g fiber), 29g pro.
Diabetic exchanges: 3 lean meat, 2 starch.

JAVA ROAST BEEF

Coffee turns a simple beef roast into a crowd-pleaser. It also adds richness to the gravy, which can be soaked up with crusty bread or poured onto mashed potatoes.
—Charla Sackmann, Orange City, IA

Prep: 10 min. • **Cook:** 8 hours
Makes: 12 servings

- 5 garlic cloves, minced
- 1½ teaspoons salt
- ¾ teaspoon pepper
- 1 boneless beef chuck roast (3 to 3½ pounds)
- 1½ cups strong brewed coffee
- 2 tablespoons cornstarch
- ¼ cup cold water

1. Mix garlic, salt and pepper; rub over beef. Transfer to a 4-qt. slow cooker. Pour coffee around meat. Cook, covered, on low 8-10 hours or until meat is tender.

2. Remove roast to a serving plate; keep warm. Transfer cooking juices to a small saucepan; skim off fat. Bring to a boil. In a small bowl, mix cornstarch and water until smooth; gradually stir into cooking juices. Bring to a boil; cook and stir until thickened, 1-2 minutes. Serve gravy with roast.

Per 3 ounces cooked beef with about 2 tablespoons gravy: 199 cal., 11g fat (4g sat. fat), 74mg chol., 342mg sod., 2g carb. (0 sugars, 0 fiber), 22g pro.
Diabetic exchanges: 3 lean meat.

ITALIAN SHRIMP & PASTA

This dish will remind you a bit of classic shrimp Creole, but it has a surprise Italian twist. Slow cooking gives it hands-off ease—perfect for company.

—Karen Edwards, Sanford, ME

Prep: 20 min. • **Cook:** 7½ hours
Makes: 6 servings

- 1 pound boneless skinless chicken thighs, cut into 2x1-inch strips
- 2 tablespoons canola oil
- 1 can (28 ounces) crushed tomatoes
- 2 celery ribs, chopped
- 1 medium green pepper, cut into 1-inch pieces
- 1 medium onion, coarsely chopped
- 2 garlic cloves, minced
- 1 tablespoon sugar
- ½ teaspoon salt
- ½ teaspoon Italian seasoning
- ⅛ to ¼ teaspoon cayenne pepper
- 1 bay leaf
- 1 cup uncooked orzo or other small pasta
- 1 pound cooked medium shrimp, peeled and deveined

1. In a large skillet, brown chicken in oil; transfer to a 3-qt. slow cooker. Stir in tomatoes, celery, pepper, onion, garlic, sugar and seasonings. Cook, covered, on low 7-8 hours or until chicken is just tender.
2. Discard bay leaf. Stir in pasta; cook, covered, on high 15 minutes or until pasta is tender. Stir in shrimp; cook, covered, 5 minutes longer or until heated through.

Per 1½ cups: 418 cal., 12g fat (2g sat. fat), 165mg chol., 611mg sod., 40g carb. (10g sugars, 4g fiber), 36g pro.
Diabetic exchanges: 5 lean meat, 2½ starch, 1 fat.

TEST KITCHEN TIP
Unless a recipe tells you to add ingredients, do not lift the lid while the slow cooker is operating. Every time you lift the lid, steam escapes and you add cooking time.

ALPHABETICAL RECIPE INDEX

BUFFALO CHICKEN MEATBALLS, 15

RED POTATO SALAD DIJON, 159

ROASTED GREEN BEANS WITH LEMON & WALNUTS, 183